Third Sector
Management

Third Sector Management

The Art of Managing Nonprofit Organizations

William B. Werther, Jr.

and

Evan M. Berman

Georgetown University Press/Washington, D.C.

Georgetown University Press, Washington, D.C.
© 2001 by Georgetown University Press. All rights reserved.
Printed in the United States of America

10 9 8 7 6 5 4 3 2 1   2001

This volume is printed on acid-free offset book paper.

Library of Congress Cataloging-in-Publication Data

Werther, William B.
   Third sector management : the art of managing nonprofit organizations / by William B.
Werther, Jr., and Evan Berman.
     p. cm.
   Includes bibliographical references and index.
   ISBN 0-87840-843-6 (cloth : alk. paper)–ISBN 0-87840-844-4 (pbk. : alk. paper)
   1. Nonprofit organizations—Management. I. Title: 3rd sector management. II. Berman,
Evan M. III. Title.
   HD 62.6. W47   2001
   658'.048—dc21   00-061024

*This book is lovingly dedicated to
my son, Bill, his wife, Mari, and their children,
Chase and Hunter Werther (WBW),*

and to

*my wife, Dira, and daughter,
Daniella Celine Berman (EMB).*

Contents

PART I. THE STRATEGIC PERSPECTIVE AND PLAYERS

List of Figures

List of Tables

About the Authors

William B. Werther, Jr., Ph.D., is the codirector of the Center for Nonprofit Management and Office Depot Management Scholar at the University of Miami. He also is a past chair for the Managerial Consultation Division of the Academy of Management, Fellow and past chair of the International Society for Productivity and Quality Research, and Fellow in the World Academy of Productivity Science. Teaching and research interests include corporate strategy, technology, and their human resource implications.

He has earned multiple teaching awards and is an award-winning author. *Human Resources and Personnel Management*, 5th edition (McGraw-Hill, 1996), and *Dear Boss* (Simon and Schuster/Meadowbrook, 1989) are two of his many books. Besides books translated into nine languages, he has authored more than 80 articles for *California Management Review, Organizational Dynamics,* and other journals. Service includes editorial board memberships for the *National Productivity Review, Health Care Management,* and the *Journal of Management Development,* for which he served as North American editor.

His experience includes work for the White House Conference on Productivity, NASA, the American Productivity and Quality Center, and scores of other nonprofits in health care, education, arts, community development, religion, and philanthropy. An experienced labor arbitrator, he chaired the Public Employment Relations Board for the City of Phoenix from 1980 to 1982. In Miami, community service includes a gubernatorial appointment to the International Currency and Barter Exchange Committee, the Executive Committee of Leadership Miami, and service on other nonprofit boards. His expertise has been sought by more than 100 organizations in Europe and the Americas, including the White House, the U.S. House of Representatives, Arizona State Senate, *Fortune, Wall Street Journal, U.S. News and World Report,* and *Nation's Business.*

He earned a Ph.D. (Phi Beta Kappa) from the University of Florida in 1971; then became a professor of management at Arizona State University for 14 years. In addition, he has taught at the Universidade do Porto (Portugal), the Universidad Autonoma Guadalajara (Mexico), and the Universidad Gabriela Mistral (Chile), where he serves as a visiting professor each spring.

Evan M. Berman, Ph.D., is associate professor of Public Administration at the University of Central Florida (Orlando) and teaches in the school's Ph.D. Program in Public Affairs. His experience includes numerous seminars to nonprofit and public managers on organizational improvement, strategy, and productivity. He is a member of the American Society for Public Administration and past chair of its section on Personnel and Labor Relations. He has worked for the National Science Foundation and has served as a consultant to U.S. Congress and the National Academy of Sciences.

He has received teaching and research awards and is a leading scholar on productivity improvement in public and nonprofit organizations. He has published more than 75 articles and several books on these topics, including *HRM in Public Organizations* (Sage, 2001), *The Ethics Edge* (ICMA, 1998), and *Productivity in Public and Nonprofit Organizations* (Sage, 1998). His research has been published in such journals as *Journal of Urban Affairs, Policy Studies Review,* and *Public Administration Review.* He has also done extensive research on community-based planning involving public and nonprofit organizations addressing important social problems. His work has been presented in foreign settings and translated in foreign languages.

Educated in Europe and the United States, he received his Ph.D. from George Washington University in 1988 in the area of public policy. Before joining the faculty at the University of Central Florida, he was on the faculty at the University of Miami.

Preface

Why do some nonprofit organizations succeed and others fail? How can leaders of nonprofits increase the likelihood of success? Why is a strategic viewpoint central to building a viable nonprofit?

This book answers these and other key questions from a strategic perspective, which assumes vision, mission, strategy, and execution are pillars on which success is built. Part I of the book explains the strategic perspective and the roles of key players—including the board of directors, leaders, staff, and volunteers. Part II addresses the execution of the strategic perspective through productivity, performance measurement, alliance building, and fundraising.

Although many third sector practitioners and researchers might argue that the single key to success is fundraising, we believe that fundraising depends on how the nonprofit is positioned and performs. Though the demands for the services provided by many nonprofits are seemingly unending, the resources available to accomplish their roles are always finite. Whether arts, education, health care, religious, philanthropic, or other nonprofit organizations, they seldom have sufficient funds to deliver all the services desired by constituents. Because there are many worthy nonprofits, why should donors, volunteers, or others contribute to one particular nonprofit versus another? Restated, how does a nonprofit distinguish itself from others?

Positioning depends on a blend of perception and practices. Does the nonprofit present a vision of the future that is both ennobling and inspiring to donors, volunteers, staff, and other constituents? Is the mission of the nonprofit well-defined and focused? Bluntly put, why should anyone but recipients care about the organization, its vision and mission? Even if the vision and mission of the nonprofit are attractive, how well does the nonprofit perform? Does it have high productivity? Solid performance outcomes and measures? Are the good deeds done by the nonprofit communicated, understood, and appreciated by constituents within and outside the nonprofit? How successful is the nonprofit in building bridges to the private and public sectors? Ultimately, perceptions and performance form a foundation that shapes the success of fundraising, the lifeblood of the nonprofit.

Our intent with this book is to address the components of building a strategically successful nonprofit. Part I addresses strategic positioning. What are the components needed to put the nonprofit in the best situation to survive and prosper? Included is a discussion of the private, public, and nonprofit sectors that form a modern society. What are the benefits and limitations of a strategic viewpoint? How do nonprofits move through the organizational life cycle and what are the implications of moving toward maturity for the nonprofit, its board, its strategies, and its structure?

The strategic view emphasizes the necessity of a clear vision, mission, and strategies for nonprofits. Why does vision matter? What is meant by a vision-directed mission? What are the basic tools of analysis when trying to understand a nonprofit's success potential? Answers to these questions drive the formation of an active, focused board and give direction to the leader's strategic role. The strategic viewpoint enables a more effective approach to staffing—whether using full-time professionals, volunteers, or a mix of both.

Part II explores efficient execution. Merely having a strategic viewpoint is an insufficient condition of success. High levels of productivity are needed to ensure that resources are efficiently used. Evidence of that efficiency must be available to donors, board members, leaders, and others in the form of performance measures and outcomes. With limited resources available to nonprofits, alliances among public and private organizations can leverage limited resources. Bridge building among other sectors of the economy enhances the effectiveness and efficiency of resource use by further leveraging the nonprofit's limited resources.

With a strategic viewpoint and a well-executed story to tell, fundraisers are armed with the right tools to "sell" the nonprofit to likely donors, board leaders, staff, volunteers, and others. Moreover, focused fundraising connects the vision, mission, strategies, execution, and evaluation to create a solid platform for future growth and success. A solid foundation is needed as nonprofits navigate an increasingly turbulent and competitive environment.

Acknowledgments

The authors would like to thank Leonard Turkel of Turkel Resource Foundation and codirector of the Center for Nonprofit Management at the University of Miami for his keen insights, encouragement, and wise counsel; Jay Malina for his community leadership and insights into board management and community development; Sandy Lane of the Greater Miami Chamber of Commerce for many years of advice and insights; Jerry Goodwin and John Rossfeld at the University of Miami's Sylvester Comprehensive Cancer Center and James Skinner of the Coral Gables Police Department for their openness and professionalism in creating long-range plans for their respective organizations; Nancy Herstand, executive director of the Performing Arts Center Foundation of Greater Miami for her fundraising and leadership insights; Ruth Schack, president of the Dade Community Foundation; and Robin Reiter-Faragalli, vice president of human resources at the *Miami Herald* for their generosity of time and ideas.

We also thank Belinda McCarthy, dean of the College of Health and Public Affairs, for her leadership; Marilyn Crotty, director of the Institute of Government at the University of Central Florida for bringing the resources of UCF to bear on community problems; and Dean Sprague, city manager of the city of Maitland for sharing his facilitative leadership and community building skills.

These people are community assets who lead by example and by doing for their communities.

Part I

The Strategic Perspective and Players

1

The Third Sector

Society consists of the private sector, the public sector, and the nonprofit sector, sometimes referred to as the "third sector." Organizations in the third sector often pursue educational, health, cultural, religious, artistic, political, charitable, philanthropic, or other social goals. They seek to serve the public at large (such as the disaster-relief efforts of the Red Cross) or the public good of a narrowly defined membership (such as a home owners' association or country club). Their aims often support the most noble features of society.

Nonprofit organizations (or "nonprofits") fulfill a unique role in society. They differ from business in that they do not seek to maximize profits. Their aims follow from their mission to serve the public good; activities are not constrained or prioritized on the basis of their profit potential. Moreover, surpluses are reinvested in the organization rather than distributed to corporate owners. Nonprofits also differ from public organizations in that their activities are not subject to processes of democratic governance. Nonprofits often take over where inadequate political will exists, such as providing additional support for the arts or education that includes religious elements. In recent years, nonprofits are also used by governments in helping to implement public policy, such as by providing services to special populations.

Nonprofits also stand on their own, regardless of the distinctions among the three sectors. Nonprofits are often unique in the values they adopt and the passion with which they operate. For example, many nonprofit schools commit to educating the child as a whole, rather than only focusing on narrow, academic skills. Some focus on helping the child perform in a web of social relationships, whereas others emphasize moral development or self-esteem. They may have a secular or religious base. Likewise, environmental organizations are often passionately committed to preserving nature as their first priority, leaving it to business and government to balance other priorities. Nonprofit organizations operate under their own set of values and have their own ideology with which they pursue their goals. Although many private and public organizations seek to make the world a better place as a part of their efforts, nonprofits tend to be strongly driven by the values embraced by the organization.

Knowledge about the third sector is fundamental to understanding the broader society in which we live. It provides contrast between the governmental and for-profit sectors; it reflects the emergent and ongoing concerns of society; and it often serves as the springboard for social change in local, national, and international arenas. Historically, many successful local and societal issues initially championed in the nonprofit sector have gained support and eventually developed considerable implications for government and business. Examples include compulsory free public education, workers' compensation, social security for elderly citizens, birth control, animal rights, pollution control, and scores of other issues. The emotional, in-kind, and financial support of those concerned are often sufficient to create a nonprofit organization that serves as a platform for the group's concerns. The third sector also provides nonprofits with shelter from the profit motive of business and the limitations of democratic governance. Starting in the nonprofit arena, ideas and causes need neither government support nor profitability to survive.

On the surface, many activities of nonprofits seem similar to those of business or government. After all, providing health care services or kindergarten through 12th-grade education are found in each of the three sectors. So why single out the management of the nonprofit sector for separate consideration? Is there not one best way to provide these services? The answer is a resounding "no." The way that services are provided inherently reflects the purposes of organizations, its leadership, and constraints that characterize their environment, causing for-profits, government, and nonprofits to act and react differently.

The Strategic Approach

To understand nonprofits, their leadership, and their constraints, this book argues for a strategic approach that views nonprofits from a broad perspective and asks such questions as, What is the nonprofit trying to achieve? What are the expectations of constituencies that support a specific nonprofit? What strategies are available to the nonprofit? What roles do leaders play? What resources does the organization have to support its aims? Surely, then, there is a need for understanding how successful nonprofits attain success, but "best practices" are only one of several factors that shape how nonprofits accomplish their goals.

The strategic viewpoint that underlies this book focuses on the "why, what and how" of organizations. When we asked nonprofit directors these questions as we prepared for this book, most responded by talking about the activities their organization performed, whether it was feeding the homeless or providing funds to other nonprofits. Certainly, understanding the day to day activities of a nonprofit is essential because these activities ultimately justify its existence. But before there was activity, the creators of the nonprofit had an idea that served as the central organizing principle, the reason they and others were willing to devote time, effort, and other resources to creating the nonprofit. That central idea—such as feeding homeless people—becomes the basis for people to rally in support of the non-profit. The key question is *"Why* should anyone care about this organi-zation?" (McLaughlin, 2000). Although a vision statement inspires, a mission statement defines the scope and purpose of the organization. It seeks to answer the question, *What* is the purpose of this organiza-tion? It defines the core activities of the organization and its aims and further carves out the scope of the organization. Finally, the organization develops a strategy, which defines how it will attain its vision and mission. An effective strategy ties together the competencies of the organization in a way that enables it to effectively and efficiently achieve the mission. It seeks to answer the question, *How* is the organization going to go about achieving its purpose? (McLaugh-lin, 2000).

The vision, mission, and strategy of an organization constitute a strategic approach that guides leaders, staff members, volunteers, beneficiaries, donors, and other constituents in understanding the goal, scope, and direction of the organization.

Benefits of a Strategic Viewpoint

Why is a strategic viewpoint necessary? Understanding nonprofit organizations from a strategic framework offers several benefits. First, it provides a unifying theme around which the many activities of the nonprofit can be understood and interpreted. It serves as a shorthand explanation of the nonprofit without becoming bogged down in details unique to different organizations. Whether recruiting staff, donors, volunteers, or board members, a strategic perspective provides the basis for informed commitment among the nonprofit's various constituents by addressing "Why?" "What?" and "How?" Simply put, the strategic approach summarizes the most compelling arguments for involvement and support (Sheehan, 1999).

Second, a strategic viewpoint offers guidelines for action. The vision, mission, and strategy serve as templates against which operational and fundraising plans are evaluated. Will specific actions move the organization toward its vision? Which decisions best support the mission? Do action plans fall within the nonprofit's strategy? Why should one course of action be preferred over another? Agreement about the strategic elements is more likely to make decisions and actions a source of unity among internal constituents (such as management, staff, and volunteers) and reinforce a consistent picture among external supporters (such as potential board members, donors, funding agencies, and allies).

Third, as explained more fully in later chapters, virtually all nonprofits form alliances among private, public, and other organizations. The ability to gain assistance of other organizations is often essential to a nonprofit's success. Without clarity of vision, mission, and strategy, it is difficult to discern which relationships are important and for what reasons. More compelling, unless the nonprofit can clearly articulate its niche, potential allies may be uncertain, and therefore reluctant, to assist the nonprofit.

Fourth, a strategic approach forms the basis for evaluating the nonprofit. Is the nonprofit doing a good job? Is the executive director effective? Are constituents being effectively and efficiently served? As will also be developed more fully in later chapters, nonprofits (by definition) do not have profits by which to gauge their success. Likewise, they are not subject to voter approval, as is the public sector. Instead, an assessment of the nonprofit must evaluate its vision, mission, and strategy. Without these strategic benchmarks, board members, outside supporters, staff, and volunteers have little against which to compare results. Because nonprofits often depend on the goodwill of their supporters, being able to demonstrate effectiveness becomes increasingly crucial for nonprofits that wish to grow and prosper (Greenfeld, 2000).

Limitations to a Strategic Viewpoint

The strategic perspective has limitations. First, developing a strategic approach may not match the desires of the leadership (Clolery, 1999).

Some nonprofits, particularly small ones, operate opportunistically. That is, revenues are raised, resources are committed, and programs are undertaken based on current possibilities—independent of any grand or strategic design. This opportunistic culture is much more common among newly formed nonprofits or nonprofits that have a strong, founding leader. Some founding leaders view the nonprofit as their fiefdom. Those that do often do not see the need for a strategic approach. In fact, they may view mission statements and strategies as *limitations* on their freedom to act. Often this view is reinforced among board members who are selected for their support, friendship, and philosophical agreement with the founding leader. Though such nonprofits would benefit from a strategic approach, as a practical matter opportunistically run nonprofits seldom change unless there is a change in the leadership or the organization faces some crisis.

Second, a practical limitation is resources. Developing a strategic approach and following through takes time and resources. Not convinced of the value behind a strategic approach, it is difficult to get boards, leaders, and senior staff to devote the energies needed to create and operate from a strategic perspective.

Third, a strategic approach may assume a degree of sophistication that the nonprofit has yet to attain. Expecting a nonprofit to develop sophisticated vision, mission, and strategy statements that serve as the templates for its actions and evaluation may be unrealistic initially. Newly formed nonprofits, much like new businesses, need time to determine their niche, expertise, and support. Prematurely locking the nonprofit into one direction or another may cripple or even destroy the organization's potential. Understanding the stages of development among nonprofits gives insights about the internal and external characteristics associated with different levels of maturity and sophistication.

The Life Cycle of Nonprofits

Not only do nonprofits vary by vision, mission, and strategies, they exist at various stages of development. Like people, organizations move through a life cycle as they mature. Each stage presents different challenges—some of which are opportunities and others of which are threats. How a nonprofit navigates these stages shapes its effectiveness and determines its very survival. This navigation of the maturation process takes place in many ways and on many levels. Two important dimensions are the strategic and operation levels.

Strategic Nonprofit Evolution

Table 1-1 uses a three-stage framework: formation, growth, and maturity. Within each stage, the relevant issue evolves. This evolution is neither systematic nor uniform. Nonprofits proceed at different rates and in different ways. Some organizations will move rapidly from formation to growth to maturity on one issue and lag behind on another. Except at the very beginning of a nonprofit's existence, it is not unusual to expect one to have characteristics associated with multiple stages as some issues mature and others remain unchanged.

Vision Driver

A vision statement is an ennobling, articulated statement of what an organization is and what it is striving to become. It answers the questions of what the world would be like if the mission were attained. The vision of the nonprofit typically reflects the glory of the purpose at the formation stage, but evolves to embrace key constituents. As the nonprofit gains success and matures, the vision may be expanded to a larger purpose or domain. This expansion typically reflects the organization's growing success and the pressures placed on it by internal constituents (such as managers, professionals, and staff) and external forces (such as funding sources, clients, board members, community expectations). Although the founder or those involved in the formation stage may view this expansion of the vision as desirable, they may also see it as a dilution of the organization's original mission. Although changes or expansion of the vision may be essential to the ongoing viability of the organization, such changes can be the basis for schism among supporters and staff.

The vision driver is typically the founder or founding group. With greater maturity the vision becomes increasingly institutionalized and is increasingly driven by staff and supporters and less by the founders. In time, the vision drivers give way to professional leaders, who add their beliefs and expectations to the interpretation of the vision and the mission. Professional, nonprofit managers typically bring with them a more systematic approach to the leadership of the organization. Sometimes this transition may substitute systems and efficiency for the zeal and passion of the founders. Improved accountability also may be injected into the vision of the organization, because founders typically focus on outcomes rather than internal processes.

Table 1-1 Nonprofit Evolution at the Strategic Level

Issue	Formation	Growth	Maturity
		Stages	
Vision	Glory of the purpose	Glory of the purpose and those involved	Glory of expanded purpose and involvement
Vision driver	Founder(s)	Founder(s) and staff	Staff and supporters
Mission	Altruistically fill a need in community	Balancing narrow community need and related agendas	Expanded community need as a means to other agendas
Organizational objective	Altruistically fill a need in community	Professionalize to gain legitimacy and effectiveness	Institutionalize and increase legitimacy
Strategic barriers	Founder's drive, financing, and supporters' dedication	Professional staff's management of mission, money, and "missionaries" (resources and supporters)	Supporters of management of mission, money, and staff (resources and staff)

Mission

The mission of most nonprofits typically is to fill a need in some defined community in an altruistic fashion. With growth of the organization comes a greater need to balance the needs of the beneficiaries with those of the larger community. The introduction of professional management complicates the mission by adding the personal needs and aspirations of managers as another element of the organizational mission. At the mature stage, nonprofits often expand the needs to be met through more complex agendas. Moreover, the success of a maturing nonprofit affects—and therefore almost always changes—the needs and expectations of beneficiaries (Drucker, 1989).

Organizational Objectives

The organizational objective (or objectives) and the mission are virtually indistinguishable in the formation stage. However, the evolution toward growth leads to a greater need for "professionalization" as a means of gaining perceived (and actual) legitimacy among multiple constituents. That is, the nonprofit seeks to "look" successful as a means of attracting greater recognition and support. A new, dynamic equilibrium among organizational objectives and the processes used to achieve those objectives must be found. The objective of the organization becomes to differentiate itself from other nonprofits. It becomes institutionalized within its service community and among its supporters, often having dedicated sources of revenue and well-oiled alliances with powerful "movers and shakers" in the community.

Strategic Barriers

Along the way to maturity, strategic barriers emerge. In the formation stage, the barriers are numerous but usually include the founder's drive and personality, which gives life to the nonprofit but may also limit its effectiveness because of myopic zeal and dedication. Overidentification by the founders with the organization or overidentification of the organization with the founders may delay the transition to the growth or maturity stages. Powerful, entrenched leaders backed by their allies on the board may view necessary change or unsettling dialog as a personal affront to their esteemed contribution. New ideas may be seen as criticism of past practices instead of improvements on the foundation created by the founders. The inability or unwillingness to challenge the leaders may cause the organization to stagnate (Maranville, 1999).

This same risk of stagnation exists when professional managers become too entrenched in their roles and place job security and power above the vision and mission of the organization. This strategic barrier of leadership can block the nonprofit's ability to adapt to its changing environment. In the same way, sources of funding and the dedication of supporters—particularly early members of the board—are both strengths and barriers. As growth moves the organization toward greater professionalism, professional managers often replace founders. How they manage the mission, money, and "missionaries" determines the organization's success in the transition to a mature nonprofit. At the mature stage, the impact of supporters may become a strategic barrier, especially if they are able to use resources to control the nonprofit's strategies for delivering its service.

Operational Nonprofit Evolution

Day to day operations also evolve as the nonprofit matures. Table 1-2 tracks some of the key operational issues as they change from the formation to growth to maturity stages.

The services provided by the nonprofit almost always begin along a narrow range because of limited resources. Growth typically brings an expansion of the deliverables. This expansion may be in the number of services, the number of clients, or both. At maturity the scope of the services provided is usually well settled.

Funding

Funding often begins during the formation stage on a hit or miss basis that is best characterized as opportunistic. Growth and increased professionalization leads to a focus on securing repetitive sources of funding. At maturity, funding may be institutionalized so that monies are more or less automatically forthcoming either because of endowment, dedicated funding sources, reliable fund-raising processes, or some combination of these. With the exception of foundations and well-endowed nonprofits, fundraising often commands the most attention from leaders and board members.

Table 1-2 Nonprofit Evolution at the Operational Level

Issue	Stages		
	Formation	Growth	Maturity
Services	Narrow and few	Expanding	Settled/expanded
Funding	Opportunistic funding services	Repetitive funding sources	Institutionalized sources
Organization design	Organic	Fragmented and functional	Functional hierarchy
Procedures	Few and informal	Some formal systems	Levels of controls and systems
Promotion	Awareness and applications	Applications and image	Image and uniqueness
Employee relations	Informal	Planned	Well-defined
Community relations (orientation)	Few and funding-oriented	Expanding constituencies	Established constituencies
Failure	Funding burnout by board/ director	Staff/purpose conflict	No self-renewing mechanisms

Organizational Design

Organizational design summarizes the structure and reporting relationships within the nonprofit. Following the formation, growth, and mature stages, Figure 1-1 illustrates common organizational designs associated with each stage typically found in domestic nonprofits (Hudson and Bielefeld, 1997). At the beginning, organizational design is often of little concern because the nonprofit is so small that traditional hierarchical reporting relationships do not exist. The design, if there

Figure 1-1 **Organizational Designs for Nonprofit Organizations**

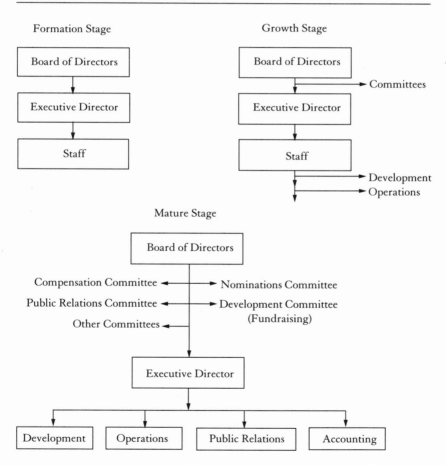

is one, might best be characterized as organic and free flowing, where the executive director might serve as chief fundraiser as well as janitor. With growth in size, the design begins to resemble traditional organizations, divided into functional departments that correspond with responsibilities such as operations, accounting, and fundraising. The more mature the nonprofit becomes, the more it will create specialized departments with vertical layers of reporting relationships, as illustrated in Figure 1-1.

Procedures

Procedures are few and informal at the beginning of a nonprofit's life cycle. To provide coordination, consistency, and efficiency, procedures grow in complexity and number, including some formal systems as the nonprofit grows. At maturity, formal systems exist, which can lead to a bureaucracy that becomes more focused on procedures than results.

Promotion

Promotion of the nonprofit is almost always by word of mouth or free public relations within the community. Efforts are directed at creating awareness of the nonprofit organization and the applications of its efforts. With growth the purpose and applications that the nonprofit will pursue share the spotlight with creating a favorable image of the nonprofit. At maturity relevant constituents are familiar with the role of the nonprofit so promotion largely focuses on image and how this nonprofit is unique.

Employee Relations

Employee relations begin as informal among a small staff. The formality of job descriptions, traditional roles, fringe benefits, and even hiring criteria are usually minimal if not absent. As the number of employees grows, their importance and visibility grow, taking more management time. To ensure equity and fairness, employee relations become more planned and systematic. With the arrival of professional management, employee relations rules and procedures typically become formalized.

Community Relations

Community relations in the formation stage are just one of many important demands on the leadership. If the community is an important part of funding or supporting the formation stage, community relations may consume an oversized proportion of leadership time and resources. The majority of community relations in the formation and growth stage are focused on fundraising—either by direct money-raising efforts or by more indirect attempts to expand relevant constituents among donors, beneficiaries, or the media.

Failure

Failure is a key operating issue in its own right. In the formation stage, failures are often many as the leadership seeks the right combination of services and revenue generation. As with new business endeavors, the early stages demand that the leader have multiple competencies because resources are often insufficient to acquire needed skills. Though organizations such as Community Foundations, the Business Volunteers for the Arts, or Chambers of Commerce can provide sources of assistance and funds, success ultimately depends on the nonprofit developing a minimum range of competencies to survive (Mayntz, 1999). Along the way toward survival, many artistic and executive directors report burnout because their early efforts are largely directed toward fundraising, not the mission they had hoped to achieve.

As the organization grows in size and complexity, another potential failure point is the transition from formation to growth stages, which may be accompanied by a transition from founders to professional management. Conflicts among founders and new board members, between the board and staff, among staff members, and over changing vision and mission requirements can lead to failure.

In the mature stage, bureaucratic hardening of the organizational arteries can lead the nonprofit down a path of gradual failure. The lack of self-renewing mechanisms may preclude periodic revitalizations of the organization. Though this risk exists among private and public organizations, profits and voters send messages about the need for change. But in nonprofits, particularly mature ones with dedicated streams of resources, there may not be an obvious corrective mechanism. Board members may feel honored to be on the board of directors and thus may not want to rock the boat with tough questions and tougher standards. Without an automatic rejuvenation of the board, this important oversight function can become captive to the executive director and staff, which typically control the information flow reaching the board. In extreme cases, the board may usurp resources for its benefit at the expense of the nonprofit's mission, furthering the possibilities of outright failure (Seibel, 1999).

Nonprofit Leadership

Ultimately, the success of a nonprofit depends on leadership. Because the leadership issue in nonprofits is so complex, a strong argument can be made that the best leaders are found in the nonprofit sector. The argument is that given the complexity they face, they must be good! In the private and public sectors, leaders have a clear, dominant constituency they must please. Business leaders must produce results that maximize the wealth of the owners and stockholders. They must be concerned about other constituents, of course, from customers and employees to government and the media. But if the owners are satisfied, their representatives (the board of directors) often grant the chief executive officers (CEO) great latitude. Likewise, politicians in the public sector look primarily to the electorate. If voters are satisfied (or at least indifferent), public sector leaders also have great latitude. But nonprofit leaders find a variety of more or less equal constituent groups that must be satisfied. For example, a university president is unlikely to last long without simultaneously pleasing students, faculty, staff, alumni, and donors. An arts organization must keep the artists, patrons, donors, and staff satisfied. Lacking a clear, definitive measure of success (such as profits or votes), most nonprofit leaders must perform a delicate balancing act, inspiring constituents, achieving results, and juggling conflicting claims on resources (Sandler and Hudson, 1998).

Multiple Roles of Leaders

Whether in the private, public, or nonprofit sector the person in charge usually has to play multiple roles. One way to understand these different roles is to narrowly define the terms leader, manager, and administrator.

A leader signifies one who is responsible for the strategic health of the organization, whether called CEO, executive director, or other title. The leader's role is to create an ennobling vision of the organization's future possibilities, clarify the mission, and develop effective strategies to achieve the mission. Though leader is a crucial role, much more time is usually devoted to being a manager. A manager is responsible for marshaling organizational resources to obtain defined objectives. An administrator seeks to balance the demands of multiple constituents.

Most heads of private, public, and nonprofit organizations play all three roles. They must inspire the organization, achieve objectives, and balance conflicting claims, moving from one role to the next as circumstances require. These efforts always take place against the backdrop of limited financial, human, and other resources. In the nonprofit sector, however, leaders often do not have the luxury of a straightforward decision criterion—profits or votes—to use when evaluating conflict demands on limited resources among constituents. Their success depends on leadership and managerial abilities along with especially sensitive administrative skills.

Thus understanding nonprofits requires a strategic viewpoint and an operational perspective demands considerable sensitivity to multiple constituencies. It is their collective assessment that largely determines the success of the nonprofit and its leader.

Nonprofit Boards

The nonprofit's success or failure is the responsibility of the organization's board of directors. They are responsible for hiring, evaluating, rewarding, and if needed replacing the leader—commonly called the executive director or president. Other responsibilities of the board are formally set forth in the articles of incorporation and its bylaws. In practice, the role of a nonprofit board often varies widely, depending not only on the officially stated duties in the incorporation papers but also on the nonprofit's stage in its life cycle. Table 1-3 summarizes some of the practical concerns facing a nonprofit board—including its role, functions, and failures.

The Board's Role

In the formation stage, a working board takes on leadership, managerial, and even administrative responsibilities. Demands on starting up

Table 1-3 **Nonprofit Evolution at the Board Level**

	Stages		
Issue	Formation	Growth	Maturity
Board's role	Working board	Managing board	Advisory board
Board's functions	Strategic guidance	Strategic guidance	Strategic reformulation
	Policy formulation	Policy formulation	Policy guidance
	Committee responsibilities	Committee involvement	Committee oversight
	Staff-line support	Issue leadership	Issue evaluation
	Operational funding	Operational and project funding	Institutionalize funding sources
	Leadership selection and support	Leadership support and evaluation	Leadership advice and succession
	Directing operations	Advising operations	Monitoring operations
Board's failures	Selecting director	Advising director	Monitoring operations
	Managing board responsibility	Managing board composition	Failure to reevaluate strategic mission and board composition
	Passive involvement in operations		Overinvolvement in operations

the nonprofit typically overwhelm both the financial and human resources available to get the necessary activities done. Board members may contribute time, money, professional, or other in-kind services to launch the nonprofit. Then they are often actively engaged in raising funds, dealing with community relations, and delivering the services of the nonprofit. Though there are considerable leadership and organizational implications for such heavy involvement, there literally may be no other choices if the nonprofit is to survive its formation stage and begin to grow.

As the organization begins to grow, the role of the board evolves from that of a working board to a managing board, which deals with policy issues and increasingly leaves day to day activities up to the executive director and the staff. A managing board expects the executive director to bring important policy, operational, and funding issues to the board for their reviews and concurrence. Though the detail with which the board becomes involved depends on the sophistication and maturity of the organization and its management team, the general rule is that the executive director proposes and the board disposes, either supporting or rejecting the executive director's recommendations. Because the balance of resources and demands is often precarious in the formation and growth stages, even a managing board is apt to be heavily involved in crucial decisions.

One sign of a mature nonprofit is the evolving role of the board. Among mature, well-established nonprofits, hands-on involvement by board members typically declines. The managing board of earlier years gives way to an advisory board, which exists primarily to offer guidance to the executive director and evaluate his or her performance.

These transitions from working to managing to advisory board are crucial to the maturation of the nonprofit. If the board does not take an active role in the beginning, the limited resources may cause failure. But if the board is too heavily involved later on, it may undermine the executive director. The result will be that the board finds strong, confident professionals quit because the board usurps their authority. Or the overly activist board may only be able to attract and retain weak executive directors unable to assert their leadership. In general, the board must provide the support needed for the nonprofit to grow and mature, slowly withdrawing hands-on involvement as the executive director and staff exhibit the ability to meet the strategic and operational demands they face.

The Board's Functions

summarizes the main board functions and their evolution through the formation, growth, and maturity stages. Without a precise definition for each stage, the exact transition point of these board functions cannot be specified with precision either. Instead, the transitions of each function from one stage to another are meant as guidelines.

Evolving Responsibilities

Even though the executive director is responsible for the strategic health of the organization, the board provides strategic guidance, which includes setting parameters and direction for the nonprofit. Strategic guidance remains an ongoing role of the board; what changes as the nonprofit evolves is the degree of specificity from the board. In the early stages, strategic guidance is apt to be very detailed and specific. As the board becomes more confident in the viability of the nonprofit and its leadership, guidance becomes more general, especially if the nonprofit is gaining in stature and success. Because the executive director can become so involved in the day to day details of the nonprofit's operations, the board often needs to initiate, even lead, the strategic reformation of the nonprofit's vision, mission, and strategies. Imprecision rules. When should the board or the executive director initiate a reformation of these strategic issues? The general answer is that it should be done *before* the nonprofit begins to lose its operation effectiveness or the support of key constituents. Because foreknowledge is unlikely, most mature, sophisticated nonprofits initiate periodic strategic reviews every year or every several years. Senior nonprofit management and board members often attend an offsite meeting at which the executive director or outside consultant works the group through rethinking its vision, mission, and strategies. Often the vision and mission remain unchanged, though strategies are often reconsidered and recast.

Policy Formulations

Policy formation includes strategic, operational, and philosophical guidelines that address day to day decisions. Policies are guides to action. They often limit management discretion because the object of the policy is too important to ignore. For example, a nonprofit may have a policy that states it is "an equal opportunity employer." This internal policy reinforces legal and increasingly societal norms. Because the human, legal, and public relations implications of discrimination are so severe, the board may impose this policy on management. Likewise, the nonprofit may want to go beyond legal or societal norms and declare that it will not discriminate against former felons or other nonprotected groups. By the time a nonprofit has evolved to the mature stage, policy formation gives way to guidance, and the management team is allowed to develop needed policies, usually subject to formal or informal approval of the board. Of course, by the time the nonprofit has become a well-established, mature organization, most major policy issues (such as equal employment) have been addressed.

Structure-Based Communications

Board-level committees are often formed to keep the board informed and involved. Some are (or should be) standing committees, such as fundraising committees. Other committees may be ad hoc, coming together for a specific purpose and then dissolving, such as an annual compensation committee that assesses the executive director's pay and benefit package. Early on in the development of the nonprofit, board members may assume committee responsibilities to chair committees and make recommendations to the full board. With greater and greater maturity, committee responsibilities usually give way to committee involvement, where board members serve on key committees that are officially or unofficially led by staff. As maturity leads to greater professionalism and complexity, board members may be assigned to committee oversight, where staff-led committees report to specific board members who serve a liaison capacity between the board and management.

Funding

Funding is the lifeblood of any organization, including nonprofits. Our interviews with nonprofit leaders and board members revealed that funding is perceived to be the single most important impediment or driver behind their success. Board involvement with funding in the formation stage focuses on operational funding, meeting the day to day financial needs necessary to keep the nonprofit paying staff and providing a service. Many nonprofits—particularly small, community-based ones—never progress beyond a constant struggle to find operating funds. Many board members who are invited to join the charter board are included because it is expected that they will give or raise operating funds.

In the growth stage, operational funding often continues to be of board-level concern in addition to project funding—where monies are sought for specific functions or activities, which may or may not repeat (usually, again, depending on funding). Those nonprofits fortunate to reach the mature stage on funding issues have largely resolved their ongoing operational funding needs. These usually larger, older nonprofits often focus on developing alliances or other connections that provide ongoing, institutionalized funding sources, which ensure future funding. For example, an arts organization might convince a local government or progressive chamber of commerce to add an annually recurring line in its budget for the arts organization or to sponsor an annual fundraising event.

Leadership Selection and Support

Leadership selection and support is a universal board function during formation. Any time the executive director needs to be replaced, the selection process falls to the board, regardless of the nonprofit's stage of development. As the nonprofit matures, the board continues to provide leadership support and evaluation. In mature settings, the board works with the executive director to provide leadership advice and succession feedback about maintaining management continuity as people resign, retire, or are fired.

Life Cycle Implications

During the formation stage, board members are often actively involved. They provide staff-like support, working beside the executive director and other members of staff, providing assistance as though they were paid employees. With a stronger infrastructure of human talent that comes with successful growth, board members may provide issue leadership, suggesting areas or activities for staff to consider or investigate. In a mature nonprofit organization, the board members perform issue evaluation, where board members evaluate the appropriateness of issues brought forward from the management staff (Newcomer, 1997).

Following the same pattern as with other issues, the degree of involvement by the board in operations shifts from directing operations in the formation stage to advising and then monitoring operations as the nonprofit matures. As mentioned earlier, this gradual disengagement from hands-on involvement to a role of guidance and monitoring is a delicate balancing act. Too little active involvement by the board in day to day operations at the outset and the nonprofit may fail; too much involvement later on and the board may undermine the effectiveness of the executive director and the management team.

The Board's Failures

There are several key leverage points at which board performance can have a decisive impact on the nonprofit's chances for success. Selecting the director may be the single most important decision the board makes. Often faced with limited funds, the selection decision may be based on finding anyone who will take the job or giving it to someone who helped create the nonprofit. Unfortunately, enthusiasm does not ensure competence. Advising the director, of course, is an ongoing responsibility. Because the executive director serves at the pleasure of the board, following the board's advice is almost certainly necessary to maintain the job of executive director—even if the advice is bad. Success of the nonprofit as it matures may cause the board to forego or fail to perform its responsibility to monitor operations. Though this lapse is almost certainly evidence of the board's high opinion of the executive director, the board remains responsible for evaluating the nonprofit's performance.

Restated, the board must also manage itself (Carver, 1997). Managing board responsibilities is done by the board or it does not get done. In the formation stage, these responsibilities are largely centered around hands-on involvement with operations. As the needs of the organization change the board must also start managing board composition—who should stay on the board, who should leave, who would bring needed talents to the board. Closely related to managing the board's composition, the board must also reevaluate the strategic mission and make board composition an ongoing issue.

Boards often fail their nonprofit organization if they take a passive stance toward operations at the formation stage or practice overinvolvement in operations during the mature stage. The degree of involvement by the board during the life cycle of the nonprofit is a delicate balance, which is maintained through an ongoing dialog between the board and the executive director, with the board helping the director when needed but offering the necessary latitude for the director to lead, manage, and administer the nonprofit.

Leadership and Staffing

The nonprofit's stage of development also affects the leadership and the staffing. The selection of the leader—whether called president or executive director—is essential. It may be the most important decision made for the nonprofit, particularly in its early stages of development. The leader must find a balance between planning and action. In the beginning of a nonprofit, the demands may be so overwhelming that action is little more than reaction. Professionalism arrives as the nonprofit develops both resources and the sophistication to use them. Not only must the leader be aware of the leadership–manager–administrator distinction presented earlier in the chapter, but he or she must strike a balance of reactive responses to current issues facing the nonprofit and proactive anticipation of future demands.

This reactive–proactive balance extends to staffing. As with leadership, staffing the organization depends on time and resources. Early on in the nonprofit's evolution, the leader may have no choice but to use volunteers, if they can be found, because of limited financial resources. Even when resources allow staff to be hired, limitations of funding and availability of qualified personnel may lead to suboptimal hiring. Hiring may be further undermined by the limited abilities and procedures used by the leader to staff the organization.

With greater maturity and resources, the staffing process becomes more professional. Not only does the leader have a better idea of the skills, knowledge, and abilities needed, the growing resources and reputation of the nonprofit attract a larger number of quality applicants. This maturity also allows a tighter connection between the strategic plans of the organization and its staffing decisions. For example, even in the presence of additional resources, unpaid volunteers may be a better use of resource than full-time staff. Not only are there obvious cost savings, but the type of unpaid volunteer that some nonprofits have access to may offer skills, networking contacts, and an enthusiastic approach not available among employees. The spouse of a wealthy or powerful community leader may offer the nonprofit access to resources, potential board members, or other leaders that would not be typical of a paid staff member, for example.

Strategic Execution

Beyond the strategic positioning of the nonprofit, ultimately the non-profit must deliver results. Execution also is affected by the nonprofit's stage in the life cycle. Again, resources play a crucial role. The sophistication of the staff and volunteers and the sophistication of the business techniques used by the nonprofit do depend on resources, which tend to become more widely available with growth and maturity.

Many nonprofits have limited resources with which to implement state of the art management techniques, and because of such unsophisticated techniques, leaders find it difficult to gain additional resources. Without high productivity, resources are squandered; without solid performance measures and the feedback they provide, the relative success of various efforts are hard to gauge; without the sophistication in strategic direction and execution, building bridges with the public and private sector becomes difficult. With all these difficulties, raising funds by which to improve in all of these areas becomes less likely, further reinforcing the nonprofit's inability to break out of the vicious cycle in which it may find itself.

Plan of the Book

The book continues in the next chapter with a closer look at the purpose of nonprofits. The vision, mission, and strategy issues and their formulation processes are examined in greater detail. The essentials of developing a board and the processes needed to support an effective ongoing board become the focus of chapter 3. Chapter 4 returns to the all-important question of leadership. Roles, boundaries, and the operationalization of the mission are the key concerns of leaders.

Building an organization marks the growing professionalization and maturity of a nonprofit. In chapter 5, staffing a nonprofit organization includes traditional, human resource considerations and issues not typically found in the public or private sectors. Chapter 6 tackles the topic of nonprofit productivity. Productivity becomes an important operational focus because the higher organizational productivity, the greater impact it can have per unit of financial and nonfinancial resources. Chapter 7 addresses performance management: How do we know when a nonprofit is doing a good job? Chapter 8 discusses the needed to create alliances with the private and public sectors.

Fundraising, the focus of chapter 9, is filled with paradoxes. We explain why fundraising is a reflection of how effective the nonprofit organization is led by the executive director, the board of directors, and the processes they put in place. Chapter 10 concludes the book by putting the third sector into perspective and addressing the issues we believe will come to dominate the concerns of nonprofit leaders in the future.

Conclusion

The private, public, and nonprofit sectors are the economic pillars on which society is built. Though their contributions to a modern economy may overlap, each faces unique strategic and operational considerations. The third sector is particularly important because it can be an incubator for ideas and societal solutions that are too limited to attract the for-profit sector and not widely enough supported to draw political attention in the government sector.

To comprehend the role and operations of the third sector requires an understanding of the strategic approach, leadership, and boards of directors. These elements are leverage points that shape nonprofits. The strategic viewpoint offers insights into the vision, mission, and strategies that nonprofits use to define themselves. The vision and mission suggest what the nonprofit is striving toward and what it hopes to achieve. The strategy suggests how the nonprofit seeks to attain its vision and mission.

How a nonprofit succeeds is strongly influenced by its stage of development. This life cycle perspective examines how the nonprofit reacts to its environment and how it addresses internal operational issues as it matures. These evolutionary perspectives affect both strategic and operation issues.

Even leadership must adapt to its circumstances. Executive directors often have to wear multiple hats—ranging from the role of a leader who defines the grand vision, to the manger who deploys resources to reach objectives, to the role of administrator who must balance the concerns and trade-offs among various constituent groups served by the nonprofit.

In a similar manner, the board of directors must adapt its approach to controlling the nonprofit. In general, the board must take an activist role at the beginning when human and financial resources are limited. As the nonprofit matures and gains capabilities, the board's role becomes increasingly advisory and evaluative.

References

Carver, J., *Boards that Make a Difference* (2nd ed.), San Francisco: Jossey-Bass, 1997.

Clolery, P., "Red Cross Gets Former NIH Chief," *The NonProfit Times* (August 1999): 1, 4.

Drucker, P., "What Businesses Can Learn from Nonprofits," *Harvard Business Review* (July–August 1989): 89–93.

Greenfeld, K. T., "A New Way of Giving," *Time* (July 24, 2000): 48–59.

Hudson, B. A., and W. Bielefeld, "Structures of Multinational Nonprofit Organizations," *Nonprofit Management & Leadership* (fall 1997): 31–48.

Maranville, S. J., "Requisite Variety of Strategic Management Modes: A Cultural Study of Strategic Actions in a Deterministic Environment," *Nonprofit Management & Leadership* (spring 1999): 277–91.

Mayntz, R., "Organizational Coping, Failure, and Success," in H. K. Anheier (ed.), *When Things Go Wrong*, Thousand Oaks, CA: Sage, 1999, pp. 71–90.

McLaughlin, T. A., "Dreams and Actions," *The NonProfit Times* (February 2000): 20.

Newcomer, K. E., *Using Performance Measurement to Improve Public and Nonprofit Programs,* San Francisco: Jossey-Bass, 1997.

Sandler, M. W., and D. A. Hudson, *Beyond the Bottom Line: How to Do More with Less in Nonprofit and Public Organizations.* New York: Oxford University Press, 1998.

Seibel, W., "Successful Failure: An Alternative View of Organizational Change," in H. K. Anheier (ed.), *When Things Go Wrong: Organizational Failures and Breakdowns*, Thousand Oaks, CA: Sage, 1999, pp. 91–105.

Sheehan, R. M., Jr., "Achieving Growth and High Quality by Strategic Intent," *Nonprofit Management & Leadership* (summer 1999): 413–28.

2

The Strategic View

A nonprofit is founded for public benefit and operates to accomplish a well-defined, articulated mission. Its programs effectively and efficiently work toward achieving that mission and it is committed to continuous quality improvement. Based on the values of quality, responsibility and accountability, nonprofit board members, volunteers, and employees act in the best interest of achieving the organization's mission at all times. (Minnesota Council of Nonprofits, 1999)

Among the thousands of business, government, and nonprofit organizations, how does a single nonprofit organization define its place? What distinguishes one nonprofit from another? How do the people inside and outside of the nonprofit organization evaluate its goals and actions? Answers to these and related questions are found in the nonprofit's mission, vision, and strategy.

Nonprofits exist to achieve a purpose. That purpose is commonly embodied in a mission statement. It tells supporters, employees, and beneficiaries of the nonprofit why it exists. A mission statement is a concise summary of what the nonprofit intends to do. A local food bank, for example, might have a mission statement as simple as "to feed hungry people in our community." The W. K. Kellogg Foundation, a major U.S. foundation, lists its mission statement as, "To help people help themselves through the practical application of knowledge and resources to improve their quality of life and that of future generations" (W. K. Kellogg Foundation homepage, www.wkkf.org). Not only does the mission statement focus the efforts of the organization on what it does, perhaps equally important it tells others what it does *not* do. In the case of the food bank, it does not provide medical care or transportation or housing for poor individuals, except as incidental to its mission to feed them. The Kellogg mission statement is so broad—as perhaps it should be for a foundation designed to help people meet unforeseen challenges—that it gives little guidance as to what it does not do.

A mission statement differs from a vision statement. A vision statement is an articulated, ennobling declaration of what the organization hopes to achieve (Hamel and Prahalad, 1993). It may have been the dream of the founder. For example, Dr. Martin Luther King summarized his vision of race relations in the United States in his famous, "I Have a Dream" speech. To take the food bank example, a vision statement might simply read, "To eliminate hunger in our community." Kellogg's vision strives toward a "common vision of a world in which each person has a sense of worth; accepts responsibility for self, family, community, and societal well-being; and has the capacity to be productive, and to help create nurturing families, responsible institutions, and healthy communities" (W. K. Kellogg Foundation homepage, www.wkkf.org).

The difference between a mission and vision statement is one of intent. The mission statement tells what the organization is going to *do*; the vision statement identifies what the organization hopes to *achieve*.

Strategy identifies how the organization is going to achieve its mission and vision. It is how the organization intends to deploy its resources to meet the needs in its environment. A local food bank may allow needy people to pick up nonperishable foods at a centralized location once a week; it may operate a 24-hour soup kitchen to feed those who show up in need; it may have a mobile food service, delivering food to elderly clients or shut-ins; or it may use a combination of these strategies to "feed hungry people."

As suggested by Figure 2-1, nonprofits operate in a "boxed canyon" of constraints. These imposed limitations narrow the strategic choices that can be used to create an effective strategy. If the strategy is effective, it furthers the mission and attains the vision within the constraints faced by the nonprofit. Constraints include resources (particularly human and financial), organizational policies (organizational dos and don'ts), and limitations imposed by the operating environment (which almost always include legal and cultural). All organizations face these same sets of constraints, with the specific limitations of each constraint varying widely among different nonprofits.

This chapter provides an overview of strategic thinking. We begin with a look at vision and why it matters in shaping the mission. Then the bulk of the chapter turns to frameworks that create and evaluate strategy. The chapter ends with a discussion of the organizational structure needed to support the nonprofit's strategy.

Figure 2-1 **Strategic Constraints on Nonprofits**

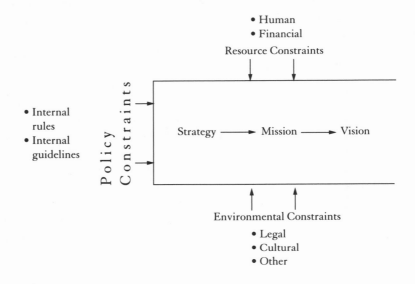

Why Vision Matters

Vision matters because it can serve as a source of inspiration and motivation for those associated with the nonprofit—including donors, employees, beneficiaries, and other constituents. Often shaped by the founders and updated by subsequent leaders, the vision can be the glue that binds people to the organization and that binds the organization itself together. As an ennobling statement of what the organization hopes to achieve, of what it hopes to be and become, the vision statement gives people an opportunity to be part of a purpose or cause that is bigger than they are. They gain status and satisfaction by being part of some noble undertaking. Donors may donate and volunteers may volunteer because they want to be associated with a noble undertaking, such as feeding hungry people. Because most nonprofits face severe resource constraints, a powerful vision statement can be an inducement that attracts resources from the community. Often fundraisers and literature describing the nonprofit draw heavily on the vision and mission to excite donors into providing financial support for the nonprofit.

As Gary Hamel and C. K. Prahalad (1993) noted, leaders shape the vision by trying to define the future that the organization should strive toward, rather than just describe the organization's most likely future. Then leaders work to control the elements of that future to ensure that they move toward the future captured by the vision. Foresight requires creativity and cleverness; implementation requires hard work. Both are needed for successful creation and pursuit of the nonprofit's vision.

Vision-Directed Mission

As discussed earlier, the vision tells what the organization hopes to be and become, and the mission states what the organization will do to achieve that vision. The purpose of the organization is to achieve its mission, of course. Achieving the mission ("feeding hungry people") moves the organization toward attaining its vision ("ending hunger"). Though the vision ("ending hunger") may be difficult or even unlikely, it serves as a guide for the mission.

Because the mission is often an overarching statement (such as "feeding hungry people"), it is operationalized by breaking it down into achievable goals and objectives. Often goals and objectives form a cascade of related targets. For example, the mission of "feeding hungry people" may give rise to a broad goal of having enough financial, human, and food resources to feed those who present themselves at the food bank's soup kitchen. This broad goal may give rise to a series of specific objectives—such as keeping a one-week supply of food at the soup kitchen, having enough staff to meet unexpected increases in new recipients, and increasing funding levels by 10 percent above the previous year's budget. No one of these objectives fulfills the mission of the organization, but each contributes toward fulfilling the broad goal of sufficient human, financial, and food resources. If each objective is met, then the broad goal ("having enough resources") is likely to be achieved. If that broad goal and others are fulfilled, then the mission would be achieved.

The aggregation of objectives into goals and goals into the mission should aim the organization in the direction of attaining its vision. At the same time, a clear mission focuses the efforts of the nonprofit. As Peter Drucker explains, nonprofits can make better use of their mission than for-profits: "Starting with the mission and its requirements may be the first lesson business can learn from successful nonprofits. It focuses the organization on action. It defines the specific strategies needed to attain crucial goals. It creates a disciplined organization" (Drucker, 1989, p. 89).

Strategic Thinking

Although a vision attempts to define what the nonprofit strives toward and the mission defines what activities it will do to get there, strategy addresses how the organization will go about its efforts (McLaughlin, 1999). As Figure 2-2 suggests, strategy seeks to match the needs in the external environment with the nonprofit's internal competencies. The external environment provides opportunities in the form of needs. All organizations exist to meet the needs of others. Nonprofits often elect to meet needs that are not addressed (or fully addressed) by the private or public sectors. There is a need in most communities to feed hungry individuals, for example. Though the government has programs to feed hungry people, nonprofits may come into existence

Figure 2-2 **Environmentally Driven Strategy Formulation**

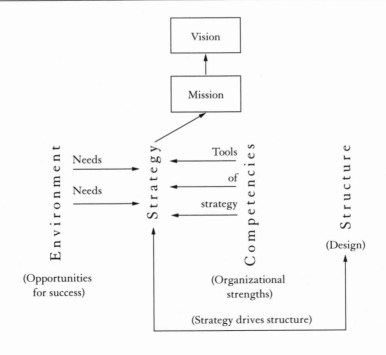

to help the government achieve its goals or simply to take care of those whom the government does not reach.

To meet these needs in the environment, nonprofit organizations develop capabilities that are often referred to as competencies. Capabilities or competencies are organizational-based strategies or abilities that become the tools or building blocks of strategy (Prahalad and Hamel, 1990). Other organizations may have similar capabilities, too, so competencies are not always unique to a particular nonprofit. However, if a nonprofit has competencies that are central to its mission and are not easily duplicated by others, these are considered core competencies. Competencies are internal capabilities; core competencies are internal capabilities that are central to the nonprofit's mission attainment and are not readily duplicated by others (Prahalad and Hamel, 1990). They are unique elements of the organization that differentiate it from other organizations. For a small neighborhood dance group, core competencies may be of little concern because such nonprofits seldom experience fierce competition with other neighborhood dance groups. However, a regional, nonprofit hospital may need to be clear about its core competencies because it competes vigorously with other health care providers. Knowing what its core competencies are can be the basis for differentiating the hospital from others, suggesting what services should be expanded or limited. For example, if the hospital runs an exceptional emergency room service that also facilitates a high census of patients in the hospital, hospital administrators may wish to strengthen this competitive advantage as they allocate financial and other resources.

Strategy attempts to match the needs in the environment (hungry people) with the nonprofit's competencies (acquiring and distributing food to needy individuals). *Competitive* strategy, as practiced among businesses or militaries, attempts to match competencies and needs in ways that give the organization a source of sustainable, competitive advantage (Barney, 1997). With nonprofits, competition among nonprofits may appear in the search for resources (especially funding) or for reputation building (particularly in providing the "best" service to constituents). In general, however, strategy among nonprofits is concerned about the most effective and efficient way of matching internal competencies with needs in the external needs. Nonprofits want to be effective (do those activities that further its mission) and efficient (do those activities with the least resources needed). Even though effectiveness and efficiency may not always be optimal, this process of matching needs with capabilities takes place within the constraints suggested by Figure 2-1.

Successful strategies do not match just any internal competencies with any external needs. Needs and competencies are matched to form strategies that are appropriate to the vision and mission of the nonprofit. Internal resources and competencies are then strengthened in an attempt to differentiate the nonprofit. Though the vision and mission formally identify the purpose of the nonprofit, strategy—how the nonprofit goes about achieving its vision and mission—helps differentiate it in the minds of its constituencies.

Few people inside or outside the organization pay much attention to the vision and mission because they are abstract. If leaders do not communicate the mission and vision to both internal and external constituents, others will fill this gap of knowledge with their own interpretations. Then instead of a common vision and mission, the nonprofit risks losing a sense of organizational purpose, cohesion, and focus as people pursue what they think the mission and vision *should* be. Even when communicated, the result can be a schism between staff and its management if pursuit of the vision and mission conflicts with the values of the staff—particularly professionals who have developed a set of values around what is right and wrong.

For example, many university leaders espouse the vision and mission to become a top regional or national institution. The vision and mission may even be widely publicized and supported. But when resources are allocated in ways that prevent professionals from doing the superior job they recognize as necessary to make their university a top school—such as cutting the library or technology budgets—the leadership may come under attack for not supporting their espoused vision and mission.

As the strategy unfolds, people notice the strategic intent of the organization is to provide a service that seems appropriate to both the internal resources and the external needs (Sheehan, 1999). What determines "appropriateness" of the strategic intent is the values that come to be associated with the organization's activities. For example, does the organization value efficiency or compassion more—or does it value both equally? Collectively, values held by the people within the organization become incorporated into the nonprofit's culture. This culture gives the organization a source of emotional cohesion in the form of shared values, which serve as a guide for what people in the organization consider "appropriate" or "right" and "wrong." Often these values are set forth in words or deeds of the founders or early leaders.

Through time, however, changing needs in the nonprofit's environment may make the strategy outdated, calling for a reformulation of the organization's vision, mission, and strategy (Rugh, 1997). Vision, mission, strategy, and environment all interact. Changes in the environment seldom lead to a change in the mission and vision of the nonprofit because the underlying need and the vision to satisfy that need seldom change. But nonprofits periodically must adapt to their changing environment by rethinking their strategy. Strategy reformulation reconsiders the organization's competencies and how they are applied to the needs addressed by the nonprofit. Whether reformulating a strategy or developing one for the first time, strategists must assess the external environment in which the nonprofit operates (Anheier, 1999).

Environmental Evaluation of Nonprofits

Nonprofits exist and operate in a larger environment. This general operating environment includes cultural, sociological, legal, technological, governmental, and regulatory dimensions. Changes in any of these dimensions can affect the vision mission, or strategy, of the nonprofit. For example, if government-enacted legislation provided guaranteed health care to all citizens, many nonprofits that exist to meet health care needs for poor individuals would need to rethink their vision, mission, and strategy. People would still need health care, so the vision and mission might change only slightly, if at all. But the strategies used to gain the needed financial resources (for example, operating a large fund-raising effort) might have to be scrapped in favor of a new department that acquired and administered federal health care funds. Periodically, typically once a year, professionally managed nonprofits need to conduct an assessment of this general environment—looking for changes in the society, economy, philanthropy, demographics, culture, technological, governmental, regulatory, or other areas that might affect the vision, mission, or strategy (Besanko, Dranove, and Shanley, 2000).

Armed with an understanding of their operating environment and its ongoing changes, strategists commonly apply SWOT (strengths, weaknesses, opportunities, and threats) analysis. SWOT analysis is a widely used framework for evaluating both the external environment in which a nonprofit operates and its internal competencies. Less sophisticated nonprofits will simply draw together key staff and board members and ask them to do this analysis based on their understanding of the organization and its environment. Best practices find sophisticated nonprofits operating by fact-based management. That is, a detailed briefing book will be compiled for those to be involved in the SWOT analysis. The briefing book will contain background research, independent surveys, and other sources of "facts" about the nonprofit and its environment.

Strengths and weaknesses are used to assess the organization. They give insights into the competencies of the nonprofit by identifying what the organization does well and not so well. Understanding strengths and weaknesses is crucial to shaping a nonprofit's strategy and resource allocation. Strategy builds on strengths, and resource allocations are used to make organizational strengths stronger. Weaknesses are not ignored. But often they are not "fixed" or strengthened because to do so does not enable the organization to better meet its mission. For example, a food bank may have a high turnover among volunteers. This turnover could be reduced, perhaps, by giving volunteers free rides to and from the food bank through use of an internally staffed bus system. Assuming a sufficient pool of volunteers, the extra expense of a bus system and driver to pick up volunteers would not substantially further the food bank's mission to feed the hungry, though it might reduce a "weakness" caused by high turnover among volunteers.

Strategic success generally relies on doing better what the organization already does well, not fixing weaknesses that may or may not be crucial to mission accomplishment. Weaknesses in the organization are monitored, but usually little is done to fix these weaknesses unless they threaten the nonprofit's ability to deliver its mission.

"Opportunities" and "threats" are found in the external environment. Opportunities are chances to further the mission of the organization. Strategic thinking seeks to identify and exploit opportunities by using the strengths found in the nonprofit's competencies (Kluyver, 1999). Consider an actual example:

> The executive director of a metropolitan food bank noticed that it rained heavily every day over the Fourth of July weekend, a holiday where many people like to plan picnics and outdoor barbecues. On Monday, the executive director called the two major bakeries in town and asked

for a donation of hot dog and hamburger buns that would be returned as unsold since few shoppers would have planned cookouts. Normally, day-old breads are used immediately because of their very limited shelf life, but the food bank had large, walk-in freezers that had been donated the previous year, so it could freeze the surplus buns and use them over the coming weeks.

The rainy weather created an opportunity for the food bank and the availability of large, walk-in freezers represented a competency that no other food bank in town had. By matching the environmental opportunity with an internal strength, the food bank was able to further its mission by meeting its objective of having sufficient food for those who needed it.

The art of strategy is matching internal competencies with external opportunities that further the mission of the nonprofit. Nonprofits can err by forgetting their mission and strategy and merely becoming opportunistic, seizing opportunities that present themselves but hold no relation to the vision, mission, or strategy of the nonprofit.

Suppose, for example, that the local government announces a sizable grant that includes capital and operating funds for one year to encourage some nonprofit to undertake the point-to-point transportation needs of the elderly individuals in the community. Because the food bank already has several panel trucks in which the seats could be reinstalled and because those trucks are only used to pick up food a small portion of their available time, a decision might be made to pursue the grant because most nonprofits are continuously looking for revenue-generating opportunities. The food bank has some capabilities (trucks) and the opportunity does exist in the environment (elderly individuals need transportation and the local government has funds).

To pursue the grant opportunity offers a source of both revenue and a way to further serve the local community. However, the transportation of people on demand presents different requirements on the nonprofit—including special licenses to transport people, new potential liabilities, expensive insurance, complex scheduling and routing needs, additional vehicle maintenance, recruitment and selection of additional drivers, and other demands.

Though each of these issues and others could be addressed and resolved, management attention and resources would be taken away from the mission of feeding hungry people. Because the nonprofit has no competencies in transporting people on demand, it might not be very effective or efficient at this new set of tasks. At the same time, this new "opportunity" might dilute the organization's effectiveness in achieving its original vision and mission of addressing hunger in the community. (On the other hand, these conflicts with the mission must be balanced by the needs of elderly individuals for transportation and the potential "public relations" benefits of greater community visibility.)

Although a nonprofit has to be opportunistic in pursuing its vision and mission, opportunism carried to an extreme that transcends the original purpose of the organization may dilute its focus, effectiveness, and its support among those inside and outside the organization. Unfocused attempts to exploit opportunities that are not bounded by the vision and mission of the organization can confuse, even discourage, those who support the nonprofit. Understanding the vision, mission, and strategy in relationship to the nonprofit's internal strengths and weaknesses is a prerequisite to developing a strategy that meets the needs and opportunities in the external environment. Armed with an understanding of these relationships and a current analysis of the external environment, leaders can plan.

Planning and Goal Setting

Nonprofits typically operate according to a predeveloped plan. Though each organization undertakes planning in a way that is uniquely suited to its history, values, and culture, most nonprofits have a one-year plan that supports longer range goals and objectives. Typically, planning begins with a reassessment of the external and internal environments, which may be ongoing or undertaken periodically (Barry, 1997). With a general environmental assessment and SWOT analysis, planners reconsider their long-term objectives for the nonprofit. Are the objectives still appropriate in light of the changing environment? Are they reasonable based on the SWOT analysis? If not, changes are made that suggest a better fit between internal competencies and environmental demands. These changes often mean that the strategy is also going to be revised to figure out how new objectives will be undertaken. If competencies fall short of what are needed, new capabilities are developed or acquired, resources permitting.

Most organizations begin with the long-term plan. They attempt to answer the question, "Where do we want to be in three (or five) years from now?" That is a tough question. It not only assumes that decision makers can approximately decide on what will be important in five years, it further assumes that a consensus exists (or can be built) around the key dimensions of that future. Even so, unexpected changes can upset even the best-conceived long-term plans.

Then working backward from that future, planners attempt to identify benchmarks or broad goals that should be targeted between now and the distant future. Ultimately they arrive at the goals that need to be undertaken during the next year. These goals become the planning premises on which other actions will depend. Specifically, each of the one-year goals is commonly broken down into supporting SMART objectives—that is, objectives that are *s*pecific, *m*easurable, *a*ction-oriented, *r*esponsible, and *t*ime targeted. *Specific* means that the objective is precise, not vague. *Measurable* assumes that others can evaluate progress toward the objective. *Action-oriented* suggests that the objective will be stated in terms of what will be done or achieved. Those who are *responsible* for achieving the objective are also identified by name, title, or group. *Time-targeted* requires that a time be associated with the completion of the objective. Ideally, the attainment of each SMART objective will result in its corresponding goal being met. If all the broad goals are met, then the nonprofit has achieved its strategy.

When each department of the nonprofit has completed its SMART objectives, these objectives usually become the basis for developing an annual budget. The allocation of monies (and other resources) force leaders to make choices. These trade-offs are seldom easy because appropriate goals and objectives often exceed available resources. Priorities must be set. Ideally, priorities are evaluated against the vision, mission, and strategy.

Goals and objectives that best further the vision, mission, and strategy are funded. Monies are assigned to each objective, and the resulting budget becomes a basic control tool for evaluating the financial and strategic progress of the nonprofit. The resulting plans—both the long-range plan and the shorter, annual one—are reviewed by the executive director and presented to the board of directors. The board reviews the long-range plans to ensure that they are compatible with the vision and mission of the organization. It scrutinizes the budget to ensure that monies will be appropriately spent. Often the board expects to see a statement of sources and uses of funds, which is a financially oriented illustration of where the nonprofit will acquire the needed funds ("sources") matched with the expenditures ("uses").

During the year, the executive director and the board review the nonprofit's progress toward achieving its stated objectives and goals. They also monitor the associated budget to ensure the fiscal soundness of the nonprofit.

These plans, budgets, goals, and objectives also serve other purposes. First, they focus the staff's and board's attention on what the nonprofit is expected to achieve and under what financial constraints. Second, these goals and objectives can be important tools for board members and others who are involved with fundraising. Not only do they point to specific activities but they also show donors the nature and amount of needed funding. Third, the process of developing the goals and plans offers an opportunity for those within the nonprofit to understand its specific aims, translated into SMART objectives with their financial implications. Fourth, plans, budgets, goals, and objectives become measurement tools with which the operational effectiveness and efficiency of the nonprofit can be gauged (Herman and Renz, 1998). If the planning process has been well-done and followed-up throughout the year, then the nonprofit will achieve its mission and move toward accomplishing its vision.

Pitfalls of Strategic Planning

Strategic planning has a variety of pitfalls that should be made explicit. First, plans are not reality; they are collective "best guesses" about what is possible. Their attainment assumes well-focused effort and an environment that acts as expected—even though environments constantly change. Changes in the environment, leadership, staffing, resources, or countless other assumptions on which the plan is based must be considered as signals to reevaluate the accuracy of the plan.

Second, the credibility of the leader and the plans comes into question if the planning process becomes little more than a document that sits on a shelf until the next planning process. The process of putting the plan together has value because it brings key decision makers together and forces them to consider the nonprofit and its relationship to the changing environment. But the time and energy to produce it are likely to be considered wasted if it is not used to guide the day to day decision-making efforts of staff and leaders. Then the subsequent year, the planning process may well be considered a sham and not evoke the insights or commitment needed to make it work. Simply put, plans and planning processes gain credibility only to the extent that they are used as an often-consulted management tool.

A third pitfall is that strategic plans are not seen as learning tools. What went right? Wrong? What objectives were achieved? Which were missed? Why? How could the planning process itself be improved? One of the innovations that the U.S. Army has included for years is called "after action reviews." After an exercise or combat mission is concluded, participants are debriefed. The purpose of the debriefing is not to find fault or place blame. Rather, the questions center on what went right and wrong and why. What can be learned that will make the organization more effective next time? Because the focus of planning is the future, decision makers seldom look back and ask, What could be learned from the last planning effort?

Leadership Roles and Decision Making

Strategy formulation and reformulation assumes leadership from the executive director and the board. The degree of board involvement depends on the sophistication of the nonprofit. As suggested in chapter 1, start-ups typically demand heavy board involvement because resources and staff are scarce. Board members may actually undertake roles (such as fundraising) that in older, better-established nonprofits are handled by staff (such as a development officer). More mature nonprofits often have internal professionals to manage the overall process and the needed details. In this instance the executive director serves to lead the process and the board serves to evaluate it. Regardless of the size or maturity of the nonprofit, board members hold the executive director responsible for the performance of the organization. They assist, advise, coach, and even replace the leader as needed.

The key function of the nonprofit's leadership is to make decisions. Decision making is at the heart of any organization (Bielefeld and Scotch, 1998). It is what leaders do. The decision-making process can be broken down into five steps. Following the steps is no assurance of a good decision. However, failing to heed the considerations listed in Figure 2-3 will almost certainly lead to an ineffective decision.

Step 1: Identify the Issue

The decision-making process begins by recognizing that a decision is needed. Though obvious, this step is crucial. Misstate the issue and

Figure 2-3 **Steps in the Decision-Making Process**

I. Identify the Issue
   A. Is it a problem or opportunity?
   B. Is it a problem or a symptom?
II. Generate Alternatives
   A. Individual versus group creativity
   B. Constituency analysis
III. Select Alternative
   A. Constructive and destructive change
   B. Rational versus emotional resistance to change
IV. Implementation
   A. SMART objectives
   B. Who? What? When? Where? Why? How?
V. Follow-up
   A. Objectives as standards
   B. Measurement
   C. Control

the remainder of the decision-making process fails. Two questions are key: Is the issue a problem or an opportunity? Is it a symptom or a problem?

Defining an issue as a problem tends to limit possibilities. Most nonprofits have insufficient funds to achieve all the goals that they would like to pursue. "If only we had more money, we could . . ." is a common refrain among leaders of nonprofits. Seeing the lack of funds as a "problem" focuses attention on how to get more funds. If, on the other hand, a lack of funds is defined as an "opportunity" to rethink the nonprofit's entire fundraising approach, attention is likely to shift from gaining more donations to how and why the nonprofit is funded.

An alternative view may be that the lack of funds is a symptom of a larger issue. Perhaps potential supporters do not fully understand the mission and vision of the nonprofit, making funding a symptom of poor communications. Perhaps the strategies to fulfill the mission and vision do not seem appropriate to potential donors, who may want more permanent solutions than simply feeding hungry people. Perhaps the methods are outdated and the lack of funds is merely a symptom of a still larger issue. If a lack of funds is a symptom of larger issues, acquiring more funds may solve the current needs but the symptom will return. In fact, the reoccurrence of a "problem" might suggest that the solutions being used are only providing temporary, symptomatic relief.

Not all problems can be viewed as opportunities; sometimes they are merely roadblocks to desired goals. In these instances problem-solving seeks to return the organization back to the same position it was in before the problem occurred. Sometimes, as with a common cold, all one can hope for is symptomatic relief until the issue returns. Exploiting opportunities, however, often suggests new alternatives for capitalizing on the issue in a way that benefits the organization. Nevertheless, how the issue is framed will strongly affect subsequent steps in the decision-making process.

Step 2: Generate Alternatives

With a clear statement of the issue, alternative solutions need to be generated. In this case, two thought processes are helpful. First, who decides—a single decision maker or those affected by the decision? Second, does the proposed solution consider those affected?

Executive directors and other leaders often see their role incorrectly as making decisions. A better perspective would be to see their role as getting decisions made. In the first case, the decision maker believes it is his or her role to generate alternatives and make a decision. In emergency situations, someone *does* need to take action, make decisions, and lead. But in most organizational decisions, life and death emergencies are rare. More often, solo decision makers believe that it is their responsibility or they fear that getting others involved may make them look indecisive. Sometimes it is simply quicker for the leader to announce the decision. Excluding true emergencies, solo decision makers deprive those affected by the decision of their involvement. In turn, this lack of involvement deprives the organization of multiple perspectives and viable, sometimes even superior, alternatives. Perhaps worse, the commitment to implementing the solution is likely to be less among those who did not participate in the decision making. Though issue identification and alternative generation may be faster with solo decision makers, the quality of the decision is likely to be lower and it is likely to encounter greater resistance to change when those affected are not involved.

Tapping the group's creativity sends several powerful messages to those inside the nonprofit. First, it says that those affected by the decision are valued for their ideas. Second, the leader is more likely to be seen as a coach or a guide rather than a dictator. Third, their involvement serves to train people in the organization about the issues being faced and the processes being used. Fourth, by creating ownership in the issue and its solution, members of the nonprofit are more likely to be committed to making the selected alternative work well.

One approach to evaluating alternatives is to do a constituency analysis. The group evaluates the advantages and disadvantages of likely alternatives from the perspective of the constituents who will be affected—how will it positively or adversely affect leaders and managers, staff, volunteers, donors, board members, beneficiaries, and the larger community? Not everyone will be happy, but this analysis seeks to determine which alternatives do the most good and the least harm.

Step 3: Alternative Selection

At some point a decision must be made from among the relevant alternatives. Those options that do not address the issue or do so in a way that is unacceptable to a key constituency are typically eliminated. In picking an alternative, decision makers need to be aware that changes can be constructive, destructive, and sometimes both. Decisions imply change. Change typically destroys previously created systems, relationships, or implied bargains. Those who found previous ways comfortable may feel uncomfortable and resist the decision actively or passively. Resistance to change can sink an otherwise good alternative. In making the final selection of an alternative, decision makers must consider the likelihood of resistance to change. If participative decision making was used and constituency analysis was applied, resistance may be significantly lessened. But resistance may be likely nevertheless.

Particularly difficult for board members, executive directors, managers, and others to understand is that the resistance to change may not be rational. When change affects feelings, emotional reactions may be "arational"—that is, resistance may be based on factors other than reason. Explaining the "reasons" for the change, the need for the change, the logic behind the change, the benefits of the change, or other seemingly rational approaches may fail.

People live in a world based on assumptions. Change violates our assumptive world, creating uncertainty, even anxiety. Emotional reactions often ensue following a violation of our assumptive world. It may be easier to constructively or destructively attack the decision as wrong or inappropriate rather than submit to the needed change. Decision makers may compound this problem by reacting to emotional concerns with logical responses. Those with emotional concerns then view the "logical" responses as uncaring, often because they feel unheard. Many managers react to an employee's emotional plea with, "Yes, but we need to make this change because. . . ." The affected person is seeking reassurances and confirmation of their emotional concerns, not additional reasons why the decision is needed.

Step 4: Implement the Decision

Successful implementation depends on objectives to pursue and plans to get there. The need for SMART objectives helps ensure that the decision is implemented. Objectives become benchmarks that provide direction for those who need to take action, and they serve as standards against which progress can be measured.

In developing the SMART objectives and plans for implementation, thought needs to be given to the newspaper reporter's questions: *Who* will be responsible for the implementation? *What* will they do? *When* will they begin and finish? *Where* do they need to begin and end? Are those affected clear about *why* this decision is being implemented? *How* will those who are responsible undertake this implementation?

Step 5: Follow Up on the Decision

A key question in the decision-making process is, How do we know that the solution that was implemented solved the problem? This last step in the decision-making process is the control function. It compares the standards created as part of the SMART objectives with the results of the implementation. Did the solution implemented exploit the opportunity or solve the problem? If the answer is yes, the decision did solve the issue identified in step 1, then the decision-making process was a success.

For important decisions, some managements will undertake a review to learn what went right and what went wrong. What can be learned from the issue and its resolution? As mentioned previously, the U.S. Army calls these after action reviews. They are considered a powerful form of action that helps those involved learn about the decisions leading up to an action and their implications in hopes of improving decision making in the future.

If the decision failed to resolve the issues identified in the first step of the decision-making process, leaders need to repeat the decision-making process.

Strategy and Structure

Returning to Figure 2-2, strategy relies on a careful evaluation of the nonprofit's operating environment (Maranville, 1999). Because the environment embraces demographic, technological, economic, social, political, legal, and other changes, it is dynamic. As these changes occur, the relative importance of the nonprofit's competencies change. Some competencies may become more useful, whereas others fade in importance. New competencies must be developed internally or acquired from others. Strategy, which seeks to blend these competencies into a coherent approach to achieving the nonprofit's mission, must also change to adapt to the changing environment.

Periodically, the leadership of the nonprofit must undertake a reevaluation of the external environment, internal competencies, and how they are blended into a strategy. This strategy reformulation process is typically done once a year or in response to sudden, unanticipated, and significant changes in the nonprofit's environment or its competencies. For example, if a major donor stopped supporting the nonprofit or if the executive director quit, a reassessment of the nonprofit's strategy might be in order.

Because strategy is built on competencies, the nonprofit must strengthen its competencies—especially its core competencies. In general, competencies are developed internally or acquired from the external environment. Internal competencies are created or strengthened by devoting resources to their development. In the case of the local food bank, for example, they may use their funds to train staff or volunteers, giving them new capabilities that add to its people-based competence. Or systems and procedures may be upgraded, making the food bank more efficient or effective in achieving its mission.

When the nonprofit's environment is turbulent, leading to rapid or unanticipated changes, nonprofits often need to acquire competencies from outside the organization. The need for the external acquisition of competencies is explained by the need for speed. In a rapidly changing environment, the need for additional competencies may arise so fast that the nonprofit does not have the time to develop these competencies internally.

Core competencies—which are both essential to the mission of a nonprofit and not readily developed by others—are strengthened on an ongoing basis. Knowing which capabilities are central to the success of the organization helps leaders set priorities. It tells them what activities or abilities are more or less important than others. For example, the food bank must maintain accounting records of its funds. However, accounting is not a core competency; it is not central to its mission of providing food to the hungry. Because accounting is not a core function, the food bank may decide to minimize the resources expended on accounting so it has more resources to pursue its mission.

The structure of the nonprofit is designed to support its strategy (Shoichet, 1998). The form (structure) of the nonprofit follows its function (strategy). Because most nonprofits are concerned about the financial well-being and because many conduct the same general activities year in and year out, most nonprofits are organized functionally—that is, the structure of the nonprofit is clustered into departments in which each person in the department does similar work, such as accounting, public relations, and the like (refer back to Figure 1-1). This functional design is generally considered to be efficient in day to day operations because it takes advantage of specialization within each function. However, a functional design can be resistant to change—especially changes that cut across multiple functions—because each functional area views the impact of change from different perspectives (Jaques, 1989).

Another approach to ensuring efficient resource use is to question whether the nonprofit should undertake certain activities or contract them out to others. This contracting-out decision is commonly referred to as the make-or-buy analysis, which evaluates the costs associated with performing a noncore function or activity and compares those costs with contracting the activity to others outside the nonprofit.

Make-or-buy depends on the relative costs. Sometimes an outside firm can perform the function both better and cheaper because of greater specialization, superior technology, or some other advantage. For example, many large nonprofits do not produce their own payroll checks. Though this activity is crucial to the employees, the production of payroll checks is not central to the mission of the American Red Cross, for example. If outside vendors can produce these checks and make direct deposits to employee checking accounts more efficiently than the American Red Cross, then it would be foolish for this charitable organization to perform this noncore activity. This same logic applies to janitorial services, building maintenance, accounting, and other activities.

The tactic of applying make-or-buy analysis can affect the structure of the nonprofit. Not only are individual activities subject to make-or-buy analysis, but entire functions can be evaluated on the same basis. Should the local food bank do its own accounting? The accounting needs to be done, of course, but the question is can the food bank contract this work to others cheaper than it can do so internally? If the answer is yes, then this noncore activity may be contracted to a local accounting firm. (Because the local accounting firm may be willing to charge subsidized rates or even undertake this responsibility for free, many nonprofits find that contracting out noncore functions can be cost-effective, leaving more resources with which to pursue their missions.)

In advanced economies with considerable business support services available, more and more organizations are contracting out noncore functions. Not only does this lead to financial economies, it allows leaders to focus more directly on the mission. The impact on structure is to "hollow out" traditional functions and activities. The result can be hollow organization that is missing some of the functions found in Figure 1-1. The key is to get needed functions and activities done appropriately at the lowest cost.

Conclusion

The vision and the mission of a nonprofit serve as guidelines to those inside and outside the organization. Vision expresses an ennobling statement of what the organization is trying to achieve; mission tells what the organization is trying to do. They are important not only to provide guidance but to attract supporters to the nonprofit's goals.

Strategy attempts to weld the capabilities and competencies of the organization into a coherent approach to meet the needs in the nonprofit's environment. Because the environment changes constantly, capabilities, competencies, and strategy need to be reviewed periodically, usually once a year.

The reformulation process includes a careful evaluation of the external environment, in which planners seek opportunities to exploit and threats to guard against. Opportunities, ideally, are within the scope of the organization's mission and vision, so that pursuit of opportunities does not distract leaders from the purpose of the nonprofit. Internally, the assessment includes identifying strengths and weaknesses. The strengths are used to exploit the opportunities in the environment. Weaknesses such as outdated equipment are monitored, with little action needed unless they actively threaten the organization. The result is a strategy that uses the strengths of its internal capabilities and competencies to exploit the opportunities in its external environment.

Planning and goal setting follow. Long-term plans are based on achieving long-term goals. These goals are broken down into SMART objectives and subobjectives, paralleling the organization's structure. If the objectives are achieved major goals are accomplished. If these broad goals are met, then the organization's strategy proves successful in achieving the mission of the nonprofit.

Although strategy seeks to ensure that the organization is effective, efficiency matters, too. As a result, most nonprofits are organized to support the strategy around a functional design that takes advantage of specialization. More and more organizations are finding that the rigid application of make-or-buy analysis to their functions and activities sometimes leads to savings by contracting work to others who are more efficient at a particular task. When this occurs among noncore competencies, the result can be a hollow organization design in which the traditional activities of the nonprofit are missing and contracted to others.

References

Anheier, H. K. (ed.), *When Things Go Wrong: Organizational Failures and Breakdowns,* Thousand Oaks, CA: Sage, 1999.

Barney, J. B., *Gaining and Sustaining Competitive Advantage,* New York: Addison-Wesley, 1997.

Barry, B. W., *Strategic Planning Workbook for Nonprofit Organizations, Revised and Updated,* Saint Paul, MN: Wilder, 1997.

Besanko, D., D. Dranove, and M. Shanley, *Economics of Strategy*, New York: John Wiley, 2000.

Bielefeld, W., and R. K. Scotch, "The Decision-Making Context and Its Impact on Local Human Service Nonprofits," *Nonprofit Management & Leadership* (9, no. 1, 1998): 53–70.

Drucker, P. "What Business Can Learn from Nonprofits," *Harvard Business Review* (July–August 1989): 89.

Hamel, G., and C. K. Prahalad, "Strategy as Stretch and Leverage," *Harvard Business Review* (March–April 1993): 76–84.

Herman, R. D., and D. O. Renz, "Nonprofit Organizational Effectiveness: Contrasts between Especially Effective and Less Effective Organizations," *Nonprofit Management & Leadership* (9, no. 1, 1998): 23–38.

Jaques, E., *Requisite Organization*: *The CEO's Guide to Creative Structure and Leadership,* Arlington, VA: Cason Hall, 1989.

W. K. Kellogg, homepage, available at http://www.wkkf.org/WhoWeAre/default.htm#mission (2000).

Kluyver, C. A. *Strategic Thinking: An Executive Perspective*, Upper Saddle River, NJ: Prentice-Hall, 1999.

Maranville, S. J., "Requisite Variety of Strategic Management Modes: A Cultural Study of Strategic Actions in a Deterministic Environment," *Nonprofit Management & Leadership* (9, no. 3, 1999): 277–91.

McLaughlin, T. A., "Elements of Strategy," *The NonProfit Times* (April 1999): 20, 22.

Minnesota Council of Nonprofits, Committee on Nonprofit Standards, *Principles & Practices for Nonprofit Excellence,* available at http://www.mncn.org/pnp_doc.nun (March 30, 1999), p. 4.

Prahalad, C. K., and G. Hamel, "The Core Competence of the Corporation," *Harvard Business Review* (May–June 1990): 80–91.

Rugh, T. E., "Remissioning Nonprofits: Two Case Studies of Membership Associations," *Nonprofit Management & Leadership* (7, no. 3, 1997): 305–15.

Sheehan, R. M., Jr., "Achieving Growth and High Quality by Strategic Intent," *Nonprofit Management & Leadership* (9, no. 4, 1999): 413–28.

Shoichet, R., "An Organization Design Model for Nonprofits," *Nonprofit Management & Leadership* (9, no. 1, 1998): 71–88.

3

Board Development

Nonprofits fill needs not otherwise addressed by for-profits or government (Alexander and Weiner, 1998). As a result, nonprofits are given tax-exempt status under the expectation that they will operate in the public interest. It is the responsibility of the board of directors (sometimes called the board of trustees or board of governors) to ensure that the nonprofit operates in the public interest. Although the board does not own the assets of the nonprofit, the members are the custodians of these assets that are held in trust for the public good.

Boards of directors are the ultimate authority in nonprofit organizations. The members are responsible for the success or failure of the nonprofit's vision, mission, and strategies. They govern the nonprofit directly through their decisions and indirectly though their advisory efforts. Practically, however, the board typically hires an executive director or president of the nonprofit and delegates to him or her operational responsibility for the success of the organization. A narrow interpretation of the board's activities would suggest the board is responsible for hiring, evaluating, and replacing the president or executive director. In practice, the involvement of the board varies with the history, maturity, and resources of the organization and the board members' personal preferences (Carver, 1997). The organization of the board varies because of tradition, a nonprofit's unique operating or mission characteristics, or requirements of the nonprofit's bylaws. The National Center for Nonprofit Boards in Washington, D.C., is the leading source of information about the variations in board activism, involvement, and organization.

This chapter addresses the role that boards of directors fill in nonprofit organizations. The next chapter will focus on the role of the executive director as the chief executive officer of the nonprofit. The following chapter will examine staffing, along with the role of staff and volunteers.

Board Responsibilities

Besides hiring, evaluating, and replacing the executive director, boards create policy and review performance. Policies serve as guidelines for the organization. They are constraints needed to focus the organization toward the results deemed appropriate by the board. In setting policy, the board needs to consider multiple constituencies. Constituency (or stakeholder) analysis seeks to identify those parties who will be affected by the board's policymaking actions. Typically, constituents include the executive director, staff, clients, donors, the larger community in which the nonprofit operates, and the board itself. Often conflicts exist among these stakeholders so that a policy deemed necessary by one group maybe be seen as inappropriate, or even wrong, by another. For example, board members often want the executive director to spend more time, money, and other resources on public relations, giving the nonprofit greater community visibility. Although this in-creased visibility may enhance the stature of those who are on the board and build wider support among the community, public relations activities cannot be allowed to consume time, talent, and other re-sources to such an extent that the mission or vision of the nonprofit is impaired.

Although the executive director, staff, and others should be sensi-tive to differing perspectives, disagreements still arise. If the board is insensitive to potential conflicts, such conflicts may erupt into a schism that splits the board and its support. Even when the board is united, it can undermine the nonprofit if the board's wishes cause the nonprofit to drift from its vision, mission, and strategy. Board decisions may be particularly damaging because it is the final arbiter of policy. There is no appeal, unless the board does something that is illegal.

The board also must review the performance of the nonprofit. Its evaluation of the executive director's performance as the leader of the organization is essential to ensuring that goals and objectives are attained within the policies set forth by the board. Simply put, the board serves as a "check-and-balance" on the performance of those within the organization for which the board is responsible (Howe, 1997).

Constituent-sensitive policies and performance reviews are two activities that the board must undertake. Nevertheless, there are a variety of other responsibilities that boards generally assume. It is responsible for periodically reviewing the vision, mission, and strategies of the organization. Though reformulation of these issues may be left to staff, with or without board involvement, the board ultimately must approve these key policy-oriented proposals. Likewise, the executive director and staff may develop goals and support budgets; undertake large purchases; and propose hiring plans, pay raises, benefits, or other human resource policies that are generally subject to board approval.

Board Involvement

Beyond policy and evaluation responsibilities, boards undertake a wide variety of activities. The scope of these activities varies from organization to organization. In general, however, the maturity of the nonprofit and the activism of individual board members are major determinants of the board's involvement (Sandler and Hudson, 1998).

As presented in Table 1-3 nonprofit organizations evolve through three stages: formation, growth, and maturity. In the formation or start-up phase, the board tends to be a working board with hands-on involvement. Limited resources—particularly financial and human—are offset, at least partially, by the active involvement of board members in fundraising, personnel decisions, operations, and other activities. It is not unusual for board members to actually perform duties that would typically be done by staff members in larger, better established nonprofits. As the organization grows, board members take a more managerial role through involvement in committees, working side by side with staff and the executive director. Although some hands-on involvement remains—especially in fundraising—board members begin to evolve toward a more advisory and evaluative role, providing ideas and recommendations rather than actually performing duties that are left to staff. By the time the nonprofit becomes a mature organization, the board is usually better described as advisory. Completed staff work is more common, with the board only needing to review and approve. Involvement is less because the resources available enable most activities to be handled by staff, leaving the board in more traditional advisory and evaluative roles.

Another driver of board member involvement is individual expectations and personalities. Most board members realize that they are on the board to "give, get, or do." That is, a board member is expected to make a donation of monies (or in-kind services), solicit resources on behalf of the nonprofit, or perform some needed function. For example, many wealthy people are asked to serve on a board in the expectation that as they come to understand and identify with the vision and mission, they will be likely to make sizable donations. Others are nominated for board membership because they can obtain resources for the nonprofit, even though they may not actually give their own monies. For example, executives of local firms may be asked to join because their firms have a foundation or marketing budget that can be a source of funding. They may have their in-house print shops produce free programs and brochures for the nonprofit as well. Also, having executives on the board makes membership attractive to those who want to interact with them in hopes of obtaining business from the executives' companies. Thus lawyers, accountants, or others who might potentially supply goods or services want to get to know executives in hopes of becoming vendors to the firm. Still others may be invited to join the board because they have special expertise, such as law, accounting, public relations, or marketing. Their role is to "do" for the nonprofit what otherwise would cost the nonprofit money to have done. For example, many accountants on boards serve as the controller, maintaining the nonprofit's books in lieu of making or getting donations of money (Levy, 1999).

Personalities of individual board members combine with the expectations of the nonprofit to determine the activities with which the board becomes involved. Some members are activists, others are more passive. Some people serve on a large number of boards, feeling that all they need to do is show up and lend their name to the organization and make (or get) donations. Others believe that unless they are personally informed and involved in every major decision, they are sidestepping their responsibilities. A good board is likely to be a blend of both kinds of member. If everyone was an activist, the demands on the executive director and staff for information and involvement could be overwhelming to the point of being counterproductive. Conversely, if all board members merely showed up and had little involvement, advice and assistance when needed would be difficult to obtain without adding additional staff or outside consultants, both of which are expensive and time consuming. As the president of the Center for Public Skills Training suggests about board leaders (Martinelli, 1998, p. 12):

- They are visionary and future focused.
- They possess entrepreneurial spirit.
- They are risk takers.
- They are good communicators.
- They are system thinkers.
- They find course of action that will exert the highest possible leverage.
- They discover creative ways to connect their organizations to the world around them.
- They value diversity.

Too often leadership of mature nonprofits finds the board chair looking to the executive director for leadership. Though that expectation of the executive director is fair, it does not exempt the board—especially the board chair—from exerting visionary leadership.

Structured Board Involvement

To focus the involvement of the board and board members, most nonprofits establish board committees (Herman, Renz, and Heimovics, 1997). Commonly, these include development (fundraising), marketing or public relations, compensation, human resources, and nominating committees, as shown in Figure 3-1. (Other committees may be formed that are unique to the particular nonprofit, such as an ethics committee at a nonprofit hospital or an athletic committee at a private university.) The reason for forming these committees is to engage the board members in these important activities (Shoichet, 1998).

In the formulation stage, committees may not yet exist, or if they do a single board member is the entire "committee." As working boards evolve into managing boards during the growth stage, the committee typically includes the head of the functional area (such as the chief development officer), one or more board members who have an interest or expertise, and the executive director along with any other staff deemed appropriate. In the mature stage, the committee structure will look much the same, with the burden of preparing for the committee meetings and achieving the goals of the committee shifting from the board members to the staff. At this stage, the board member's role is largely advisory and evaluative, serving as a communication linkage to the board.

Figure 3-1 **Traditional Committee Structure of Nonprofits**

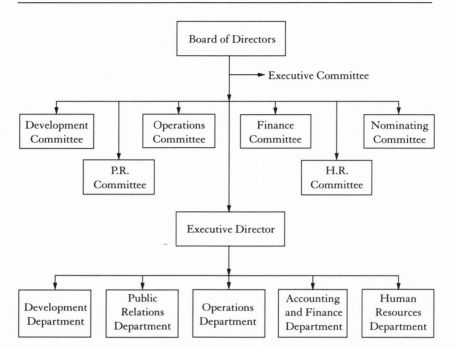

Each of the committees exists to oversee the operations of their corresponding functional area. The human resource committee of the board, for example, establishes the broad human resource policies under which the nonprofit deals with staff. It then reviews proposed personnel policies, promotions, terminations, and related human resource matters in varying degrees of detail, depending on the traditions of the organization and its level of sophistication. Major operational decisions—such as purchasing a costly piece of equipment or significant changes in future activities of the nonprofit—are reviewed by the operations committee. The public relations committee of the board is the vehicle by which the board shapes the public image of the nonprofit. This image is crucial to recruiting new board members and staff and to raising funds. The finance committee concerns itself with the all-important cash flow, income, and expenses of the nonprofit. Nonprofits often seek a board member who has professional expertise in this area, usually someone who works with a local accounting firm or holds a high-level corporate position in this area.

The development committee is a euphemism for the fundraising committee. Most nonprofits face more demands on their resources than their limited funds can address. Thus there is often a sense of urgency, even desperation, about the need for more funds. There just never seems to be enough money to do all the things that the board, executive director, and staff deem appropriate. This lack of resources is particularly acute in new nonprofits or those that have not been able to secure dedicated sources of funds through established fundraising events or reliable appropriations from endowments, governments, corporations, wealthy individuals, or philanthropic organizations (Saidel and Harlan, 1998). Often, an informal rule—seldom stated— is that the successful chair of the board's development committee is considered next in line to become chair-elect of the full board.

Board members' efforts are a blend of hands-on contributions and sharing expert knowledge or providing contacts related to the objectives of each department. Two exceptions to this pattern are the executive committee and the nominating committee.

The executive committee is a subcommittee of the entire board. When a nonprofit has a large board, frequent meetings may be cumbersome and difficult to arrange. Moreover, there may be people on the board who are there because of their names or contributions but who add little else to the policy, advice, and evaluative activities of the board. In fact, some nonprofits have huge boards consisting of people who are largely inactive but kept on the board because they contribute. Simply put, a large board of 20, 30, or more members may be more indicative of the fundraising strategy of the nonprofit than its governance structure.

Needed is a subset of the board authorized to take action, so an executive committee of the board is created to oversee the business of the nonprofit between board meetings of the full board. It typically consists of the chair of the board, the executive director, and the heads of each board subcommittee. Depending on the bylaws of the nonprofit, the executive committee's powers to act may be limited to specified emergency situations (such as approving expenditures not previously budgeted).

Because members of the executive committee are active, involved board members, they have a strong—often decisive—say in shaping key policy decisions. For example, the chronic lack of funds to undertake all activities within the nonprofit's mission means priorities must be set. The executive committee addresses the prioritization of issues, either deciding the priorities for the nonprofit or making recommendations that are likely to be approved by the full board.

The purpose of the nominating committee is to identify and evaluate potential board members for nomination to the full board of directors. It typically consists of the past board chair, the current chair, and the executive director. Others, because of their insights or contacts, also may be included. In most nonprofits, the nominating committee is ad hoc, convening once or twice immediately before new board nominations are needed. Among more sophisticated and mature boards, the nominating committee is a standing committee that meets throughout the year to discuss potential board additions. Prospective board members are preliminarily evaluated as to their likely contributions—such as time, money, in-kind, or skills. Then the top prospects may be approached to learn of their potential interest in joining the board. For the very wealthy and hard-to-get community leaders, for example, they may be courted with facility tours, invitations to cocktail receptions, or treated as guests at other events of the nonprofit for months or even years.

When boards have fixed terms with mandatory term limits, new members are typically added each year. Although the exact duration of the term limits varies according to the board's bylaws and articles of incorporation, it is common for each member to be elected by the full board for a period of three years, perhaps with the possibility of being renominated for additional terms. Then, with staggered terms, about one third of the members needs to be replaced or renominated each year, if the bylaws specify mandatory term limits. The staggered terms provide both continuity (because two thirds of the members of the board are experienced and familiar with the nonprofit) and "fresh blood" (new people with, presumably, new ideas and energy).

Without term limits and mandatory rotation, the board can become stagnant, lacking new directions and eagerness to make needed changes. Exceptions in mandatory term limits are typically made for the chair-elect, current chair, and the immediate past chair. Thus once a board member becomes chair-elect, she or he is exempt from the term limits until having moved through the chairs and completed a year as past chair. This exception helps ensure an orderly transition of leadership, continuity, and backup should anything happen to the current chair.

A final part of the committee structure among long-lasting non-profits is often informal, not appearing on the official organization chart. It consists of past chairs of the group and, perhaps, the founder. Among academic-oriented nonprofits, for example, these people are called "Fellows." In other nonprofits they may be referred to as honorary chairs or the "leadership council." This exclusive "committee" is a means of keeping past leaders in contact with the nonprofit so that their insights, contacts, and resources are not lost. Though they typically have no defined duties, they are valuable to the board and executive director because they are a source of the history of the organization. They know how previous problems were solved. In times of crisis they can be rallied to come to the aid of the nonprofit with ideas, help, and even funds.

With board members serving on committees, the structure keeps the board informed of the nonprofit's efforts. It also exposes staff members to the board so that pay, promotion, and other human resource recommendations can be better understood. Informed board members are better able to perform both their evaluative and advisory functions. Of course, this design does have the potential drawback of undermining the executive director's authority. As one executive director observed,

> Occasionally, when I make a decision that impacts a particular department, the department head will use his or her involvement on the board committee to re-argue my decision with a member of the board. Though I have admonished the board to avoid taking sides on these issues, occasionally a board member will agree with a department head and then I am put in a difficult position. These "end-arounds" are like watching a child shop a decision between mother and father. It sure does undermine my authority.

Board Evaluation

An evaluation of the current board members is kept by the executive director and reviewed by the nominating committee. This information allows for a rational approach to prospective committee assignments and to potential board leaders. It also allows members of the nominating committee to approach other board members about their role and contributions. Figure 3-2 suggests likely areas in which board members are evaluated. The Miami City Ballet, for example, assigns points to

Figure 3-2 **Board Evaluation Criteria**

Criteria	Actual (Prospective) Board Members							
	Adams	Baker	Cava	Delany	Emerson	Finly	Gaven	Harris
Financial contribution (potential) Direct— Raised—								
In-kind contribution (potential)								
Skills contribution (potential)								
Available contacts (potential)								
Leadership (potential)								
Attendance at board meetings								
Ability to attract other board members (potential)								
Other contributions								
Overall value to board (points)								

Key: 1—Low score; 5—high score.

each item of evaluation, requiring a minimum predetermined score for a member to be renominated to the board (Newcomer, 1997).

Most nonprofits face a seemingly endless demand on their often limited resources. Thus the need for funding is typically a high priority in deciding who should be kept (or added) to a board of directors. Although access to unrestricted funds via contributions are most attractive, whether made as a donation by board members or raised by them, in-kind contributions are highly valued too. These may include accounting services, use of company facilities to hold meetings, or other assistance. Likewise, a public relations expert on the board may offer his or her skills in lieu of (or in addition to) the nonprofit's in-house public relations capabilities. Personal contacts, the ability to attract others to the board, leadership skills (that may lead to board chair or other leadership positions within the nonprofit), and even attendance at meetings are all criteria considered in evaluating board members.

Whether applied to current or prospective board members, the executive director and the nominating committee need objective and systematically collected information with which to evaluate board seats. Collecting and evaluating this information, along with the need to identify potential board members and leaders, strongly argues for a standing nominating committee—particularly in large, multifaceted nonprofits. Otherwise, board selection and retention is based too often on subjective criteria of personality, friendliness, and status rather than on meaningful contribution.

Board Recruitment

Nonprofit organizations are created with the expectation that they will last in perpetuity. The purpose for which the nonprofit was formed may disappear, as would be the case if a nonprofit hospital was sold to a for-profit hospital chain or if the disease for which the nonprofit was formed was cured. Nevertheless, when a nonprofit is created it is assumed that the organization will perpetuate itself. Central to that process is renewing the board (Kile and Loscavio, 1996).

As mentioned earlier, board members are typically elected for a fixed term as specified in the bylaws. Even if the bylaws allow renomination to the board for second or subsequent terms, people leave and must be replaced. At this point, board recruitment becomes a crucial activity in the survival of the board and the organization.

Board recruitment involves identifying, evaluating, and soliciting potential board members. Some boards—particularly those for new or low-prestige nonprofits—must be opportunistic. That is, they cannot be too selective and need to get the best board members they can attract. More established or prestigious boards can be more selective. In either case, the executive director and the nominating committee need to be clear in what they are looking for in a prospective board member. Do they want a "name" to enhance the prestige of the board? Are they looking for someone who will bring money or in-kind resources to the board? Are they looking for someone with specific technical or leadership talents?

The easy answer for most boards would be "all of the above." Realistically, however, the executive director and the nominating committee can be compared to a coaching staff trying to recruit new players from the annual college draft. The nonprofit needs to know what specific needs are most important. Although an "all-of-the-above" answer might be accurate, seldom is a board able to recruit a person who fills multiple board needs. The smaller, less prestigious the board, the more likely that the nonprofit will need every type of board member. At the same time, a prestigious board is likely to have fewer needs and those needs are easier to fulfill.

Clear on what roles the prospective board members will need to fulfill, the identification of potential members begins. Some of the characteristics that might be sought among prospects are the time, willingness, and enthusiasm to serve. Initially, many ideal candidates will plead a lack of time or willingness. Their pleas are likely to be truthful, because this type of board nominee is likely to have limited time and even a limited willingness. Nevertheless, successful people who ultimately agree are likely to honor their commitment willingly and are likely to find the time needed to serve. In part, their initial reluctance is part of the "courting ritual"; the prospect wants to find out how desired he or she is. If they do not feel truly needed and wanted, they may decline the offer to serve. Other desired characteristics include knowledge of the organization; knowledge of how nonprofit boards work; and their personal or professional knowledge, skills, abilities, resources, and contacts (Kile and Loscavio, 1996).

The nominating committee is ostensibly responsible for matching board needs with potential talent. In reality the job often falls to the executive director, especially when the nominating committee is ad hoc and not a standing committee. The risk is that those asked to join the board by the executive director may feel loyalty to him or her. This loyalty may compromise a board member's willingness to critically evaluate the executive director's performance.

Though the nominations to the board generally occur only once year, the executive director or the standing nominating committee identify potential community leaders throughout the year through their personal and business contacts as well as via suggestions by board members, staff, or self-nominations. Another fruitful source is active volunteers who support the nonprofit's projects but who are not yet on the board. They may be further evaluated by asking them to serve on board committees before actually asking them to serve on the board. These candidates have shown through their behavior that they are committed to the mission of the nonprofit. Carried to an extreme, where many board members are recruited from volunteers, the composition of the board may not be what is needed. As one author observed,

> Notice that with this method, which is not uncommon, the board is designed to be composed of people recruited by staff for their ability to perform staff work. Such a design raises questions. For example:
>
> - Is board work the same as staff work?
> - Is ability at staff work a good predictor of ability at board work?
> - Is it possible that there are people who would be good board members who are not available to the board through this recruitment method?
> - Is it possible that staff may be deprived of good volunteers by virtue of the co-option by the board? (Carver, 1998, p. 47)

Other proactive recruiting approaches might include contacting the community relations or public relations departments of major organizations in the community. Large corporations, government agencies, universities, religious, and other organizations often have a pool of potential leaders who may be interested in active community involvement with a nonprofit. Likewise for professional firms, such as law, accounting, consulting, advertising, marketing, and others who may see board involvement as a source of community visibility and potential client contacts. Professional and trade associations are often willing to take on "good causes" by providing talent and potential leadership. Local area optometrists, for example, might be willing to volunteer one morning a month at a low-income health clinic or the head of the local professional organization may be interested in serving on the board of the clinic.

New arrivals in town—such as executives, professionals, or their spouses—may be a productive source of potential recruits. Although little is known about these people, they may see an opportunity to be on a nonprofit board as a way of getting involved in their new community. Even existing community leaders who serve the constituency—such as doctors or other professionals—may be interested in taking their personal efforts and uniting with an existing nonprofit that serves the same population.

Another source of potential leaders is among other volunteer organizations. People who are active in the local chamber of commerce, church or school fundraising efforts, or other civic groups may also have an interest in working with a different nonprofit, particularly if they are attracted to the nonprofit's vision and mission. A particularly good source of energetic talent is often found among committee chairs in community groups. Often these are the people who become the future "names" among community leaders, and they are interested in the chance to make a mark.

Soliciting prospects to join the board often involves more than just asking potential recruits. "Frequent problems arise because board members' expectations and responsibilities often are not clearly defined" (Green, 1997). Passive board members might be honored merely to be on the board and the nonprofit may be glad simply to have a high-visibility board member. But active, involved board members want to know what is expected of them. They may have to be sold on joining, especially those who are the most attractive prospects and who already may have multiple commitments. Simply put, those involved with board recruitment must be able to answer the question, Why should I join? Potential board members have questions, such as:

- What is expected of board members?
- How do you see me fitting in?
- How much time will I be expected to spend at meetings and on board matters?
- What skills are needed on the board?
- What fundraising responsibilities will I have?
- What types of legal actions are outstanding against the organization?

Though persuasive arguments can (and should) be made at the time the potential board member is solicited to join, most people will want to think about the nature of the commitment and the nature of the nonprofit. Needed are take-away materials that further sell the idea of joining the board through information about the nonprofit.

A board recruitment package comprises persuasive materials that argue the benefits *and* responsibilities of joining the particular nonprofit board. This package of materials should include a statement of the nonprofit's vision and mission. Sponsors and sources of donations might also be provided. The package would likely identify other board members and senior staff, along with providing brief biographical information and even telephone numbers for each person. Marketing brochures (or descriptive excerpts from grant applications), listings of upcoming activities, and programs of recent fundraising or performance events also may be included. Although bylaws, articles of incorporation, planning documents, budgets, other financial statements, and job descriptions of senior staff may all be relevant, they may be too ponderous, even overwhelming to be included in the first set of materials given a prospective board member. Besides these documents might make a good justification for follow-up contact or correspondence with the prospect.

Responsibilities of board members must also be discussed. The types of people one would want on a board are not stupid; they realize that they are being asked for a reason and that they will have to meet some expectations. Better to spell out those expectations at the beginning so neither party wastes further time or resources if the match is not a good one. Included would be expectations about "giving, getting, or doing" on the board. Are there financial expectations that one will contribute or raise a given amount of funds? What roles would a prospective board member play on the board? How often and how long does the board meet?

Orienting and Integrating New Board Members

Though the executive director and the nominating committee need to be diligent in identifying, evaluating, and soliciting potential board members, the job does not end with a "Yes, I will serve." Merely having someone on the board is not the goal. The goal is to have appropriately productive, energetic, and involved board members who will function effectively in advising and evaluating the nonprofit's performance. This means that the new board members must be oriented and integrated into the board. As one scholar observed,

> My research into 16 nonprofit social service organizations indicates that boards of directors and the Chief Professional Officer (CPO) should be more involved in board development including efforts to recruit board members, train them, evaluate the board's performance, and set specific duties for the board. Typically this training consists of a meeting with the executive director, a review of a packet of

information such as the bylaws and minutes of prior meetings, and a tour.

Many board members did not recognize that they had received any training. (Green, 1997, pp. 60–61)

Orientation of new board members involves explaining the vision, mission, strategies, and operations of the nonprofit. Unfortunately, these issues often seem obvious to senior staff and existing board members because they are intimately familiar with the nonprofit. As a result, the orientation of new board members tends to be nonexistent or superficial at best. Besides a formal, staff-driven orientation, one or two members of the board (presumably members of the nominating committee who want their latest recommendation to be successful) need to take the new board member in hand. That is, the new member should be teamed up with a "buddy" who gives the needed insights behind the formal orientation to make the new member feel like a part of the nonprofit.

Then quickly after joining the board, the new member should be put to work. For a new board member to feel fully integrated into the board, he or she should become actively engaged on a board committee or special project. The involvement shows that the organization does not merely want a "warm body" on the board but that board members are expected to contribute through their efforts. As the new board member makes an effort on behalf of the nonprofit, he or she is likely to feel a growing commitment to the organization. To put in effort on a project and not feel a growing commitment would create the dissonance of "Why am I doing this if I do not care?" More likely, the degree of future commitment is often dependent on the amount of effort invested.

Board Renewal

Because the board is central to the success of nonprofits, renewal of its membership has been at the heart of this chapter. A standing nominations committee and term limits on board members are two key practices that further the ongoing renewal of the board. A standing nominating committee (as opposed to a last-minute ad hoc version) is less likely to be dependent on the executive director and staff for recommendations. The recommendations of the standing committee also are likely to be more carefully weighed, rather than just "finding someone to stand for nomination" a few weeks before terms expire.

Term limits are a two-edged sword. On the one hand, key leaders are lost as their term expires. This problem is partially addressed by having a succession plan, such as chair-elect, chair, and past chair who are automatically exempt from being retired from the board until they have moved through each of these positions. This promotional hierarchy suggests the ability of potential leaders to get guidance before and during their term as chair, which usually lasts one year. The fixed term allows leaders to make their mark on the organization without being burdened by multiyear terms in office. Remember, even though leadership service may be prestigious and even beneficial to one's career, board members are volunteers with other, often more important commitments in their lives.

The difficulty of telling a well-intentioned board member that his or her services are no longer desired is lessened by limits on board service. For those who made only a marginal contribution, they can be honored, recognized, thanked, and moved off the board without incident. Those who proved valuable receive the same treatment, too. However, they can be temporarily exempted by nomination for a second term or by moving them through the leadership hierarchy. Even if the person is not appropriate to become chair, most nonprofit bylaws permit someone to be reappointed to the board after being off it for one year.

Finally, as part of staff-led planning efforts, which typically take place each year around the same time, a critical examination of other actions that are needed to strengthen the nonprofit and its board are appropriate subjects. (The strategic leadership roles of the executive director and board chair will be explored in the next chapter.)

Liabilities of Board Members

Being a board member is not just an honor. Nonprofit board members have responsibilities that also carry obligations. Although the standard of care expected of board members varies with state laws and precedents, directors are expected to exercise their fiduciary responsibility with the sound judgment expected of a reasonable person. The "reasonable person" rule, as it is called in legal circles, assumes that a board member will act as any reasonable person would under similar circumstances. Determination of "reasonableness," however, may be decided through a legal proceeding when board actions result in a suit.

Suits may arise from a variety of sources, including

- Government agencies, for violations of federal, state, or local laws and regulations;
- Beneficiaries, who believe their rights are not being recognized by the nonprofit;
- Donors, who believe that their wishes are not being fulfilled;
- Employees, present and past, who believe that promises, employment contracts, or employment laws are not being honored; and
- General public, who disagree with actions of the nonprofit.

Suits typically arise over issues of fiscal mismanagement, conflict of interest, wrongful termination, or violations of laws—such as violations of wage, social security, tax-reporting violations, or civil rights and other employment-related laws.

To reduce the impact of such potential suits on the organization or board members, some (mostly large and prosperous) nonprofits carry directors' and officers' liability insurance. Commonly referred to as D & O policies, these forms of insurance provide legal assistance and indemnify the organization and board members up to stated policy limits. Most nonprofits find the cost of such insurance to be prohibitive and do not have them. At a minimum, the nonprofit should agree to "hold harmless" board members and reimburse them if such cases arise. (Of course, a financially weak nonprofit's offer to do so might be well-intentioned but worthless.) In reality, suits against nonprofit boards are relatively rare because few have assets that would make them targets of lawsuits. Nevertheless, the degree of liability for board members is a topic that should be reviewed by both the board and individual members.

Conclusion

The board of directors is the ultimate authority within a nonprofit. The members are charged with pursuing the public good in return for the organization's nonprofit status. At a minimum, the board is responsible for hiring, evaluating, rewarding, and replacing the executive director or president of the nonprofit. In practice, the involvement of the board varies widely. In newly formed nonprofits, the board will be heavily involved, with members even assuming operating responsibilities, as discussed in chapter 1. As the organization matures, the board moves toward a more supervisory and then advisory roles. Central to its function, however, is that of an evaluative role.

To engage board members, it is common for them to be assigned to various board committees. The executive committee usually consists of the board chair, the executive director, and heads of the key committees. The nominating committee is likely to include the current and immediate past board chair, along with the executive director or others. The development committee is so crucial to many nonprofits that its chair often becomes chair of the board, especially in nonprofits that require board chairs to rotate after one year of service.

Because the board has overall responsibility for the nonprofit, recruiting board members is central to perpetuating the board and the nonprofit. The nominating committee—whether ad hoc or standing—needs to identify, track, evaluate, and recruit potential board members. Prospects need to be advised of what is expected of them on the board, oriented and integrated into the board (typically by a task force assignment or a position on a board committee), and their contributions monitored and evaluated. Board members should also be aware of their liabilities.

References

Alexander, Jeffrey A., and Bryan J. Weiner, "The Adoption of the Corporate Governance Model by Nonprofit Organizations," *Nonprofit Management & Leadership* (spring 1998): 223–42.

Carver, John, *Boards that Make a Difference (2nd ed.),* San Francisco: Jossey-Bass, 1997.

Carver, Miriam Mayhew, "The Board's Very Own Peter Principle," *Nonprofit World* (January–February 1998): 20.

Green, Jack C. "Nonprofit Misconduct: Board Members Take Heed," *Business Forum* (winter 1997): 60–61.

Herman, Robert D., David O. Renz, and Richard D. Heimovics, "Board Practices and Board Effectiveness in Local Nonprofit Organizations," *Nonprofit Management & Leadership* (summer 1997): 373–85.

Howe, Fisher, *The Board Member's Guide to Strategic Planning,* San Francisco: Jossey-Bass, 1997.

Kile, Robert W., and J. Michael Loscavio, *Strategic Board Recruitment,* Gaithersburg, MD: Aspen, 1996.

Levy, Reynold, *Give and Take,* Boston: Harvard Business School Press, 1999.

Martinelli, Frank, "Encouraging Visionary Board Leadership," *Nonprofit World* (July/August 1998): 11–14.

Newcomer, Kathryn E., *Using Performance Measurement to Improve Public and Nonprofit Programs,* San Francisco: Jossey-Bass, 1997.

Saidel, Judith R., and Sharon L. Harlan, "Contracting Patterns of Nonprofit Governance," *Nonprofit Management & Leadership* (spring 1998): 243–59.

Sandler, Martin W., and Deborah A. Hudson, *Beyond the Bottom Line: How to Do More with Less in Nonprofit and Public Organizations,* New York: Oxford University Press, 1998.

Shoichet, Richard, "An Organization Design Model for Nonprofits," *Nonprofit Management & Leadership* (fall 1998): 71–88.

4

Strategic Leadership

Perhaps the most important decision facing any nonprofit is the choice of leader. Whether called executive director, president, or some other title, the leader is central to the nonprofit's success. Hired by the board of directors, the executive director serves as the chief executive officer (CEO) of the nonprofit. As such, the CEO is responsible for all aspects of the nonprofit, excluding those responsibilities reserved to the board (McFarland, 1999). Dr. Bernadine Healy sees her role as president of the American Red Cross as a diverse mix of responsibilities, "First and foremost, of course, is representing this grand institution, being a steward of this organization, a humble steward in the face of its mission, its goals and what that means to all constituents, to the governors, the volunteers to the staff and of course to the pubic we serve" (quoted in Clolery, 1999).

As discussed earlier in this book, an executive director of a nonprofit plays multiple roles. Though leaders in other organizations also must play different roles, the need for attaining objectives, building consensus, and relying on uncontrolled resources in the form of volunteers and donations makes the job of CEO for a nonprofit particularly challenging. As with all general management positions, CEOs of nonprofits must be leaders, managers, and administrators. The term *leader* refers to the CEO's ability to articulate an ennobling vision and help define the appropriate mission and objectives that will lead toward that vision. In an ideal situation, the leader can inspire others, inside and outside the organization, to support his or her vision (Gardner, 1993). Given the need to attract volunteers, donors, and board members who typically serve without compensation, the ability to lead and attract others with a compelling vision is very important (Drucker, 1992).

In the managerial role, the CEO must be able to marshal human, financial, and other resources to attain objectives. In turn, attainment of these objectives ensures that the purpose or mission of the nonprofit is achieved. In pursing objectives, however, the CEO of a nonprofit often relies more on the goodwill of donors and volunteers than on the ability to command traditional subordinates. The executive director must do all this with attention to efficiency and outcomes that make sense for multiple, and sometimes conflicting, constituents.

The role of administrator, as the term is used in this book, is one that is focused on achieving a workable balance among the nonprofit's various constituencies. All organizations have multiple, often conflicting constituencies whose demands must be balanced. However, in government and for-profits, administrators can point to the voters' wishes or the need to make a profit as a final arbiter of tough decisions. Nonprofits have neither of these relatively clear-cut measures. Instead, the nonprofit only has its internally generated standards against which to measure performance, which often rests on a delicate balance among the board members, clients, staff, donors, volunteers, and other groups with an interest in the nonprofit's activities (Austin, 1998).

Unlike the CEO of other types of organizations, the executive director is limited and challenged by the need to maintain harmony—especially among volunteers, donors, board members, and sometimes even staff who may be paid below market rates. Where revenues in government or business may rely on taxation and performance, nonprofits are often largely, if not completely, dependent on the goodwill of those who support them through their contributions of money or effort. An administrator must consider these different stakeholders and find solutions that are more or less acceptable to each, which is seldom an easy task. Otherwise, valued sources of support may evaporate. At the same time, the board must measure the CEO's performance against the vision, mission, strategies, and objectives discussed in chapter 2.

Evolving Boundaries and Expectations

As with the evolution of the board and the nonprofit itself, the role of leaders also evolves across the nonprofit's life cycle. Early in its evolution, leaders are not only responsible for results, but with the lack of financial and human resources inherent in the early stages of a nonprofit they may have to undertake many of the activities typically associated with staff duties in larger nonprofits. As a result, leaders' efforts may be diverted from strategic issues to more mundane activities—including clerical duties such as filing, correspondence, and the like. In these early stages, the board of directors is often a working board (as discussed in chapters 1 and 3), so some help may come from board members who roll up their sleeves and pitch in.

As nonprofits mature, leaders become increasingly managerial. They must supervise staff and eventually staff managers who are in charge of different functions, such as operations, marketing, and development. With increased sophistication, more and more activities are delegated to staff, and the CEO's time and energies are increasingly devoted to planning, follow-up, coordination, and other management duties.

At the same time, the CEO must operate within a set of boundaries that are often not well-defined. Essentially, the CEO is responsible for all aspects of the nonprofit that are not reserved to the board. Hiring and developing staff, fundraising, delivering the nonprofit's service or performance, conserving and protecting the nonprofit's assets, and running the day to day operations are just some of the CEO's concerns. Moreover, as the nonprofit matures, these boundaries and expectations change. With greater maturity, staff assumes responsibility for more and more of the activities, and the role of the board becomes increasingly advisory and evaluative.

Perhaps the most fundamental change, besides expanding resources, is the relationship between the board and the executive director. Early in the development of the nonprofit members of the executive committee and the CEO jointly explore likely avenues for the CEO to consider in fundraising, organizational design, and mission-related objectives. This give and take between the CEO and a working board often takes place as informal advice and assistance, given in the spirit of a common commitment and involvement. These informal interactions help to ensure support of the board and give a sense of direction to the activities of the CEO. As the nonprofit matures, the board tends to become less involved in the day to day activities of the nonprofit. The result is that CEOs move from a collaborative role to one in which they need to initiate new ideas and proposals. As a result, they make more and more formal recommendations to the board for fundraising, programs, and other activities. This shift puts a burden on the CEO to be proactive, recommending new directions, objectives, and actions to the board.

Regardless of these evolving roles, the CEO remains responsible for the successes and failures of the nonprofit. He or she may delegate responsibility to others for operations, fundraising, or other aspects of the organization. However, in delegating the authority to others, the board still holds the executive director responsible. Delegation does not lessen the CEO's responsibility.

The CEO's Strategic Role

Because most board members, including the chair, typically rotate off the board according to a time schedule found in the bylaws, the initiative for creating and maintaining a strategic focus falls to the CEO. Usually, it is the CEO that provides the leadership continuity from year to year. Even in a large, well-endowed nonprofit, such as the American Red Cross, formulation (or reformulation) of the nonprofit's strategy is seldom delegated to others (Maranville, 1999). The CEO takes charge of this responsibility for several reasons. First, the strategy and related objectives determine how the nonprofit will function. Others in the nonprofit typically have jobs with a narrow focus; the CEO, however, has an overall view and an overall responsibility for the nonprofit. Second, the CEO will have to direct the implementation of the strategy, so it makes sense that he or she is involved with its creation. Third, the final strategy, typically embedded in a long-range plan, constitutes an agreement between the CEO and the board about what goals and objectives will be pursued. The attainment of these goals and objectives will be the basis for evaluating the CEO, renewing his or her contract, and providing raises or bonuses. Fourth, the leader must be committed to the strategic intent of the organization (Sheehan, 1999).

CEOs understand that their strategic role is to end up with a blueprint for the nonprofit's future. As Porter and Kramer (1999, p. 121) observed about foundations, that blueprint "will require developing a strategy, aligning operations with that strategy, and revising the foundations' governance so that the strategy can be monitored effectively." However, experienced CEOs also realize that the process they use to develop the plan may be as important as the final document. This balance between process and results is critical because the final plan must be feasible.

To be feasible in the face of limited resources means that those who will be involved in the plan's execution need to have a commitment to that plan. Informed commitment assumes that those responsible for achieving the goals and objectives understand the purpose behind the goals. Informed commitment also assumes that those responsible have been involved in the planning process. To present staff or the board with a finished plan—regardless of how elegant or well-thought-out—is unlikely to win their commitment. Involvement in the process is much more likely to create a sense of ownership in the final plan and, thus, a commitment to achieve it.

By getting people involved in the planning process, CEOs make choices about which goals and objectives are to be pursued and how. They understand the effort and resources that will be needed to attain the goals and objectives. This involvement is particularly important when the organization wants to undertake a significant change, such as redefining its vision or mission or embarking on a major new project. Consider an extended example that highlights the implications behind a decision by an arts or cultural organization to build a new facility.

Many nonprofits devote considerable efforts to raising the necessary operating funds to pay salaries, utilities, and other expenses. A decision to build a multimillion dollar facility means that all the operating expenses still have to be raised and a capital fund needs to be started.

Typically, the process begins among a small group of insiders—the executive director, the chief fundraiser (whether on staff or the board), and key members of the executive committee. They discuss the need for a facility and reach agreement that something needs to be done. A commitment is made among this small group to go forward, even though none of them may be clear about the scope, cost, and effort involved. To comprehend the full scope of the project, a planning committee is formed, which usually consists of the CEO, chief fundraiser, and a member or two from the board's executive committee. Two key tasks become immediately obvious: The need for a design and a means to pay for it. The result is often a design subcommittee and a fundraising planning committee (Levy, 1999). Though the design is crucial, the key to success, ultimately, is the funding. But before designs and money is the need for board approval. Without it, the CEO cannot go forward.

Often by means of a long-range planning retreat, the board and key staff will meet to create a new five-year plan. As part of the planning process, the idea of a new facility will be introduced and discussed. Ideas will be solicited from the board, and a step-wise program of action will be suggested. These action steps may well include community discussion or focus groups that are created to learn of the community's wishes and objections. Moreover, by creating an outreach to the community, the hope is to build a broad base of support and knowledge about community needs related to the nonprofit's mission and vision. Moreover, the community needs may be used to solidify board support for the idea of building a new facility. Community wishes learned through the open, long-range planning meetings may become another reason to suggest a new facility. Through several iterations of community and board meetings, the long-range plan emerges with the goal of a new facility as its centerpiece and with the board's and community's support.

Board support is necessary on two levels. Without board support, the new facility remains a dream. With board support for the idea, the implication is that those who approved it will help get it built.

Sometimes even before a design committee seeks an artist's conception, the commitment-building process continues. Switching from community meetings about the nonprofit's long-range plan, staff, docents, current and past board members, and donors might be invited to small group discussions to talk about the need for facilities and how that need might be met. Large-scale community involvement by those most likely to have an interest in the project builds support and creates a base for future fundraising and political allies. The design subcommittee may then ask for artist's renditions from local or national architecture firms based on some rough and very preliminary ideas that the CEO, the artistic director, and the focus groups have expressed.

These rough ideas are shared with the board in hopes of keeping, even expanding, their commitment. The preliminary concept is then shown to those who are likely to be key donors. The hope is to get a few major, lead gifts promised, perhaps including a very large gift that will be secured in exchange for naming the facility or some part of it after the lead donors. Receptions to unveil the plans or models of the facility are used to extend the circle of people who are part of the process and will, it is hoped, give to the project above and beyond their traditional support.

Finally, often a year or two later, a formal fundraising campaign is announced, along with the large lead gifts. With 20 to 40 percent or more of the funding promised before the announcement, the intent is to create excitement in the community and remove doubts about the fundraising success by beginning with substantial progress already under way.

The catalyst behind a new facility program or the drive to create a permanent endowment or other major undertaking is typically the executive director. Though it may appear that a board member or others are leading the charge, very often it is the CEO who has planted the seeds of the idea and nurtured them to fruition through the long-range planning process.

Long-Range Planning

What are the accomplishments the nonprofit wishes to achieve over the next three or five years? What new goals, directions, or programs are needed for the nonprofit to pursue its vision and perform its mission? A simple response to these two questions is for the nonprofit to continue doing what it has always done. Though there may be important needs met by this course of action, without new directions the nonprofit may fail in its mission. The nonprofit risks becoming irrelevant if it does not redefine itself periodically.

Reformulation of the vision—such as ending hunger in our community—seldom occurs. The vision of what the organization is striving toward is seldom achieved. If it was accomplished, the vision would have to be redefined, as was the case with the March of Dimes when polio was virtually eliminated by vaccines in the 1950s (McFarland, 1999). The mission is so closely allied with the vision—feeding hungry people, for example—that it too seldom changes. Regardless of whether one looks at food banks, educational institutions, health care providers, religious organizations, or most other nonprofits, the original vision and mission—though they may be recrafted to be more articulate or to have more impact—seldom change. Educational institutions continue to provide education; nonprofit hospitals continue to provide for sick individuals; and so on.

What does change periodically is how the organization is going to pursue its vision and accomplish its mission. That is, what goals and subsidiary objectives will be set and how will the nonprofit marshal its resources to achieve those goals and objectives? Figure 4-1 offers a conceptual framework of the elements that need to be considered in crafting a long-range plan. The long-range plan evaluates the competencies of the nonprofit and the needs in the environment. With an understanding of the internal strengths and weaknesses and the external opportunities and threats, the planning process develops a strategy that enables the nonprofit to pursue its mission and vision. Changes in strategy may require a reorganization, changing the structure of the nonprofit.

Long-range planning operates under the umbrella of the organization's vision and mission, as seen in Figure 4-1. The entire purpose of the long-range planning exercise is to further the nonprofit's ability to attain its mission and pursue the vision. One study suggests the

Figure 4-1   **Conceptual Elements in Creating a Strategy**

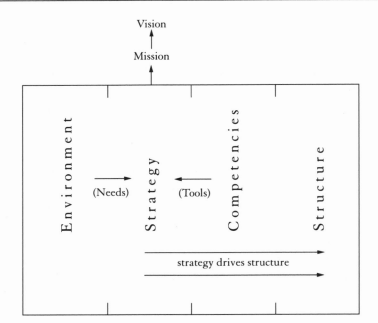

importance of long-range planning to YMCAs. The results are likely to be applicable to an even wider range of nonprofits.

A study of 240 YMCA organizations revealed that regardless of organization size, those organizations that used a formal approach to strategic planning had higher levels of financial and social performance. The better performers also assigned the responsibility for planning to a strategic planning subcommittee of the board rather than to the board's executive committee or to an outside consultant. (Siciliano, 1997)

The long-range planning process begins with an external and internal analysis.

External Analysis

Nonprofits operate in the larger context of the environment, as shown on the left of Figure 4-1. Though obvious, the nonprofit must define its environment—in other words, is it concerned about local, statewide, regional, national, or international issues? Then within that environment, who are the constituents it intends to serve, given the nonprofit's vision and mission? What are the relevant needs of those constituents? What are the opportunities for service in the environment and which ones are most relevant to the nonprofit's vision and mission? Are there threats in the environment that might weaken the nonprofit or impair its ability to deliver the needed services it deems appropriate? These are not simple questions.

Determining the environment is often best done by asking the nonprofit's constituents how they see the nonprofit. Small discussion or focus groups might be set up with the board, staff and volunteers, clients, and donors. The executive director or an outside facilitator needs to understand what these constituents perceive as the needs that the nonprofit should address. The nonprofit may not be able to respond to all the needs in the environment, even though those needs may be within the scope of its mission statement; resources are always limited. Nevertheless, it is important to get multiple perspectives on the multiple needs in the environment so that the nonprofit can use the long-range planning process to prioritize its actions.

Multiple perspectives put a burden on the CEO to stay informed of trends other than those that affect clients. Effective CEOs continually educate themselves about changes in the social–cultural environment. What are the trends in attendance at the types (art, music, religious) of activities conducted by the nonprofit? What are the expectations of donors? Board members? What demographic trends are favorable or unfavorable to the nonprofit? Many religious groups, for example, recognize that their parishioners are graying, so youth outreach programs are begun. Are the racial, ethnic, economic, or other demographic characteristics of the nonprofit's constituents changing? If so, how? How do technological, economic, or legal developments affect the nonprofit's plans and future? Though a widely diverse board of directors can be used as a focus group to partially answer these questions, the executive director must be conversant enough with broad external trends to raise these important questions as part of a general environmental analysis. A nonprofit may fail for a variety of reasons, including poor management and poor funding in particular. But a lack of sensitivity to the always changing external environment can undermine, even make obsolete, the nonprofit's mission. Take the following example:

In the early 1980s, South Miami Beach (or "South Beach," as the natives refer to it) was populated primarily by elderly retirees and recent immigrants to the United States. Both groups tended to be poor and needed a variety of social services from government and nonprofits. The retirees primarily needed gerontology-related services, particularly home health care; the immigrants needed language and skills training along with guidance on how to navigate through the maze of government and social services. The immigrants also needed these services primarily in Spanish and secondarily in Haitian Creole.

Social service-oriented nonprofits that did not understand and track these demographic trends became increasingly irrelevant. Even though the immigrants desperately needed training and education services, if these services were in English, this assistance was of marginal use, at best. Likewise social-oriented services provided to the retirees in the 1970s—social gatherings, dances, lectures, and the like—became increasingly irrelevant as this retiree population transformed from the "young old" (recent retirees) to the "the very old" who had limited mobility for shopping, health care, and other life functions.

Then in the late 1980s, the demographics changed radically, as a much younger population discovered the funky art deco district, great beaches, and fine weather. Now there was considerable need for AIDS education and awareness as elderly residents and immigrants were pushed out of the area by rapidly rising rents and living costs.

In general, nonprofits deliver their services locally. Therefore, changing area economics and demographics powerfully affect the mission of nonprofits. As a result, the CEO and staff need to stay aware of these trends, track them, and estimate their future impact on the organization. Thus a general environmental evaluation is another key to the external analysis that is needed before developing long-range plans and strategies. Simply put, the external analysis must identify the threats and opportunities that are present or emerging in its environment.

Internal Analysis

The CEO must also conduct an internal analysis to understand the nonprofit's strengths and weaknesses. Strong capabilities are often called competencies, as shown in Figure 4-1. Core competencies are capabilities in which the nonprofit excels and other nonprofits would find difficult and time consuming to duplicate. For example, a food bank that had a mobile food kitchen, food storage capabilities, dedicated funding sources, and agreements with area grocery stores, bakeries, and restaurants to get surplus food would have multiple core competencies. Though the mobile food kitchen and the food storage facilities would be fairly easy to duplicate, any other nonprofit involved in feeding the hungry would be at a considerable disadvantage in obtaining a dedicated source of funding (say from the United Way or an area Chamber of Commerce). Likewise, agreements to take day-old bakery goods or other surpluses would not likely be given to another organization.

Weaknesses need to be identified also. What internal features of the nonprofit hinder (or potentially hinder) it from meeting its mission? What can be done to limit the impact of these weaknesses, preferably without a major commitment of resources? Often weaknesses take the form of limited resources—too few cooks or drivers in the food bank example. The initial reaction of staff and the CEO might be to get more resources to shore up that weakness. Often, however, a better approach is not to devote major resources but to develop a contingency plan that offers a solution to the "what if" situation in which the weakness threatens to disrupt the delivery of the mission. For example, a thinly staffed nonprofit food bank might be concerned if it lost its cook or driver suddenly. Rather than overstaff with backup personnel, the executive director might work out a contingency plan in which volunteers agree to be on call when a staff shortage occurs. Or other staff members might agree to get a chauffeur's license or a health card to fill in if needed.

The internal and external analysis captures a SWOT evaluation of *s*trengths, *w*eaknesses, *o*pportunities, and *t*hreats. This common form of organizational analysis allows strategists to identify the organization's strengths that can be applied to the opportunities in its environment. Weaknesses and threats are addressed minimally to ensure that they do not grow to the point that they undermine the nonprofit's ability to pursue mission-related opportunities. Then they are carefully monitored to detect when internal weaknesses or external threats need to be more forcefully addressed.

Strategy

Strategy seeks to marry the competencies of the nonprofit with the targeted needs in the environment, as suggested by Figure 4-1. The intent is to build on existing strengths or competencies, even reinforcing them, as a means of meeting clients' needs and achieving the mission of the nonprofit. The strategy used by the nonprofit is not only the plan of how it will deploy its capabilities and competencies to meet needs in its environment but it also helps to differentiate the nonprofit among donors, recruits, opinion leaders, and the larger community. Not only should the vision and mission be attractive to these constituencies, but these constituents should find the strategy appropriate. The "ends" of vision and mission sought by the nonprofit must be appropriate, and the "means" of strategy and process should be appealing too.

The potential trap for strategists is not to exclude an otherwise viable strategy because a competency needed to make the strategy work is not readily available. Part of the logic of long-range planning is to assess the internal and external environments to determine where the organization can be most effective. If a particular resource or competency is missing, a decision needs to be made about whether securing that competency or resource should be a goal to be pursued during the long-range plan. Consider the following example:

> Assume our food bank has recognized the need for a mobile kitchen to reach out to homeless individuals. This strategy should be seen as appropriate by potential donors, recruits, opinion leaders, and the general community before it is implemented. If not judged appropriate, support is not likely to be forthcoming.
>
> Even if seen as appropriate, the lack of money, vehicle, driver, cook, and supplies present formidable barriers. Lacking the necessary competencies to fulfill the need in its local environment, the idea might be dropped. However, it might also become a goal, stated as a fundraising challenge: If we can find a sponsor willing to underwrite the mobile kitchen, salaries, and supplies, we will implement this new service. This goal becomes a contingent strategy for how the nonprofit will deliver its service and fulfill its mission—contingent on acquiring the needed resources.
>
> Then if a local car dealer or corporation is willing to fund the new mobile kitchen—perhaps in exchange for using the vehicle as a mobile billboard publicizing the firm's generosity—the strategy can be implemented. Or conversely, if the growth of general funding is sufficient, the nonprofit may be able to gradually add this service in coming years.

Nonprofits, like their for-profit counterparts, face a choice when they lack the resources or competencies needed to implement a desirable strategy: They can make or buy the needed competency. As discussed previously, this means that they can internally develop (make) the needed competency, as with expanding traditional funding approaches until the resources are available to get another mobile kitchen and to hire another driver and cook, or they can "buy" the needed competency by creating an alliance or joint venture with other nonprofits, for-profits, or governments. Perhaps the nonprofit can subcontract (buy) some of their activities—such as getting the local school board to agree to produce surplus lunches to supplement a meal-on-wheels effort during severe storms that trap many elderly people at home. (The use of alliances as a strategy for nonprofits will be discussed more thoroughly in chapter 8.)

Organizational Structure

After a strategy is developed to match organizational competencies (present or future) to needs in the environment, the structure of the nonprofit is considered. As Figure 4-1 indicates, strategy affects structure. The purpose for the organizational structure is to support the nonprofit's various strategies. As a result, the structure should be dependent on and aligned with the nonprofit's strategies: Form should follow function.

The typical nonprofit is organized around a functional form. That is, a typical nonprofit is structured to look like the diagram presented in Figure 4-2, in which similar activities or functions will be grouped together so that all those working in accounting or development will be in the same department. This design is a "good news, bad news" arrangement.

The good news includes several noteworthy features. First, a functional design tends to be very efficient. Because the design takes advantage of functional groupings, the nonprofit takes advantage of specialization. Second, this specialized focus suggests more narrow jobs that are quicker to learn and more widely recognized when recruiting new staff (discussed in the next chapter). Third, alliances and other forms of bridge-building between the nonprofit and other organizations (detailed in chapter 8) are more readily facilitated because most people are familiar with the functional design. These

Figure 4-2 **Functional Organizational Design**

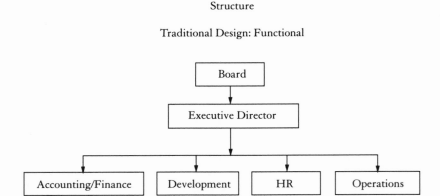

Structure

Traditional Design: Functional

benefits suggest why the typical nonprofit is almost always structured around a functional design.

The bad news of a functional design is its often slow and cumbersome responsiveness to internal changes or external demands made on the nonprofit. Within the functional structure, different functions have different priorities. Development is concerned with developing relationships with donors and increasing funding. Accounting, however, is often most concerned about accuracy. Thus an urgent plea to "do a better job" is likely to be interpreted in accounting as being more accurate, more precise, or even more efficient because these are common values among those in accounting, within or outside of nonprofits. However, the development office may interpret "doing a better job" as establishing more prospective donor relationships, leading them to be *less* concerned about the accuracy of accounting-related records.

Though this conflict is often a minor one, it symbolizes the resistance to change that is common among departments of a functionally designed structure. Moreover, the attitudes of departmental leaders tend to reinforce departmental values and to emphasize the importance of the functional department as critical. Because each functional department *is* important, some functional specialists may come to believe that his or her department's values and wishes should be supreme. At this point, interdepartmental cooperation and teamwork break down, undermining the overall effectiveness of the nonprofit (Herman and Renz, 1998). These criticisms of the functional approach are more likely to apply to large nonprofits with extensive staff support. In smaller nonprofits, people in different functions are often expected to pitch in, as when clerks in the accounting department are expected to staff registration tables at an annual gala, for example. Nevertheless, the functional design properly persists because it is widely understood and efficient—and, as chapter 6 argues, efficiency and productivity are essential to nonprofit success for a variety of reasons.

The relentless drive for efficiency has led many organizations to consider "hollow" and "virtual" organization designs. As discussed previously, hollow designs occur where the nonprofit takes some traditional function, such as accounting, for example; applies make-or-buy analysis; and then elects to have that function performed by others. The executive director's mindset must shift from the traditional "we need to do the accounting" to a recognition that the true objective is "we need to get the accounting done," whether internally or externally.

Virtual organizations are a mirror image of hollow organizational thinking. Instead of asking the hollow organizational questions—"What can we get others to do?"—the virtual organization decides what is central to its strategy and focuses its efforts on that one function, externalizing to others the remaining functions that the organization must accomplish. A classic example is a nonprofit that wants to serve as an electronic community billboard. The nonprofit's website may be supported by the nonprofit's staff, but publicity, selling ad space to event organizers, accounting for it, issuing paychecks, and countless other necessary organizational functions may all be handled by others outside the nonprofit on a fee-for-services basis or gratis.

Other Leadership Responsibilities

From a strategic perspective, the leader must guide the long-range planning process, the analysis of the nonprofit's internal and external environments, and strategy formulations. Though board members, staff, and external consultants may assist, it is the leader who remains ultimately responsible for the long-range planning process and the execution of its plans. Beyond this central strategic concern, the CEO has other concerns. Again, whether the leader actually addresses these concerns personally or delegates them to others depends both on the leader's approach to his or her job and the maturity of the non-profit. Though a list of the CEO's concerns would form the backbone of a book on nonprofit leadership, our intent is to briefly identify key concerns that can affect the leader's ability to exercise strategic leadership.

Vision Enthusiasm

If the leader does not believe enthusiastically in the nonprofit's vision, why should anyone else? To lead, the leader must have someplace he or she wants to take the followers—whether those followers are staff, volunteers, board members, donors, clients, or others. The vision defines the destination and ennobles the followers. Without it, mission attainment is unlikely to leave anyone feeling ennobled or empowered. The efforts of the nonprofit may still be needed, appreciated, and even supported: Hungry individuals still need to be fed and sick people still need to be healed, for example. But without a compelling and ennobling vision, the leader may not be able to tap the strong, emotional enthusiasm for the good that the nonprofit seeks to accomplish.

Even with an articulated and ennobling vision, if the CEO cannot muster an enthusiastic support of it, then the commitment and motivation of others on whom the nonprofit must rely is likely to be less than it otherwise would be. Some staff, board members, and volunteers may be attracted to the vision and mission. But a leader who does not exhibit enthusiasm for the vision and mission is unlikely to inspire others.

Community Sensitivity

Nonprofits exist at the willingness of society to exempt these organizations from taxes because they are fulfilling a community or societal need. In other words, nonprofits exist, at least in part, because of community support. Nowhere is this support more obvious and necessary than in funding the nonprofit (Sandler and Hudson, 1998).

Effective leaders need to be sensitive to their community and its expectations. This may not be easy, especially when the dogma of the group is to insulate itself and advocate an "us-against-them" mentality. Leaders of such groups may articulate the vision and mission of their organizations, but by exhibiting their insensitivity to the values or beliefs of others, they may win the support of their followers at the expense of a wider group of people than those with whom they disagree. This apparent friction or open conflict of beliefs may drive away support from others who do not want to be embroiled in the controversy. Even if such people support the vision and mission of the nonprofit, they may withhold expressions of that support, preferring to help other nonprofits that seem more willing to benefit the entire community.

Representation and Public Relations

In the eyes of many, the leader *is* the nonprofit organization, or at least the embodiment of it. The CEO represents the nonprofit. His or her behavior, personal attitudes about the issues of the day, and general demeanor reflect on the nonprofit. Fair or not, the leader's personal and public life tend to merge because the leader's actions are likely to reflect directly on the nonprofit. Though perhaps trite to observe, the leader needs to project a positive, self-confident attitude to both internal and external constituencies. Internally, the leader needs to lead by example. The leader is a model of how staff should treat clients, donors, volunteers, other staff, and the assortment of various individuals and groups that interact with the nonprofit. Externally, the leader's behavior needs to project an image that is congruent with the image being cultivated for the nonprofit.

So crucial is the image of the nonprofit that many nonprofits will seek out someone from the public relations or marketing community to serve on its board and help showcase the nonprofit and its CEO in a favorable light (Rados, 1996). Though some people might believe that the nonprofit should not be concerned about its image and instead should let its good deeds speak for it and shape its community image, this view may be naive. Among all the nonprofits in a community clamoring for key board members, donors, financial support, and volunteers, each has a need to be viewed favorably. Although the deeds of the nonprofit ultimately will shape its image, that image can be more effectively and favorably formed if those good deeds get community visibility. The good image helps morale within the nonprofit, enhances the status of the organization and, thereby, encourages recruitment of board, staff, and volunteer members.

Perhaps the most crucial impact of public relations is in the area of fundraising. Generating funds—as will be discussed more thoroughly in chapter 9—is crucial to most nonprofits' ability to execute their plans, mission, and strategy.

The constituents' perceptions of the nonprofit—and how the leader represents that image—are closely intertwined. The leader's overall strategic effectiveness, therefore, depends in some measure on how the leader leads the organization and how the leader interacts with constituents. Simply put, perceptions of the leader and the nonprofit shape people's attitudes and response to it.

Execution

Nevertheless, a nonprofit's deeds do speak volumes about the organization. What gets done and how it gets done tell the nonprofit's story. Good public relations can enhance that story and constituents' perceptions of it. Ultimately, internal and external constituents expect results. In the long run the cumulative results of the nonprofit will be its image. Therefore, execution is central to strategic success.

Execution means results, as will be discussed in more detail in Part II. Accomplishing goals and objectives is central to the executive director's credibility as a leader. Support from the board, staff, volunteers, donors, and others depends not only on the perception that results are being achieved but the actual attainment of objectives. One way of viewing the long-range planning process is as an implied contract between the CEO and the organization. The plan states what will be done and the execution carries it out. If the execution repeatedly falls short of the goals stated in the plan, the board's responsibility is to replace the leader with someone who can set *and* attain goals that move the nonprofit toward achieving its mission.

What makes execution against stated goals so crucial to nonprofits is that these goals are often the only measure of the nonprofit's performance. For-profits can show profit, governments get reelected, but nonprofits succeed or fail against outcomes implied by their goals and objectives. Moreover, as we will see in Part II, merely achieving goals and objectives is not enough. These goals and objectives must be accomplished in ways that are efficient, to conserve the nonprofit's resources. The process of attaining those goals should enhance the nonprofit and its relationships with constituents and allies. Ultimately, the goals and the process to attain them should make a strong case for continued community support from donors, board members, volunteers, staff, clients, and other relevant constituents.

Conclusion

Strategic leadership demands that the CEO or executive director create a vision, mission, strategy, goals, and objectives that give the nonprofit a clear direction and a basis for evaluating its performance (Newcomer, 1997). The process should engage those internal and external constituents who will be necessary to execute the nonprofit's long-range plan. The goal of engaging those crucial to the plan's success should be inclusive to win the support and commitment of those involved.

The long-range planning process begins with a clear, well-articulated, and ennobling vision of the nonprofit's mission. Then an internal and external analysis needs to be performed to identify its internal strengths and weaknesses along with its external opportunities and threats. This SWOT analysis becomes the basis for identifying the nonprofit's capabilities and competencies. It is from these capabilities and competencies that the organization weaves a strategy to meet client needs in the larger environment.

The strategy is needed to guide how the nonprofit is going to achieve its goals and objectives and thereby its mission. Moreover, in a world crowded with nonprofits that are competing for resources, the strategy further helps to differentiate one nonprofit from another.

Based on the resources and strategy, the structure of the nonprofit needs to be considered. Typically, the structure is a functional design. That is, the nonprofit is organized so that like activities are grouped with like functions. Though the functional design has the benefit of being efficient, which allows for specialization, it sometimes creates internal barriers to change because each function may have a slightly different understanding of how it should contribute to the nonprofit's strategy.

Driving the strategy formulation (or reformulation) process is a key strategic leadership concern. Others exist. The leader needs to be concerned with vision enthusiasm, community sensitivity, representation and public relations, and the execution of the long-range plan. Each of these concerns potentially holds strategic implications for the success of the nonprofit. Staffing issues are critical to execution; they will be a major focus of the next chapter.

References

Austin, J. E., "Business Leaders and Nonprofits," *Nonprofit Management & Leadership* (fall 1998): 39–52.

Clolery, P., "Red Cross Gets Former NIH Chief," *The NonProfit Times* (August 1999): 1.

Drucker, P. F., *Managing the Non-Profit Organization*, New York: Harper Business, 1992.

Gardner, J. W., *On Leadership*, New York: Simon and Schuster, 1993.

Herman, R. D., and D. O. Renz, "Nonprofit Organizational Effectiveness: Contrasts between Especially Effective and Less Effective Organizations," *Nonprofit Management & Leadership* (fall 1998): 23–38.

Levy, R., *Give and Take*, Boston: Harvard Business School Press, 1999.

Maranville, S. J., "Requisite Variety of Strategic Management Modes: A Cultural Study of Strategic Actions in a Deterministic Environment," *Nonprofit Management & Leadership* (spring 1999): 277–92.

McFarland, F. W., "Working on Nonprofit Boards: Don't Assume the Shoe Fits," *Harvard Business Review* (November–December 1999): 65–80.

Newcomer, K. E. (ed.), *Using Performance Measurement to Improve Public and Nonprofit Programs*, San Francisco: Jossey-Bass, 1997.

Porter, M. E., and M. R. Kramer, "Philanthropy's New Agenda: Creating Value," *Harvard Business Review* (November–December 1999): 121–30.

Rados, D. L., *Marketing for Nonprofit Organizations* (2nd ed.), Westport, CT: Auburn House, 1996.

Sandler, M. W., and D. A. Hudson, *Beyond the Bottom Line*, Oxford: Oxford University Press, 1998.

Sheehan, R. M., Jr., "Achieving Growth and High Quality by Strategic Intent," *Nonprofit Management & Leadership* (summer 1999): 413–27.

Siciliano, J. I., "The Relationship between Formal Planning and Performance in Nonprofit Organizations," *Nonprofit Management & Leadership* (summer 1997): 387.

5

Staffing Nonprofits

Obtaining, maintaining, and retaining an optimal workforce is essential to any successful enterprise, whether nonprofit, for-profit, or government. Although a strategic orientation, capable board, and effective leadership are necessary building blocks, staff ultimately achieves the mission and vision of the nonprofit (Herman and Renz, 1998). Staff, whether paid employees or volunteers, actually delivers the results. Although effective staffing of nonprofits seeks the right mix of human talents, as in the private and public sectors, the nonprofit sector faces some unique challenges.

The most obvious difference is the use of volunteers. Because nonprofits pursue noble causes, people are often attracted to work free as volunteers or, if as employees, they may accept smaller compensation packages because of the nonprofit nature of the organization. Although for-profits and governments seldom rely on volunteers, many nonprofits would fail if not for the gratis assistance they receive from their volunteer workforce. At the same time, Peter Lynch (1999, p. 107) observes,

> Volunteerism is always said to be as American as apple pie. Without it, much of what we hold dear in this country, from Little League teams to church choirs, would simply cease to exist. And many of our grandest, most important cultural and charitable organizations can attribute their success as much to the donation of brains and brawn as to the collection of gifts and grants.

But volunteerism has gone through some rocky times of late. Although initiatives like the 1997 President's Summit for America's Future have helped bring about an increase in the amount of hours committed to charitable activities, this progress just barely offset the losses recorded earlier in the 1990s. In 1995, America actually had five million fewer people donating their time than seven years earlier in 1988.

Since 1995, volunteerism has picked up considerably. "An estimated 109 million people—or about 56 percent of all American adults— volunteered some of their time last year..." (Greene, 1999, p. 16). Ironically, one survey revealed that 93 percent of nonprofit executives viewed volunteer satisfaction as a major issue, and yet nearly one half have no systems to evaluate or ensure that satisfaction (Points of Light Foundation, 1997). At the same time, some for-profit organizations recognize the crucial role volunteers play.

According to the *Philanthropy Journal Alert* (Hyatt, 1998, p. 2):

> Bank America has organized a volunteer effort among its employees in which more than 15,000 of the workers have pledged to give time to schools and nonprofit groups. The bank ... allows employees up to two hours a week of paid time off each week to volunteer in K–12 schools, public or private. The program is an extension of a ... volunteer program that has been in existence for 10 years. The announcement of the volunteer drive comes just after the formation of the Bank of America Foundation, which will have a grant budget of approximately $100 million per year.

Though major corporations may have resources to install sophisticated volunteer programs, the sophistication of nonprofits to attract volunteers and paid employees varies widely and is strongly influenced by the size and maturity of the nonprofit. Nonprofit start-ups tend to have few resources, limited human resource policies, and a need for generalists who can handle multiple roles, often simultaneously. Usually the result is a small pool of applicants from which to hire, because new organizations lack the reputation, funding, or professionalization of management to obtain, maintain, and retain top talent. In some cases the primary criteria for being hired are a willingness and ability to fill the job opening.

As the nonprofit grows in resources and sophistication, its decision makers develop more standardized staffing procedures, the need for greater specialization among human resources, and a more visible reputation with which to attract a larger number of better applicants and volunteers. Likewise, policies to maintain and retain current employees and volunteers also become more professional and more systematic. Often as the nonprofit reaches the growth stage, it begins formalizing its human resource policies and procedures by creating a human resource department, or at least assigning human resource issues to a specialist if a full-blown department is not yet appropriate or financially feasible. Although volunteers may remain an important element of the staffing equation for a mature nonprofit, key positions are likely to be filled by full-time employees.

Thus staff (whether paid or volunteers) is one of the strategic elements of any nonprofit's resources. The professionalism and sophistication of staff will cover a broad range, influenced most strongly by the resources and maturity of the nonprofit. Likewise, the staffing policies and procedures that obtain, maintain, and retain human resources will also vary widely. Nevertheless, sound human resource policies and procedures assume a human resource information system (HRIS); an understanding of recruiting and selection processes; orientation and training programs that help integrate and develop human resources; staff evaluation; compensation systems; and general human resource policies. These topics outline the scope of this chapter.

Human Resource Information System

The human resource information system (HRIS) is the foundation of managing the nonprofit's human resources. When the nonprofit first begins, the size and complexity of staffing issues may be simple enough for the executive director or president to do all human resource duties. But when the nonprofit expands and the number of people and the complexity of jobs grow, a systematic information system is needed so that human resources activities can be delegated to appropriate managers and specialists.

The cornerstone of the HRIS comes from job analysis information. Job analysis provides written documentation about the jobs and the human characteristics needed to fill those jobs. Job analysis information is collected through paper and pencil or online questionnaires, interviews, or in rare situations by observation. (Observations are used when employees do not speak the language or are unable to articulate each task they need to perform, as may be the case with halfway houses helping those with limited mental capabilities.) Job analysis information collects data about the human skills, knowledge, and abilities needed to perform a job. It also identifies the tasks, duties, and responsibilities associated with each job in the nonprofit, as well as the working conditions under which the work is performed.

The result is a job description. The job description details the duties, skills, knowledge, abilities, working conditions, and other job characteristics—often stating these needed actions in behavioral terms that describe what the person must do to be successful. Armed with a job description, human resource specialists can undertake recruitment, selection, training, performance evaluation, compensation, and related decisions.

Staff Recruitment

The quality of the people working for a nonprofit may be the single most important determinant of the nonprofit's success. Simply put, an organization is no better than the people who work for it. The quality of hiring decisions, however, is greatly influenced by the number and quality of recruits that the nonprofit can attract, whether these are volunteers or people seeking paid employment. Recruiters seek a large recruitment ratio—the number of recruits obtained compared with the people hired. But recruiting employees in tight labor markets or volunteers who face many demands on their time can be difficult (Daspin, 1999), especially when "the number of nonprofit corporations operating in the United States increased by 50 percent" (McLaughlin, 1999, p. 20). Although many nonprofits have systematic procedures for recruiting paid staff, few have such methods for recruiting volunteers. As a result, research indicates that the typical volunteer is a well-educated, affluent, older, married, Caucasian women, which does not reflect the diversity found in society or found among the users of nonprofit services (Points of Light Foundation, 1997). Effective recruitment, therefore, occurs when qualified candidates for paid and volunteer positions apply in quantities large enough to give decision makers sufficient choices (Coolsen and Wintz, 1998).

Recruitment begins with a decision to add a new person and ends when recruits complete a written application. The process relies on several different channels of recruitment for prospective employees or volunteers because they seldom use just one method to find work. One of the most common and effective techniques for recruiting volunteers or paid workers is through referral. Referrals by employees or volunteers are particularly appropriate if the current workforce is effective. People tend to recommend people with similar work attitudes, education, and skills. Moreover the people referred already have some knowledge about the organization, its purpose, and its working conditions. Those not interested have sufficient insights to self-select themselves out of the recruitment process.

Though effective, referrals have two concerns that merit attention. First, when employees recommend their friends, cliques can develop in the organization along with the attendant morale problems. At the extreme friends and relatives may be reluctant to report wrongdoing, leading to an increased possibility of fraud or embezzlement, especially when employees have access to cash or other valuables. A second problem is one of discrimination. A workforce that is dominated by a single religious, racial, ethnic, or other classification tends to perpetuate itself when employee referrals are relied on heavily. People tend to refer people like themselves. When the nonprofit has a hard-working, effective workforce, this referral pattern is a plus. If, however, a workforce dominated by men or women refers people of the same gender (or race or religion or age or national origin or other protected classification as defined by the national equal employment laws) the imbalance will be perpetuated. Then when others who are not part of the majority pattern apply, they may be excluded as "different" and either not be recommended or, if hired, not stay. In turn, this can lead to charges against the nonprofit of discrimination, even if there was no intention to discriminate. Besides potential law violations, the attendant negative publicity can harm future recruitment efforts, damage the nonprofit's reputation, and harm future board development and fundraising efforts. Nevertheless, with these cautions in mind, people who come with personal recommendations can lead to effective hiring decisions, especially because they already know something about the nonprofit's vision and mission.

Advertising is another commonly used recruiting channel. Classified ads in local newspapers are an effective tool for finding people with general skills—such as drivers, clerical workers, cooks, counter help, and others. When specialized or professional skills are needed, classified advertising works best when directed at specialized publications that are likely to attract these unique abilities. For example, when hiring grant writers or fundraisers, many large nonprofits advertise in the *Chronicle of Philanthropy*, which reaches many such professionals. Likewise, there are specialized publications aimed at accountants, doctors, lawyers, and others that might be needed by a nonprofit.

State unemployment agencies are an appropriate channel, especially for those who are unskilled. Although many professionals disdain state unemployment offices as being for low-level workers, placing notification of job openings with state agencies does ensure a wide distribution and helps protect against accusations of selective recruitment that discriminates. Because many job searchers use multiple channels when looking for a job, it may prove effective. Moreover, supported by tax dollars, state unemployment offices are free.

Private placement firms are similar to state-run unemployment offices. These organizations charge a fee to the employer or the employee to cover their placement expenses and to make a profit. "Fee-paid" jobs are those for which the employer pays; otherwise, job seekers have to pay to use these for-profit firms—often costing 10 percent of the first year's salary or one month's pay. These firms advertise to attract recruits and may even do some prescreening according to the wishes of the nonprofit.

Closely related are temporary help agencies. These firms provide full- and part-time workers, often on short notice, to fill temporary openings—for example, to cover vacation schedules or employees on extended leaves. They are a source of recruitment because temporary employees may be interested in converting to full-time employees. In fact, today it is common for most temporary-help firms to have a contract with users that specify fees if temporary to permanent conversions take place.

When highly skilled and hard-to-find employees are needed, large nonprofits may turn to professional search firms, also known as headhunters. These firms, for an employer-paid fee, will seek out professional or technical workers who are often already employed and not seeking employment. Though an effective tool for finding an executive director or other high-level position, for example, the fees and related expenses preclude most nonprofits from turning to headhunters. Though useful, the nonprofit's leadership must monitor the search and stay firmly in charge. The responsibility for staffing the nonprofit always remains with the nonprofit, not the professional search firm.

Other recruitment channels for volunteers and job applicants range from notices on websites, bulletin boards, and even the front doors of high traffic locations. Monster.com and other web-based job posting sites offer instant access to a wide range of potential recruits, speeding up the recruitment process often at low cost. Bulletin boards and notices on front doors are other low-cost recruitment methods. However, like those candidates found via websites, often little is known about such candidates, suggesting a need to carefully verify background information.

For job applicants, recruitment at colleges, military bases, and community self-help groups that provide career skills training to economically disadvantages individuals under government, church, or welfare-to-work projects are other entry-level channels. As with any recruitment channel, recruiters must balance the cost of using the channel with the success they have in getting qualified applicants to apply.

The recruitment process ends when potentially qualified candidates make application. Most sophisticated nonprofits have a formal application form or application blank, as they are also called. The application blank provides a standardized source of information about applicants, and this information should be collected for volunteers, too (though it may be called a volunteer's information form). Though those applying may send letters and resumes that tout their skills, an application blank ensures a minimum uniformity of information gets in front of decision makers. Typically an application blank will request name, mail and e-mail addresses, telephone numbers, and background information such as education, previous work experience, and salary history. Most application blanks also contain a signature line that gives the employer the right to make background inquiries and asks the applicant to attest to the accuracy of the information provided.

Staff Selection

The selection process starts when someone completes an application and ends when the employee is hired or the volunteer is put to work. There is no one best approach to selection. Figure 5-1 shows the most common steps in the selection process.

When an applicant appears at the nonprofit seeking a job or a volunteer position and has completed an application blank or a volunteer's information form, he or she may be given a brief, courtesy interview. The purpose of this interview is to provide the person with needed information and to determine his or her overall suitability. Volunteers may be signed up right on the spot and told when they

Figure 5-1 **Steps in the Staffing Process**

1. Recruitment	5. Background checks
2. Courtesy interview	6. Realistic job previews
3. Supervisory interview	7. Hiring decision
4. Tests	

can come to an orientation or volunteers' meeting. For employees, the hiring decision often involves additional steps, central of which is the supervisory interview.

Supervisory Interviews

Supervisors are responsible for the success or failure of new hires, so most organizations give the supervisor the ultimate hiring authority, although someone in the human resources area may communicate the actual decision.

Interviews are a two-way conversation with a purpose. The interviewer uses a mix of structured and unstructured questions. Structured questions are predetermined ones that are asked of each applicant. Unstructured questions are made up as the interview goes along. The ideal interview uses both approaches, sometimes called a mixed-interview format. Structured questions are useful for comparing one applicant with another. They are particularly helpful when several interviewers get together to evaluate a particular candidate. Asking some of the same questions ensures a greater degree of uniformity in decision making. Unstructured questions make the interview more like a conversation and not a rigid interrogation. In addition, the unstructured questions allow the interviewer to probe into interesting areas or to explore answers that merit further clarification.

In general an effective interview has five stages.

Preinterview preparation. The preinterview stage requires the interviewer to evaluate the application blank or the volunteer's information form, resume, cover letter, or other materials about the candidate to determine the questions the interviewer needs to ask. What does the interviewer need to know about the candidate to make a rational decision to use the person? What questions will be asked and in what order? But the selection process is not just one way: It is a two way street—the applicant is deciding on the nonprofit and the nonprofit is deciding on the applicant. The interviewer needs to be prepared to answer questions about the nonprofit, perhaps even selling the candidate on why he or she should come to work for the nonprofit.

Creating rapport. Creating rapport with the job candidate or volunteer is the next stage of the interview. Many people are anxious in job interviews and may not interview well. That is, their anxiety may block the interviewer from seeing the real potential of the candidate. To put the applicant at ease and establish rapport, then, is the responsibility of the interviewer.

Beginning on time with a friendly greeting starts the process. Casual body language and nonthreatening questions at the beginning can help open up the discussion. For example, many interviewers will begin with questions about the weather or parking or will even ask the candidate if he or she has any opening questions. This latter approach can reduce anxiety while giving the interviewer insights into the candidate based on the questions that are asked. With a particularly anxious candidate, the interview may be conducted as part of a walk-around tour of the facilities, avoiding the face-to-face rigidity of a formal, sit-down interview.

Exchanging information. Exchanging information is the third stage, and it is at the heart of the interview process. The applicant wants to learn about the job; the interviewer wants to learn about the candidate's potential to do the job. At the same time both sides are in a selling position: The applicant needs to sell his or her abilities to the nonprofit, and the nonprofit needs to sell itself to the candidate so that if an offer is forthcoming it will be accepted. With volunteers, the selling is more one-sided, with the nonprofit trying to attract the volunteer to sign up. This exchange requires preparation as well. The interviewer needs to know about the work, its standards and expectations, the working conditions, advancement opportunities, and related concerns that are likely to be raised by the candidate. Both need to leave the supervisory interview with enough information to make an informed choice.

Questions are derived from the job application or the volunteer's information form, resume, and areas of hesitancy or uncertainty among references. With prospective employees, areas in the application blank that seem unclear or exhibit unusual background experience, job titles, salary history, and the pattern of responsibilities are key areas of interest. Particular attention needs to focus on obvious incongruities among titles, salary history, experience, and education. Most experienced interviewers expect to see a high degree of congruence among these pieces of information. With questions that are likely to be anticipated by applicants—for example, "Why did you leave your previous job?"—clever interviewers may ask the same question at different stages of the interview to see if the answers are consistent. An interviewer may rephrase the questions to probe more deeply— for example, "What could your last employer have done differently to prevent you from leaving?" and "Why?" The purpose is not to trick the applicant but to gain insight into the applicant's motivations and interests. For volunteers in this phase of the selection process, the interviewer needs to learn about the volunteer's skills, but the emphasis is still usually on selling the nonprofit.

Termination. Ending the interview is the fourth stage and is typically communicated with body language and sometimes with questions that clue the candidate that the time is up. "Do you have any final questions?" is often a common close. Or "Do you have anything else you would like to have considered?" Or "Is there anything else I should have asked before we end?" Not only do these signal the end of the interview, but they give the candidate a chance to summarize or add any other relevant information. Normally, the interviewer does not tell the job applicant the hiring decision, if it is known, because other actions (such as interviewing other candidates or checking references) may still be needed and may change the outcome. Although job openings are limited and the nonprofit seeks the best job applicant it can get, volunteers are often thanked and put to work immediately.

Postinterview follow-up. The fifth stage involves postinterview actions. These should include written notes by the interviewer recorded promptly after the interview while the impressions are still fresh. Often several candidates are evaluated days or even weeks apart. When the decision is eventually made, notes help interviewers distinguish among the various candidates and their attributes. An important caution is to avoid making notations about information that is not job-related. Comments about age, gender, race, religion, national origin, pregnancy, disabilities, or other categories may be damaging if they are subsequently discovered as part of an employment discrimination suit. Beyond being a source of potential future lawsuits, such notations are inappropriate and counterproductive to encouraging a diverse workforce.

Other Selection Steps

Tests, background checks, and realistic job previews are other steps often found in the selection process. Tests are not commonly used because most nonprofits hire too few employees to warrant developing and validating tests. A typing test for a word processor operator or a driving test for a driver seldom create problems because of their obvious direct job relevance. However, test of attitudes, intelligence, or personality are sometimes irrelevant because they lack consistency (called reliability) or they lack a relationship between the test and job performance (called validity). Tests that lack reliability and validity are worse than a waste of time. They may lead to results that discriminate against a protected group and lead to allegations of discrimination. (Even when such charges are groundless, they may be damaging to the image of the nonprofit.) For example, a reading test in English given to truck drivers who receive their instruction orally would almost certainly discriminate against foreign-born drivers, potentially leading to a discrimination suit on the basis of national origin.

Background checks are usually authorized by the candidate's signature on the application blank or the volunteer's information form. At a minimum they include reference checks, which are typically designed to validate application and other information already compiled about the candidate. Though written recommendations are most common because they create a written record, people may be more candid— intentionally or not—when asked over a telephone to give their evaluation of the candidate. Voice inflections, hesitancy, hedging, and other responses that would not be obvious in a written comment may show up in a telephone reference check, giving the interviewer areas to probe more deeply. For example, in response to a question about a drinking problem with a potential driver, for example, a written response might be a flat "no." But over the telephone, the same no might be said with hesitation or less than firm conviction: "No, not really."

Background checks should verify educational and license claims by applicants. Likewise, those who will be driving as part of their job should have their driving records checked. Credit and even criminal background checks may be appropriate for those who have access to cash or other valuables. Criminal background checks are increasingly necessary when employees have access to small children, sick individuals, or others who could be taken advantage of. Failure to make such background checks could lead to claims of negligent hiring if an employee (or volunteer) with a criminal record commits a crime while with the nonprofit. Victims often win suits when the employer appears negligent, not to mention the unfavorable publicity for the nonprofit, which probably survives only because of its good deeds and reputation. Beyond concerns about lawsuits and damage to the nonprofit's reputation, the nonprofit would also seek to protect those people who are served by their programs and thus want to be careful of their hires.

Realistic job previews give applicants an opportunity to see the job and the job setting. They are used primarily when the job or the working conditions are unusual—such as working in a psychiatric ward or working with criminals. The idea is that those who find such conditions unacceptable will self-select out of the employment or volunteer process. Though the time and effort up to this point will be wasted, it is better to have someone self-select out of consideration than to have them leave a few days or weeks after they are formally hired, oriented, and trained.

Staff Orientation

Once a volunteer is selected or an employee is hired, orientation follows. Orientation helps integrate the person into the organization by giving him or her information about the nonprofit. The orientation should cover the four "P's" of people, place, policies, and procedures from the perspective of the organization, department, and coworker levels. The result is a matrix, as shown in Figure 5-2. All effective orientation covers each of the 12 cells of the matrix shown.

The organizational level of orientation seeks to give the newcomer an overview of the entire organization, people, place, policies, and procedures. The same topics are then covered but from the perspective of the department. So at the organizational level, employees would have learned about the top leaders of the nonprofit. At the supervisory level, employees are actually introduced to their coworkers or other

Figure 5-2 **Orientation Process Matrix**

Levels	TOPICS			
	People	Place	Policies	Procedures
Organizational				
Supervisory				
Buddy System				

volunteers by the supervisor. The supervisor can tell the newcomer something about each employee's or volunteer's duties and interests to create the basis of further social conversation. The place, policies, and procedures that apply at the departmental level are also explained.

Because the newcomer is facing so much information, many supervisors will then turn the new person over to a senior volunteer or coworker. The "buddy" is selected for his or her knowledge of the organization, positive attitude, and personal characteristics (such as whether he or she is married, a parent, or likes to fish), which are similar to the newcomer's. The buddy completes the orientation by giving the newcomer insights into the informal organization and helps sponsor the newcomer's introduction to the informal work group. Acceptance by the informal work group is critical for the new person to feel like he or she fits in.

Not only does the orientation program reduce the likelihood that the person will quit, it speeds up the learning of the job. With fewer anxieties about fitting in, the newcomer is better able to focus on learning the job. The informal part of the program lets the employee ask personal and job-related questions of the buddy that he or she may be reluctant to ask of the new boss. An effective orientation not only benefits the newcomers by integrating them into the organization, but it also benefits the nonprofit's performance because the newcomer is able to learn his or her role faster (Farmer and Fedor, 1999).

Within a month of starting, sophisticated nonprofits will do a follow-up on the orientation, sometimes in the form of an evaluation of the orientation process, on the assumption that those areas rated poorly are in need of follow-up by management or the human resources function.

Training and Development of Human Resources

Training focuses on helping people do their present job better; *development* addresses the ability to perform in the future. In practice, training and development meld into a growth experience for the volunteer or employee. If one assumes that a nonprofit is only as good as its people, then training and development represent key tools for improving the performance of the nonprofit. Though it is hard to argue against the strategic value of training and development, at the tactical level many nonprofits (especially new and small ones) perceive that they do not have the resources to devote to these activities. The result is, perhaps, a "Catch 22": because a nonprofit cannot afford to invest in its people, it is difficult to improve the performance of the nonprofit; and because it is difficult to improve the performance of the nonprofit, resources are not available for training and development. This circular problem is compounded when dealing with a staff that includes volunteers. Because volunteers are "free" to the nonprofit, their potential contribution may not be as valued. To spend precious resources on training and development for volunteers is even less likely than for full-time employees. Compounding the need for training and development even further is the limited number of specialized educational degrees in the area of nonprofit management (Haas and Robinson, 1998).

Nevertheless, training and development represent a point of leverage for executive directors of nonprofits. When it comes to staff, the president or executive director of a nonprofit faces a make or buy decision. Should the nonprofit make a better staff through developing the talent—employees and volunteers alike—it has, or should it simply replace current staff members with better ones? When it comes to the volunteer component of the nonprofit, there is really little choice. Because volunteers are free, the nonprofit cannot "buy" better ones even though it may always be on the look out for energetic, able volunteers. But with paid staff, there exists the possibility of replacing current employees by "buying" new hires who are better. However, even if there were resources available to buy better staff, the costs, morale impact, and the lack of continuity may make such a systematic decision prohibitive, except, perhaps, in individual cases when current employees leave.

Thus for the bulk of nonprofits, improving staff means developing staff members. To implement a developmental program, however, requires resources. At this point, many nonprofits decide that resources might be better spent on delivering its mission or other demands and do not pursue training and development. Some leaders recognize that there are innovative ways of meeting the nonprofit's training and development needs (Smith, 2000).

Grants

Many foundations will provide funds only to nonprofits, and many prefer to give on a project basis rather than to general operating funds. Training and development monies are generally taken out of operating funds, so many leaders incorrectly assume that raising funds for such purposes through grants is unlikely to succeed. However, grants specifically targeted to provide training and development can be sent to foundations, not as a request for general operating funds but with specific program objectives to improve the staff's capabilities in delivering the mission. Not all foundations will accept this distinction, but grantors that want to avoid becoming a source of ongoing operations can view training and development grants as one-time efforts to strengthen the grantee.

Bootstrapping

Bootstrapping off the private sector or other nonprofits can lessen, even eliminate, the costs. For example, many nonprofits have senior business people from the local community on their boards. Many of these companies have long since made a commitment to training and development for their employees. The incremental cost to such firms of having members from the nonprofit attend as guests is essentially negligible. All that is required by the business is a policy decision to allow a limited number of members from the nonprofit to attend and then putting the nonprofit on the training and development distribution list. Not all the company training would be relevant to a nonprofit, but basic supervisory, management, and leadership programs along with computer skills training classes and other topics could be appropriate.

Likewise, when firms or other nonprofits bring speakers or trainers to town for their purposes, the nonprofit may be able to gain access to this person for a small honorarium, because travel-related costs are presumably already covered. Closely related are training coalitions. Two or more nonprofits can pool their limited training and development resources and create sessions designed for their needs. Take the following example:

> At the University of Miami's School of Business, the Center for Nonprofit Management was created by a local social entrepreneur, who approached the school with a willingness to give and raise funds. Then each month, for a heavily subsidized and somewhat nominal fee, scores of representatives of nonprofits attend. The half-day sessions address a variety of topics attendees have suggested. To further leverage the funds and available talent, the Center partners with others in the community, such as the National Society for Fundraising

Executives and local social services coalitions. For those who cannot afford the nominal fee, scholarships are made available from the foundation grants that support the effort.

Staff Evaluation

Many leaders believe they know how well each employee and volunteer is performing. To engage in formal performance evaluations seems an unnecessary task and it is not always pleasant, especially when a manager needs to tell an employee or a volunteer that he or she is not performing up to standard. In addition, the process consumes valuable time of the management and can lead to ill feelings if not handled well. As a result, some nonprofits miss this employee-improving and organizational-improving opportunity.

Employees and volunteers need feedback. They need to know how they are doing. Although good managers will give this feedback on an ongoing basis, the feedback tends to be situationally oriented around specific tasks. A big picture view is also needed. How is the employee or volunteer doing overall? What actions are needed to improve performance? What areas are deserving of positive feedback? What does the person need to do to grow in his or her present position? To be promoted? To ignore these questions is to imply that everyone is doing well, with the exception of tactical criticisms that arise on a day to day basis. The lack of formal feedback also implies that management is not seriously interested in helping people improve their performance. As a result, loyalty and dedication may fade and turnover increase.

Formal appraisals serve three important functions: They evaluate past performance; they are the basis for planning future improvements in performance; and they give the organization feedback on its human resources processes.

Past Performance Evaluation

Individual performance appraisals give feedback on performance. These evaluations should focus on behaviors, not personality attributes or attitudes, except insofar as these affect performance. All but the smallest organizations usually have a systematic methodology that centers on an evaluation form. Though there are scores of different approaches and forms, the specific instruments are less important than the process.

Many managers like to have the employee or volunteer fill out the form before the appraisal meeting. These self-ratings have several advantages. First, the person is forced to think deeply about his or her actual performance. Second, by committing the evaluation to writing, it adds a degree of formality and impact beyond the informal, oral feedback employees and volunteers typically receive on a daily basis. Third, when the person arrives for the feedback session, the completed form can be the basis for the discussion. Typically, the evaluation instrument will cover a variety topics, including accomplishments, current skills, and perhaps good and bad critical incidents that took place during the previous 6- or 12-month period covered by the evaluation. In the dimensions of the evaluation on which the person and the supervisor agree, there is likely to be little discussion. Where the person has been overly harsh or lenient, the supervisor can discuss these perceptions with the intent of reaching a mutual agreement about those areas of performance. Although there may be a need to redirect misbehavior or poor performance, many evaluators take the view that they are coaching the employee or volunteer by pointing out what changes are needed to achieve better performance (and evaluations) in the future. With an agreement on past performance, the evaluation process often turns to future performance goals.

Future Performance Goals

The problem with evaluating past performance is that it cannot be changed. It is in the past. Many performance review sessions end by focusing on what actions the person will undertake to attain even better performance in the future. This discussion may address the need to change behaviors in the future. Often, however, the discussion addresses what affirmative actions he or she will undertake to improve existing, or develop new, skills, knowledge, and abilities. Reassurances that the person can attain these new levels of performance along with offers of how the supervisor or the organization can help are usual elements of future-oriented performance discussions. Then effective supervisors follow-up on the employee's improvement efforts during the next rating period.

Organizational Feedback

When individual performance evaluations are aggregated, patterns may reveal themselves. Widespread absenteeism, poor attitudes about clients, low levels of understanding about the vision or the mission, and even dissatisfaction with work rules or other organizational elements may surface. When any of these or other issues form a pattern across a variety of departmental or organizational areas, the pattern may suggest an error or weakness in the nonprofit's human resource system. Widespread poor performance, for example, may mean defects in the recruitment, selection, orientation, or training efforts. Or poor attitudes about dealing with clients or patrons may call for customer service training. Simply stated, systematic weaknesses revealed by individual performance appraisals may point to areas in need of management attention and follow-up programs. On an individual basis, good or bad performance often holds implications for career advancement, training needs, and compensation adjustments.

Staff Compensation

Compensation is often a sensitive topic among the staff members of nonprofits. Strategic thinkers define compensation broadly to include salaries and wages, benefits, and other terms or conditions of employment.

Pay and Benefits

On the pay and benefits side, most nonprofits lag behind the private sector, even among the mature, well-established nonprofits. Boards, donors, and the general community do not expect nonprofit executives (and lower level staff) to be compensated as their private-sector counterparts. At the same time, responsibilities of nonprofit staff may be every bit as pressing as those found in the private sector (Oster, 1998).

At a minimum, compensation plans must seek internal and external equity. Internal equity assumes that jobs that are worth more, that contribute more, and that have greater responsibilities are paid more. That is, within the nonprofit, the chief grant writer is paid more than the secretary is and the executive director is paid more than both. Notice that these pay differences are not based on who works the hardest, which may be the janitor or the van driver. The internal focus is on the relative contributions, especially the skills, knowledge, and responsibilities, of the staff members. Even though the van driver's work might be physically more strenuous, she or he does not need to possess the skills, knowledge, or responsibilities required of the executive director. For most nonprofits, internal equity is relatively easy to address through sophisticated job evaluation programs, detailed in basic human resource textbooks (Werther and Davis, 1996).

Much more difficult is to achieve external equity, where pay for nonprofit staff is equivalent to what similar jobs make in the private sector. For example, a secretary may be paid substantially less than what secretaries with similar skills and responsibilities make in the private sector. Yet budgetary limitations may not allow the nonprofit to increase the secretary's salary to market rates. Though one person's raise may be affordable—because the person is paid at a lower rate—such a raise might upset the pay structure and create an internal inequity. Then to adjust everyone's pay upward to ensure internal equity might prove to be unaffordable with current resources. Even when more resources come to the nonprofit, those monies may be restricted to program delivery or endowment and not available for raises. Moreover, giving a raise assumes that funds will continue in the future to sustain that new salary. The result in many cases is that the nonprofit staff is underpaid.

Much of the same reasoning can be applied to benefits, which typically lag behind the private sector. For nonprofits, the addition of new or improved benefits almost always means a trade-off between raising wages and salaries or improvement in fringe benefits. Some nonprofits have reduced the pressure for more by offering staff flexible benefits that allow each staff member to select the benefit combination that best fits his or her personal and family needs. For example, a working mother may want health insurance with small deductibles whereas a senior staff member nearing retirement might want a large deductible to dedicate more funds toward retirement. Flex benefits, as these programs are sometimes called, allow both staff members to pursue their needs—reducing the pressure on the nonprofit to provide every type of benefit to everyone to please a few.

Other Terms and Conditions of Employment

Beyond traditional pay and benefits, a job may have other attributes that can partially offset external pay and benefit inequities. Only the executive director and the board's creativity limit the possibilities. High on many staff members' lists is the autonomy implied in flexible work rules. For example, rigid starting and ending times are particularly difficult for working parents who may have child care issues. Being able to attend a school play or a sporting event may help offset lower pay. As a result, a flex-time schedule may allow employees to decide which 40 hours during the week they are going to work— staying late one evening, perhaps, so that they can leave early on another.

A special benefit may be added because it makes the job more attractive. Many working parents, for example, would accept lower pay levels if they could bring their preschool children to on-site, employer-sponsored day care.

The working atmosphere in the nonprofit may offset concerns about pay and benefit levels (which can be major contributors to employee turnover). Is the nonprofit a fun place to work? Does management genuinely care about employees? Do employees feel that they are making a contribution to a noble vision?

Motivating Volunteers

By definition, volunteers do not get paid. So how are they compensated for their efforts? Though each volunteer is unique, with unique motivations, most volunteers are seeking an opportunity to make a contribution. They volunteer to do good. Thus one of the key "compensations" a nonprofit gives a volunteer is purpose. Meaningful contributions allow the volunteer to feel that he or she is making a difference. Feelings of accomplishment, contribution, achievement, and self-satisfaction come from helping. Many volunteers feel good about their association in direct proportion to the contribution they make to the nonprofit. Thus the burden of having volunteers is to put them to work at a necessary and meaningful task. Not all tasks volunteers do end hunger or right social wrongs. However, if their contribution moves the nonprofit toward its vision, its mission, then the volunteer can feel that he or she is part of something noble.

Putting the volunteer to work on a meaningful project gives a sense of purpose and accomplishment. Those efforts and accomplishments, however, need to be recognized. Although recognition may range from a simple thank you to a note of recognition at the board meeting or annual volunteers' appreciation dinner, recognition and appreciation are the currency of volunteer compensation. Closely related is the need to create an overall work environment that is satisfying.

Building a Human Organization

Staffing a nonprofit is more than just hiring people. How the human resource system performs and how the organization obtains, maintains, and retains its human resources is at the heart of how well the nonprofit performs (Brudney, 1999). The visions and mission of the nonprofit is achieved—or not—by its people.

Just as the nonprofit may have a fundraising strategy, it needs a human resource strategy. How is the organization going to build a high performance team from its unique blend of employees and volunteers? Although each organization will come to a unique conclusion, the answer lies in some balance between meeting the needs of the people and the mission-related objectives of the organization. At times, trade-offs will be made, sometimes sacrificing employee needs or mission objectives. But what the human resource strategy seeks to do is to create win–win combinations in which the needs of the staff and the objectives of the nonprofit are met simultaneously. The staff member wins and so do the organization's goals and objectives.

Though no single formula exists to create such an environment, several elements seem to be common to successful organizations. At a minimum, the human resources strategy attends to issues of awareness, involvement, and feedback (Andrew and Orwig, 1998).

Awareness

Board members and staff need to be aware of the vision, mission, strategy, and objectives of the nonprofit. Particularly important is to infuse employees and volunteers with a sense of purpose that underlies the vision. Vision statements in for-profit businesses often center on making the owners wealthy. Although there is nothing wrong with that purpose, it tends not to be particularly ennobling for most people in the organization. However, with a nonprofit, dedicated to doing some social good, leaders have the ability to inspire employees and volunteers to strive for that goal. People want to feel that they are part of something larger than they are; they want to feel connected to something worthy and noble. This awareness assumes that management undertakes concentrated and ongoing efforts to communicate the vision, mission, strategy, and goals—starting with the new employee orientation and continuing through a variety of training and educational communications. Perhaps the greatest way to create that awareness is through the personal involvement of staff members in defining (or redefining) the vision, mission, strategies, and goals of the nonprofit.

Involvement

If volunteers, employees, and board members are to be motivated to pursue the vision and mission and these are to be more than mere platitudes, they need to internalize the purpose of the nonprofit. That is, staff members should have a sense of personal ownership of the vision and mission of the nonprofit. They get this sense of ownership by being involved in the processes that examine the vision, mission, strategy, and goals. People who participate in setting goals are more likely to be committed to those goals. Moreover, participation reinforces understanding. Together, involvement and awareness reinforce one's commitment, dedication, and motivation.

Feedback

Awareness and a sense of personal involvement are maintained through feedback. Board members and staff get feedback that connects their efforts and involvement to the nonprofit's accomplishments. Formal and informal progress reports give life to the abstract ideas of vision, mission, strategy, and goals. Accomplishments are victories in which people can take pride, especially if those same people help define the goals and work toward their achievement. Bluntly stated, people want to associate with a winner. Like a sporting event, the only way people know that they are winning is when the score is reported.

Conclusion

Effective nonprofits manage staff and the human resource systems that support those people to obtain, maintain, and retain an optimal workforce. Staff members—whether paid employees or volunteers—

deliver the mission of the nonprofit. They are central to the non-profit's success.

Growth and staff turnover demand that the nonprofit recruit new members of the organization. The recruitment process seeks to give decision makers a choice of candidates from which to choose. To do this, the nonprofit pursues potential staff members through a variety of channels. Once recruits have completed an application, the selection process begins. Selection is a multistep process that seeks to determine which of the recruits is the best fit for the staffing needs of the nonprofit. Central to this decision-making process is the supervisory interview.

Once on board, new hires or new volunteers need to be oriented to the people, place, policies, and procedures of the nonprofit. Typically this orientation takes place at the organizational, departmental, and coworker levels. Training and development are then added to the human resource equation as a means of strengthening the nonprofit's effectiveness. Performance evaluations are another useful method to enhance the nonprofit's staff, while detecting human resource activities that might benefit from further efforts.

Performance evaluation also gives insight into compensation adjustments in the form of raises. Pay and benefits are often a weak element of nonprofits because resource scarcity often means compensation levels do not always equal those in the private sector. Effective management and a good working atmosphere can help offset modest compensation levels.

A nonprofit organized around its vision, mission, and strategies has direction. To that sense of direction, add a strong board of directors and strategic-oriented leaders and the nonprofit gains leadership. The addition of an optimal staff provides the vehicle through which the nonprofit leaders can attain the vision and mission. But these elements are not enough. As we will see in Part II of the book, successful nonprofits are expected to achieve their aims efficiently. Thus managing the nonprofit's productivity is essential to ensure that measured outcomes are attained with the fewest resources possible. Sometimes mission attainment is best pursued through alliances with other nonprofits, government, or the private sector. Only when all the conditions of Parts I and II of the book are addressed can the nonprofit pursue fundraising from a strategic and operational high ground. These issues of productivity management, measured outcomes, alliances, and fundraising are the topics covered in Part II of the book.

References

Andrew, M., and R. Orwig, "Generation X: How to Manage, Market, & Motivate Them," *Nonprofit World* (January/February 1998): 36–41.

Brudney, J. L., "The Perils of Practice: Reaching the Summit," *Management & Leadership* (summer 1999): 385–98.

Coolsen, P., and L. Wintz, "Learn and Grow Change: Adapting Service Organizations to a Changing World," *Nonprofit World* (January/February 1998): 44–48.

Daspin, E. "Volunteering on the Run," *Wall Street Journal* (Eastern ed.), November 5, 1999, pp. W1, W4.

Farmer, S. M., and D. B. Fedor, "Volunteer Participation and Withdrawal: A Psychological Contract Perspective on the Role of Expectations and Organizational Support," *Management & Leadership* (summer 1999): 349–68.

Greene, S. G., "Ranks of Volunteers Swell to a Record but Donations Dip, Survey Finds," *Chronicle of Philanthropy* (October 21, 1999): 16.

Haas, P. J., and M. G. Robinson, "The Views of Nonprofit Executives in Educating Nonprofit Managers," *Nonprofit Management & Leadership* (summer 1998): 349–62.

Herman, R. D., and D. O. Renz, "Nonprofit Organizational Effectiveness: Contrasts between Especially Effective and Less Effective Organizations," *Nonprofit Management & Leadership* (fall 1998): 23–38.

Hyatt, J. B., "Bank of America Gives Time to Employees for Volunteering," *Philanthropy Journal Alert* (October 14, 1998): 2.

Lynch, P. "Lost Time," *Worth* (June 1999): 107–08.

McLauglin, T. A., "Nonprofit Jobs Go Unfilled," *The NonProfit Times* (November 1999): 20, 23.

Oster, S. M., "Executive Compensation in the Nonprofit Sector," *Nonprofit Management & Leadership* (spring 1998): 207–21.

Points of Light Foundation, *Will the Best of Intentions Be Enough? A Report on Volunteerism among the Nation's Voluntary Health Organizations,* Washington, D.C.: Author, 1997.

Smith, J. P. , "Nonprofit Management Education in the United States: Management Is Not Management," *Vital Speeches of the Day* (January 1, 2000): 182.

Werther, W. B., and K. Davis, *Human Resources and Personnel Management* (5th ed.), New York: McGraw-Hill, 1996.

Part II

Strategic Execution

6

Nonprofit Productivity

Productivity improvement is the effort to make the best use of resources. It is defined as the "efficient and effective use of resources to achieve outcomes" (Berman, 1995, p. 5). He also argues that productivity in nonprofit organizations is characterized by a balanced emphasis on both effectiveness and efficiency. *Effectiveness* is about achieving the right outcomes. Nonprofits deal with many stakeholders, and they must address their needs well. Organizations must live up to their reputations for being effective in view of ever-changing expectations and community challenges. *Efficiency* is about reducing the cost of activities, typically by using fewer resources and doing some work faster or cheaper. This traditional emphasis is commonly found among for-profit companies, which seek to do more with less. Thus nonprofit productivity requires both effectiveness ("doing the right things") and efficiency ("doing things the right way").

Productivity improvement is of concern throughout the nonprofit's life cycle, though the emphasis will vary. Efficiency is commonly sacrificed for effectiveness, when the two conflict. Though resources are typically scarce at the start-up stage of nonprofits, productivity is typically less important than building a track record of effectively achieving the mission-related goals. Likewise, periods of rapid growth suggest that resources are available to fund that growth, relegating productivity to a secondary role. However, as the nonprofit becomes mature and established, its niche in the community is defined and accepted, both board members and the larger community expect nonprofits to operate efficiently, finding a tight balance between "doing the right things" and "doing things right." For a mature nonprofit to exhibit inefficiency through low productivity raises questions about the competency of the executive director, staff, and board oversight. Worse, flagrant inefficiency suggests the existence of ample resources—perhaps unintentionally undermining community support and fundraising efforts.

117

Nonprofit organizations may seem to lag in their productivity improvement efforts, at least relative to large private and public organizations. Often the focus of the nonprofit is on the mission, not on how the mission is delivered. Theorists have speculated that this may be because nonprofits face less competition than corporations and less scrutiny than public organizations. At the same time, nonprofits must balance demands from multiple constituents. Support for this proposition is readily found in countless hospitals and arts organizations that improved only in the face of threats to survival or public embarrassment. However, it is certainly also true that forward-looking leaders are often drivers of improvement efforts, regardless of the presence of competitive threats or public scrutiny. In these cases, productivity improvement of nonprofits is neither inevitable nor an insurmountable challenge. It is about the managerial decision to seize the opportunity.

Leaders have many options for improving productivity. In recent years, information technology is increasingly used to reduce time spent on paperwork and to improve exchange of information. Information technologies themselves benefit from falling costs. Feedback-based strategies are also used to improve performance by seeking client input to improve the focus of interventions and to better deal with obstacles to success. Reengineering is used to improve the productivity of delivery processes. However, productivity improvement does not rely only on new approaches that come into widespread use. It also depends on diagnosing existing problems in organizations—including unnecessary paperwork, poorly structured supervision, improper employee expectations, inadequate planning and follow-through, inefficient allocation of staff resources, and so on.

When Less Is More

When asked about conditions that hinder productivity most, many staff members would probably identify burdensome rules and questionable management decisions. When managers are asked the same question, they often point to staff incompetence and conflicting demands from funders, public agencies, and others, which dilute mission orientation. The inability to mobilize resources and focus on doing things well is a huge frustration to many who work in organizations. Three frequent, important problems commonly impair the effectiveness of organizations: too many rules, poor supervision, and acceptance of shoddy performance.

Too Many Rules

Every organization needs rules to ensure uniformity, efficiency of action, and also accountability. But when is enough, enough? Rules can quickly become barriers to mission attainment. Prohibitions (for example, to minimize the possibility of fraud or abuse) and the need to police them can focus on management and employee efforts rather than mission attainment. Indeed, new rules often create the need to expend considerable energy trying to figure out how they can be made to work. Moreover, when organizations engage in a flurry of endless concern with accountability, paperwork requirements (which often are the by-product of increased accountability) just build. When new rules are added on top of old ones, distraction and demotivation set in and the nonprofit becomes increasingly bureaucratic. Consider the impact of rules on a mental health agency:

> Faced by growing concerns about the quality and performance, mirrored by regulatory inspections of staff documentation, the agency implemented a new patient intake form to ensure that its therapists were conducting proper assessments and providing appropriate treatment plans. As one counselor observed,

> The new form and accompanying paperwork are 20 pages long and takes about three-and-a-half hours to complete. The old form was about half this length and still double of that used by other agencies. I understand the concern for quality and documentation, but this is overkill. It takes away from patient care. I work here because I care about our clients, and I really enjoy the therapeutic work. I do not like paperwork all day long: never did, never will. Yet, paperwork is exactly what I now end up doing. Many of us are thinking about leaving.

This particular example shows another problem. At this agency, counselors work on a fee-for-service basis. The extra paperwork is not compensated, causing yet further staff demotivation. The problem of rules and regulations is not limited to paperwork. Other frequent complaints are about too many rules for hiring or purchasing.

In many instances, the use of rules and regulations are actually just symptoms of more fundamental problems: inadequate performance and distrust. Because management distrusts employees to do the right thing and avoid unsatisfactory outcomes, more rules are created. This mistrust often arises from past mistakes, not malevolence on behalf of either party. Ironically, enacting more rules seldom ameliorates these problems. Rules that do not focus on improved performance and relations distract from the main mission. They reduce decision making and reinforce distant relations with management, thereby harming the motivation of staff and leading to further decreases in performance. The proliferation of rules harms productivity, and the growth of rules are more likely the more mature a nonprofit becomes.

Poor Supervision

Poor supervision is a second source of great frustration. Poor supervision can occur at any stage of a nonprofit's development. The demands of survival and mission are so pressing during start-up and growth, however, that poor supervision may seem more oppressive in a mature organization than a start-up, particularly as rules and bureaucracy shift staff's focus from mission to procedures.

As employees know, inadequate supervision comes in many forms, depending on their supervisors. Supervisors stand accused of giving either too much direction (that is, micromanaging), or too little. They are also accused of playing favorites, telling lies or half-truths, and setting employees up for failure. Some fail to show they care about their employees; they lack giving positive reinforcement and coaching. Others are seen as meddling into employees' lives. Some of the terms that have been used to label supervisors are *schizoid, ostrich, the puzzle, bully,* and *sycophant* (Bramson, 1992).

But the real effects of poor supervision are found in behaviors that are absent. Poor supervision harms motivation. A rational response by employees is to avoid interactions with supervisors ("Nothing good comes from my boss—I've tried"). Then employees are less likely to address obstacles to effective performance or take up opportunities for improvement when they surface. ("It's not my job" is a common rejoinder to productivity improvement opportunities when working under poor supervision.) Faced with an uncaring supervisor, the previously discussed employee might well be advised to shut up, do the paperwork, and look for a new job, although other outcomes are also possible. Performance suffers. Communication and employee goodwill are stopped dead in their tracks. The loss of productivity to the organization is invisible but real.

It is not our task to go into the causes of poor supervision in nonprofit organizations or to speculate about whether nonprofits are any worse off than other types of organizations. Supervisory training and mentoring often are absent in nonprofit organizations, and many nonprofit managers lack formal management training or education. Limited resources suggest that money spent on management training is money not spent on the nonprofit's mission. The result: Management training is often sacrificed, making for a false economy. For example, a recent survey of directors of social service organizations with more than 50 employees finds that only 27 percent have any management training compared, for example, to 78 percent of city managers who had such training (Berman, 1999). Supervisors usually base their actions on their own orientations and experiences, which in its inadequate and dissatisfying way are then experienced by employees. Supervision often is learned on the job, a process that is slow in the absence of mentoring and formal structures for providing feedback.

Acceptance of Shoddy Work

In many nonprofits, members are bounded by their commitment to the mission, rather than performing at high professional levels. Fearful of losing volunteers or underpaid staff members, some managers are unwilling to push their staff to do better. Other managers accept low performance, fearing the disruptions and pressures of conflict.

But there is no reason why nonprofit organizations cannot be excellent, and many of the examples of organizations in this book come from nonprofits that have made excellence their priority. In short, members of nonprofits can help each other reach new heights *and* be committed to their common cause *and* still be nice colleagues. The unwillingness to demand high standards also lowers the effectiveness of nonprofits. When health care providers are not required to master recent advances in medicine, their patients receive poor treatment. When arts organizations fail to take advantage of information technology, the costs of marketing efforts soar. When homeless shelters fail to enforce medical standards, infectious diseases spread faster through communities. Low standards can harm motivation, depriving organizational members of the pride that comes from high performance.

This problem is seldom self-correcting. In business, shoddy performance often results in loss of market share. But benchmarks may be lacking in nonprofits. Many clients and funders are seldom in a position to judge the performance of nonprofits. They may even tolerate subperformance, thinking that they have no alternative. Nonprofits often defend their actions by pointing out that their services are cost-effective. In any event, shoddy performance in nonprofits can muddle on for a long time.

Less is more: Less rules, which detract from missions, less bad supervision, which demotivates, and less reluctance to excel all increase productivity. Yet the pathway to improvement is not only found by addressing these problems head on but also by adopting new efforts.

A Winning Attitude

During the past decade, new research has identified the characteristics of outstanding nonprofit organizations. Typically, these nonprofits have made exemplary contributions to the populations they serve, for which they have received awards and recognition. Scholars have studied the characteristics of these nonprofits in minute detail, hoping to unlock the secrets of their success. From these many case histories, a pattern of striking similarities emerges (Drucker, 1992; Steckel and Lehman, 1997). Outstanding nonprofits share in the following features. They

- Focus on the mission,
- Seek opportunities for improvement,
- Consistently do the "right" thing,
- Make sure that employees feel supported,
- Are open to criticism,
- Are accountable, and
- Seek continuous improvement.

These "attitudes" increase productivity in the following ways. First, success requires dedication and commitment to doing a job well. Focusing on the mission prevents resources from being diluted in too many different directions. It is impossible to be all things to all people: Choices must be made. Second, nonprofits live in a rapidly changing world, and leaders cannot always foresee ways in which their systems may fall short; they need feedback and other inputs from clients, staff, and others to improve their decision-making and delivery processes. Third, supporting employees and being accountable builds and maintains the full commitment of resources to the organization. Productivity requires no less. Fourth, doing the right thing builds trust and pride. It is a basis for explaining to others the purpose of the organization and the rationale for productivity improvements. Doing the right thing also provides a compass in dealing with the inevitable moments of conflict and distress.

One can imagine the previously mentioned bulleted items as plaques hanging on office walls, under which cynical employees muse about the ways in which their managers' real attitudes differ. But in excellent organizations these bulleted items *do* represent the actual values adopted by top leaders, who try to transmit them to every aspect of the organization. Leaders know that pressures are great to deviate from these values and that they need to engage in an ongoing effort to help others live up to them. These values, like energy, dissipate in time. They need to be reinforced. Leaders also know that doing so requires what politicians call "retail politics"—that is, one-on-one persuasion. These values cannot be adequately mandated from the top, through memos, plaques, and the like. Rather, managers must insist that those who work directly with them follow these values and that these people instill them among those who work under them, and so on in an ever-cascading fashion throughout the entire organization. Then people begin to reinforce these values to each other. At that point, values are transformed into the cornerstones of the organization's culture. They are internalized among staff and can become self-perpetuating.

Organizations in which these attitudes of excelling exist are far less likely to suffer productivity-robbing problems. Rules will still exist, but they are no longer the most important means of achieving accountability. People are still held accountable for results. They are repeatedly told of conduct that they must avoid and are helped in avoiding it. Rules and regulations are repeatedly reviewed for their effect on mission orientation. Supervision will be focused on ensuring that employees feel supported and are given positive reinforcement for their efforts. Opportunities for improvement are sought out, not criticized. It will be assumed that supervisors must be trained. They will also be routinely evaluated so that feedback can lead to better management. The willingness of management to improve will be revisited on employees; managers will be evaluated on their willingness to engage in self-improvement, too.

The challenge of changing attitudes cannot be overlooked. The problem of knowing what to do is often met by daunting challenges of implementation. AIM—or awareness, involvement, and measurement—is a method that guides nonprofit managers in instilling these values in their staff (Werther and Berman, 1993). The first step is increasing awareness about the need for change. It is axiomatic that people cannot accept what they do not understand: People must be aware that productivity improvement is important. They specifically need to know what is expected of them and how they can accomplish these goals successfully. The second step is involvement. Involvement gives people the opportunity to question new ideas, to shape management decisions through their inputs, and to confront their assumptions through feedback. Staff involvement is needed to improve the quality of decisions. It is axiomatic that people do not resist their own ideas. The third step is measurement, which is necessary to ensure that the strategies that are put in place actually yield measurable results. As the saying goes, "What gets measured gets done." These measures usually demand the involvement of those who will be affected, which increases awareness. Measurable results provide ongoing feedback. Efforts to value employees and to find new improvements are tangible ways in which managers show their commitment to these values. The web of values creates a culture by which organizations hold themselves accountable for implementing their new strategies. Consistent and persistent actions are key to successful implementation (Coates, 1997).

Together We Can

In recent years, managers have been urged to redefine their missions based on stakeholder needs. They are also asked to measure the success of their performance based on stakeholder feedback. A great deal is learned from listening to clients, employees, communities, funders, and other constituents, especially about their wants, needs, and suggestions for improvement. Stakeholders often are a wealth of new information about how well an organization is doing and whether it is making a meaningful difference to them. By working with stakeholders and making them partners in improvement efforts, organizations increase their effectiveness and their efficiency, too.

In no area has this been more evident than in dealing with the clients of nonprofits. Emphasis on client satisfaction is strongly associated with total quality management (TQM), the management philosophy that swept through corporate America in the 1980s (Katz, 1997; *Nonprofit World,* 1993). This philosophy encompasses increased customer satisfaction, as well as other efforts such as reengineering, empowerment, and performance measurement. Although client satisfaction does not affect the survival of nonprofits in the same way as it does for-profits, it does affect the willingness of private and public funding organizations to continue their support. In this discussion we focus on relations with program clients, and other chapters (8 and 9) discuss strategies for building close relations with funders and communities.

An illustration of how client orientation can make a difference is found in the following example of a nonprofit transportation services organization.

A local transportation service serves people with disabilities. Before its client orientation effort, the members of the organization viewed its mission as providing transportation services. Residents called and scheduled appointments. The availability of service was subject to demand and the availability of drivers and vans. People waited several hours before they could be picked up from their destinations. Often, vans would arrive late, as drivers responded to last-minute demands and changes in itineraries of other clients.

Client-orientation led to adapting a mission of increased mobility for citizens. Based on the input of its users, it scheduled services into different areas of town, focusing on different areas on different days. With this new system, people dependent on these services schedule their trips accordingly, and no longer spend hours in limbo waiting for the bus to come. People who wish to have service to some part of town not served on that day must find an alternate means, such as a taxi. Last-minute changes are not made if that would inconvenience another passenger. Transportation schedules reflect the needs of clients, and satisfaction ratings are up.

Increasing stakeholder satisfaction is a four-part process. First, nonprofit organizations must identify their stakeholders: service clients, funders, and community groups that are affected by their programs. Second, managers must identify the needs of these stakeholders. Service providers often assume that they know their clients' priorities, only to be proven wrong in time. For example, many doctors assume that their patients' priority is to cure their illnesses, whereas many patients have a balanced mix of objectives: to be cured, to feel cared for, and to have convenient services. A key activity to increasing stakeholder satisfaction is bringing stakeholders in direct contact with managers and service providers. This contact can be done through periodic focus groups or town hall-type meetings. Sample questions for such activities are listed in Figure 6-1. Suggestion boxes are sometimes used to obtain a sense of client needs, but this is insufficient. Stakeholders often have unarticulated needs and may be unaware of what services organizations are able to provide to serve their needs. It is therefore necessary to create a communication process in which clients directly express their needs (Larson and Ellis, 1998).

It is well known that client needs can conflict with those of other stakeholders. For example, increasing services to homeless persons

Figure 6-1 Client Focus Group Items

- What services are most important to you?
- How often do you use them?
- Are you satisfied with these services? Why or why not?
- What three things do you like least about our service?
- What three things do you like most about our service?
- How would you like us to improve these services?
- What do you think of the following suggestions (give list)?
- Which other services do you use?
- With which other of our services are you familiar?
- Which other needs do you think we should try to address?
- Should any new services be added to meet your needs? Which?
- With which similar services of other organizations are you familiar?
- On average, is our staff courteous to you?
- On average, is staff effective in addressing your questions?
- How long does it take staff to answer your questions?
- How can we improve your customer service experience?
- How did you learn of our programs?
- Would you recommend our service to others? Why or why not?

may go against the objective of government funding agencies to minimize these expenses. These dilemmas require nonprofit organizations to develop a balanced approach to their objectives that can be explained to their clients and other stakeholders (Herman and Renz, 1997).

Third, managers must be specific about the ways in which they improve client satisfaction, recognizing their constraints. What should the nature of the client experience be? What is it today? To attain stakeholder satisfaction, what should staff say or do? What should never be said or done? Answers to these questions require a detailed vision of the client experience. Staff behaviors are important, starting with the receptionist and other frontline staff. The credibility of services often rests with employees. Some employees hold ideas about customer service or customers who are at odds with management; hence organizations must articulate specific staff behaviors and attitudes and communicate these to staff through supervisors. Typical concerns are dress codes, tone of voice and eye contact, following up on what is said or promised, and dealing with client disappointments. These practical matters are seldom addressed through incidental seminars and the like; rather, they must be a continuous concern of supervisory management by acting on client comments, direct observation, and performance appraisal processes.

However, client satisfaction often requires changes that have nothing to do with staff attitudes but with work processes and other matters. For example, what message about care and consideration does the waiting area convey? Is it noisy and messy or clean and comfortable? Are there any beverages? If not, why not? Is there something to read or see about the organization and its services? If so, is it displayed in a manner that would invite clients to read it? In other instances, work processes are a source of client frustration. Untimely invoices and long waiting times are common frustrations. They require rethinking of existing processes to make them more client friendly.

Fourth is assessment of stakeholder satisfaction. Managers often have a sense of overall satisfaction levels (for example, "Some people complain, but we get plenty of kudos, too"). Effective organizations increasingly demand more objective approaches. Customer complaints are an important source of ideas for improvement and can be counted on a periodic basis. Many improvements come from following up on their complaints. However, they are not a valid measurement of client satisfaction because many complaints are not recorded, and complaints do not measure satisfaction. Also, suggestion-box-type responses rely on self-selection, and there is no way of knowing whether those who fill out these cards are representative of all clients. There is no reason to assume that they are.

To objectively measure customer satisfaction, it is often necessary to randomly choose one or more days or events in which all clients then present are surveyed or interviewed. This approach ensures a representative sample and a reasonably high response rate. Mail surveys are seldom used for this purpose because they result in low response rates (hence casting doubt on the generalizability of the findings). In many cases, clients can be required or otherwise persuaded to complete the survey by telephone or in person. Nonprofit organizations that lack survey and statistical expertise for data analysis will find it necessary to contract for this aspect of the client satisfaction assessment effort.

This four-part process is consistent with the AIM process mentioned earlier. Management will find it necessary to increase awareness about the need for increased client satisfaction, such as through client complaints, benchmarking against the exemplary service of competing organizations, concerns expressed by finding agencies, and client focus groups. Thereafter, managers obtain the involvement of employees to generate strategies for increasing client satisfaction. Their involvement often generates good ideas for improvement. Finally, organizations must find ways to maintain and measure their customer satisfaction levels.

It is obvious that nonprofit organizations need to build close relations not only with clients but also with communities and funding agencies as well. These aspects are addressed in chapters 8 and 9. Communities expect that nonprofits operate in partnership with them; the spirit of seeking customer satisfaction is consistent with sustaining viable working relations. Funding agencies expect that nonprofits are attentive to their objectives. Though focus groups and client surveys are often inappropriate in dealing with communities and funding agencies, these four steps are still important. Successful nonprofit organizations consciously determine who their allies are, and they periodically ask them about their priorities. They also develop new responses to help communities and funding agencies meet their aims and engage in candid and constructive dialogue about nonprofit performance. Doing so improves their effectiveness and build bonds that are critical to their success.

A Little Leeway

The question of how organizations can get more productivity from their employees is central to the field of productivity improvement. One response is to give increased empowerment to employees. Often, employees feel constrained by micromanagement or too many approval processes that slow down their effectiveness. Empowerment is defined as the delegation of decision making to employees while holding them accountable for outcomes. Empowerment is no longer solely defined in terms of self-fulfillment or skills enlargement, although these are frequent byproducts of empowerment. Employee empowerment is driven by the need for results. Many managers can no longer accept employee efforts that fail to produce results, nor do they have enough time to micromanage them and still produce the results that are expected of the managers (Sandler and Hudson, 1998).

The logic of empowerment assumes that it is often more efficient to hold employees accountable for what they have produced than to supervise them in the varied aspects of their jobs (Glasser, 1994). Giving employees this extra leeway can bring forth creativity in problem solving. It often also develops a sense of ownership that comes from seeing results that are significant to the organization's clients or operations. Consider the following example:

> Before we changed, my job included that I check that request forms for travel and training were complete as submitted by other departments. If something was missing, I sent them back to these departments. Of course, I also worked with our departments to help them work the system and get what they needed. But now the departments are responsible for their own travel and training expenses. This gives me more time to work on more important matters. I still do the invoicing, but I feel more satisfied now.

Of course, not all employees welcome more responsibility. Some may see it as management trying to get something for nothing. Some leaders fear giving up control, which they see as a defining aspect of their job. Not all aspects of nonprofit work lend themselves to empowerment, either. The success of empowerment often depends on identifying suitable tasks, suitable employees, and adopting a suitable implementation strategy.

Tasks that require highly differentiated solutions or that benefit from high levels of responsiveness are good candidates for increased employee empowerment. Many nonprofit tasks are of this nature. For example, helping clients back on their feet after episodes with homelessness, addiction, financial calamity, or job loss requires custom solutions. Although many organizations develop standardized or preferred ways of dealing with these problems, clients benefit when frontline workers are allowed or even encouraged to go outside of the box of "standard or preferred operating procedures" to develop approaches that may be more effective (Eadie, 1997). Employees can be held accountable after the fact. Similarly, it makes sense to hold fundraisers and grant writers accountable for results rather than for efforts. (Of course, they must not commit any violations of policy in the process. Many organizations are therefore explicit about procedures that must not be followed without prior approval.)

A common problem with empowerment is failing to lay the groundwork. Employees must be clearly informed of what is expected from them and how they will be held accountable for results. They must agree with management that they have adequate resources and skills to succeed. A distinction is to be made between new and old responsibilities. New responsibilities have a heightened risk of failure and require a sense of partnership between staff and managers. They are pilot efforts requiring trial-and-error learning and uncertain time and resources for completion. When managers assign new tasks without this sense of cooperation, resentment and failure are nearly certain. Empowerment works best when employees develop a common set of expectations. Some useful items are found in Figure 6-2.

Reengineering has gained much currency in recent years as a potent productivity improvement strategy. It is defined as redesigning existing delivery processes by (1) organizing around outcomes, (2) reducing steps and using parallel processes, and (3) making better use of information and information technology. Many of these efforts involve empowerment. Organizing around outcomes means that units and employees are expected to produce client-centered outcomes. For example, many departments now have one-stop shopping or a single point of contact for clients: Employees at these positions are given wide authority (that is, empowerment) to make decisions that ensure

Figure 6-2 **Checklist for Empowerment**

- Did I clearly explain why I am asking employees to do more?
- Did I clearly explain what employees are expected achieve?
- Are the selected tasks appropriate for empowerment?
- Which other tasks should be targeted for empowerment?
- Do workers have adequate resources to succeed?
- Are any conflicts with other policies addressed and resolved?
- Do workers have sufficient authority to deal with events that they will encounter?
- Are workers clear about the limits of their authority?
- Do workers have access to necessary information?
- Is there a feedback plan to make adjustments?
- Do employees have the skills and experience to succeed?
- Are employees comfortable with the contingency and evaluation plans?
- Do workers feel adequate control over their ability to achieve results?

Source: Adapted from Berman, 1998.

client-focused outcomes for which they are held accountable. Similarly, managers are put in charge of departments that are designed to ensure client-related outcomes, not merely efforts toward that end. For example, transportation services often handle all matters affecting transportation, including scheduling and repairs. Managers, then, are held accountable for client satisfaction of transportation efforts.

Empowerment is also used to reduce steps in delivery processes, especially by eliminating paperwork and approval processes. Such elimination reduces the number of steps and times that work is handed off, which in turn reduces delays, errors, and accompanying client dissatisfaction. Responsibility for delivery is in large measure assigned to individual employees. Supervision is then limited to immediate superiors, thereby preventing further delays by other units or managers. Organizations also work with employees to ensure that they have information to make their decisions, which has led many nonprofit organizations to increasingly conclude that information technology is indeed necessary to ensure the timeliness and effectiveness of services.

These examples show that concepts of empowerment are not limited to employee–supervisor relations but that they are also applicable to the relationship between units and the rest of the organization.

The trends toward mission orientation and empowerment are evident in many nonprofit organizations. However, empowerment is welcomed by some, but certainly not all, employees. It is readily observed that many employees are quite comfortable with their current assignments and level of responsibilities. They do not seek change, and they certainly do not wish more of either. Even if more salary could be had, they would still welcome the status quo. The "25-50-25 rule" states that for any change effort, 25 percent of employees enthusiastically embrace it, 50 percent are fence sitters who might support it in time when and if it is beneficial, and 25 percent will oppose any change on principle. This rule, although not empirically proven, seems to fit our experience and that of many managers, as well as research showing a wide range of employee attitudes in the workplace (Kanter and Mirvis, 1989).

This rule suggests that managers should start empowerment with employees who embrace change rather than the ones who resist it. By starting empowerment with those who welcome it, using AIM principles, managers can hope to move forward and create successes, which eventually draw fence sitters to the empowerment effort. Resisters eventually accommodate the change, either through dialogue and persuasion, increased accountability, or separation. It is the road of "show me" persuasion and least resistance. The hope is that in time, through repeated efforts, empowerment becomes part of the normal expectations between employees and their managers. Indeed, as accountability is increasingly used, so, too, do opportunities increase for encouraging employees to put their best efforts forward (Brown, Hitchcock, and Willard, 1994).

Technology Management

Information technology is increasingly, albeit unevenly, used in nonprofit organizations. Technology offers the opportunity to reach more clients, serve them better, and decrease service costs. Computers are frequently used for word processing, though a recent survey shows that only 45 percent of 1,400 responding nonprofit managers state that their organization uses e-mail (National Council of Nonprofit Associations, 1998). Information technology includes specialized applications for marketing, scheduling, billing, and documentation, and some nonprofits are currently experimenting with new uses of the Internet for interacting with their clients (see Figure 6-3 for some examples). However, our focus is not with applications of technology but rather on the effort to embrace it and use it. Simply put, many nonprofit organizations view information technology as a struggle just to keep up. Many nonprofits are pushed into its use by demands of funders, clients, or employees. Often, nonprofits have no explicit plan to take advantage of the productivity improvement opportunities (Elliott, Katsioloudes, and Weldon, 1998; Wallace, 1999).

Technology often is not viewed as being central to the nonprofit mission. For example, museums are not normally thought of as leaders in technology but rather as institutions that put on exhibitions. How-

Figure 6-3 **Applications of Information Technology: Selected Examples**

- Kids' HealthLink in San Francisco is helping poor children with serious illnesses to use e-mail and the Internet to communicate with their friends and with other sick children and to keep up with their school work. The project helps their families use technology to communicate with the children's doctors, find medical information on the Internet, and participate in on-line support groups.
- Medical Training Worldwide in Novato, California, teaches surgical techniques to doctors in developing countries, is building an on-line database to coordinate information about its volunteers, and donated medical equipment and training sites.
- The National Library for the Blind, in Stockport, England, provides Braille reading material to people around the world. The library plans to add more information about its books to its website—which is designed for people who have vision problems and uses speech-synthesis software, screen magnification, or soft Braille displays to gain access to the Internet—so that library members can choose their own books, rather than having to rely on the recommendations of others.
- Bethphage, an affiliated ministry of the Evangelical Lutheran Church in America, works to provide community-based services for persons with developmental disabilities in 14 U.S. states, England, and Latvia. Using an extensive registration form and survey instrument tied to a database program, Bethphage created an effective organizing and tracking mechanism for grassroots volunteers and advocacy campaigns. This allows the organization to gauge the strength of its support in each state.

Sources: Wallace, 1999; Nonprofits' Policy & Technology Project, 1998.

ever, museums that make conservation a priority often develop very specialized technology in this area. Museums that make financial solvency and community participation a priority are quick to use modern marketing and Internet software to reach potential visitors. Websites now offer a wide range of information and products to visitors. When nonprofits make technology a priority, they often excel at it. Sometimes, technology is imposed as a priority. For example, many health care providers have been forced to adapt to information technology in their patient documentation and billing practices to satisfy new demands by insurance and billing companies. Thus whether by design or default technology increasingly affects the non-profit mission (National Strategy for Nonprofit Technology, 1999).

Technology requires management. A key step is to integrate it with the planning of the nonprofit mission. Nonprofit managers are increasingly asking (1) how technology shapes their missions and goals, and (2) how technology can assist in the implementation of them. For example, museums develop specialized exhibitions or en-hance their exhibitions by using the Internet to provide additional information on certain topics, including interesting photographic im-ages. Another example comes from education television, which has been in the forefront of tying websites to program content. To improve client relations, they can use e-mail to reach them more frequently. The ability to reach out to new clienteles in this manner can both shape the mission of a museum, educational television, or other nonprofit, as well as improve the productivity of such efforts. A necessary condition for this is, of course, the presence of technology expertise at senior levels as well as capacity to implement technology-led strategies in the organization.

Many large organizations recognize these needs and have created "chief information officer" and other technology positions. The pur-pose of this position is to bring technology-based options to senior managers and to be responsible for technological capabilities. Small nonprofits often lack the resources for funding such positions, but the principle remains the same: It is necessary to have a staff person or board member who takes leadership to increase technology aware-ness and to make information technology happen. Typically, this person is both an advocate for technology resources as well as an enabler who helps professional and administrative staff with their technology problems and questions. Although this expertise is some-times contracted out (or even based on the generous donation of time and effort of volunteers), increasingly even small organizations find benefit from having such expertise in-house.

Technology is ubiquitous, but it does not come cheap. It demands budgeting. At issue are not only hardware costs. Today, the average lifetime of a personal computer is about two to three years, and software is updated on an annual or semiannual basis. For many agencies, this implies the need for separate information technology budgets. But studies suggest that the organizational costs are even higher. Hardware and software costs are often only 25 to 40 percent of total direct costs; other expenses are training, purchasing, installation, maintenance, convergence, modification, and consulting. People must be hired to make new technology a reality and to keep it running. In addition, technology often disrupts standard operating procedures of professionals and administrative staff. They must learn, and sometimes acquiesce, to new ways of doing things. This requires considerable management, too.

Information technology is often anxiety ridden for staff who have not been trained in it. This is frequently the case, although increasingly uncommon among recent college and high school graduates.

For example, when a mental health agency adopted an electronic patient documentation system, it remained unused by all but a few staff, even though it offered significant productivity gains. Half of the staff had never used a computer before. Those who did lacked on-site assistance from a technical expert who could help deal with bugs and glitches. The system eventually found wider use after a contractor was hired to provide training and assistance. These problems show that information technology is not perceived as problem free.

Technology also exacerbates problems of confidentiality. Unauthorized access to databases can compromise the mission of any organization. In one instance, a confidential file of the names of an agency's clients with their ailments and medical conditions (e.g., whether they were HIV positive) was being sold in a nightclub. This is obviously wrong.

With so much being spent on technology, it is reasonable to ask about the return on this investment. However, a consensus exists that it is very difficult to evaluate information technology in quantitative terms because of its multifaceted and strategic nature (Remenyi, Money, and Twite, 1993). The effect of reaching more clients cheaply has efficiency as well as strategic implications for the scope of operations. Rather, when prospective analysis is sought to make investment decisions, organizations often ask the following questions:

- How is it central to our mission or implementation strategies?
- How does it help clients?
- How does it help maintain or expand our client base?
- How does it relate to other technologies, and is it feasible?
- How is it consistent with furthering professional standards?
- How does it increase the speed, timeliness, or accuracy of operations?
- How does it help us save money?

Answers to these questions help shape discussion about investment in new technology. Although not yielding a single "bottom line" answer to investment quandaries, they help to position nonprofits to the technology future and to ensure that technology is integrated in its mission.

The Accounting Approach

Accounting strategies are increasingly central to modern productivity improvement efforts. They aim to create a modern, forward-looking organization. But accounting strategies can also help nonprofits increase their productivity. Many organizations will find these efforts indispensable (*Nonprofit World,* 1999).

Cost Management

Organizations incur many expenses that managers, from time to time, examine for possible savings. Employee compensation and benefits often make up a majority of nonprofit expenditures, and in recent years health care insurance companies continue to offer new benefits packages that can reduce costs, even to small companies. Management costs of tax-deferred retirement contributions have also decreased. Many employees welcome tuition benefits, and organizations can reduce these costs by limiting tuition costs rather than the number of classes. Limiting expenditures discourages employees from choosing expensive private universities and colleges over less expensive public ones. Temporary services have become increasingly expensive but are still an attractive way of meeting peak demands affecting administrative staff without the long-term budget burden of new employees.

Office rents are also a significant expense. Many managers periodically review these to take advantage of changing local market conditions. Organizations may find it advantageous to negotiate with multiple property owners and also familiarize themselves with local ordinances that give tax advantages to landlords who lease a significant part of their building to nonprofit organizations. Some socially concerned businesses will lease nonprofits space for reduced rates, even free. Nonprofits should also consider ownership of buildings because real estate is an important collateral for business loans. Energy, mailing, and telephone costs are also significant, and providers of these frequently change their rate structures.

Risk Management

Nonprofit organizations are finding new ways of protecting their assets. Traditional risk management concerns matters of litigation, and many nonprofit organizations have general liability insurance that covers most injury and damage claims, as well as directors and officer's insurance that protects board members. Organizations often require employees to carry their own car insurance and, as appropriate, their own professional liability insurance. Like other costs, the insurance market is volatile, and managers periodically check and compare these costs, too.

Modern forms of risk management also include other assets. Information contained in computer systems is often critical to operations and revenues. Many managers have learned from experience that when computers and local area networks go down, full recovery is not always possible. Therefore, they now back up their data on a weekly or biweekly basis. Recent changes in tax laws are another area of risk management, such as activities that have become taxable. This is the case for activities that the Internal Revenue Service rules are unrelated to nonprofit missions (such as sales from enterprise activities, like a museum's gift shop).

Staffing Analysis

The way in which work is staffed is an important productivity issue. Managers improve productivity by periodically examining whether their work processes are staffed for maximum efficiency. One problem is that people operate at less than their abilities. This is frequently the case for professionals whose organizations fail to provide adequate administrative support. It does not make much business sense for therapists to lose time calling patients to remind them of their appointments; that task is best left to lesser paid personnel, while therapists engage in other, revenue-generating activities. Another problem is that tasks are completed that do not have the involvement of those who should be involved or that too many people are involved in a task. For example, database updates should not be done by many people, as this may invite errors and confusion. But the design of databases should involve its users to avoid inefficiencies that may become transparent later. Finally, staffing analysis helps identify tasks that are insufficiently being staffed. Agency growth may create the need for more bilingual administrative staff or increased demand for security. Staff turnover and agency development often create needs that are unmet.

Many organizations face peak demands, and inadequate staffing for these demands is the source of great employee discontent. For example, social services for family and children sometimes face high demands at the beginning of school terms. They also deliver a majority of services after school hours, usually in the late afternoon and early evenings. During these periods, agencies need additional staffing. When managers fail to plan for peak demands, staff become overwhelmed and overworked, causing dissatisfaction that may result in absenteeism and turnover. A common approach is to schedule staff time to coincide with peak demands. To deal with peak demand, a 1,000-bed hospital created a pool of "rapid response" volunteers who are called on to meet peak demands.

Conclusion

Productivity improvement is both a mindset and a set of strategies. Nonprofit organizations vary in the extent that they make productivity part of this mindset: Some organizations make it clear to their members that they are always trying to seek out better ways of doing things; other organizations send the signal that it is best to get along by not rocking the boat. Managers are important to determining which signal gets sent; indeed, they are chiefly responsible for setting the productivity tone of organizations.

Once managers have decided to what extent they promote productivity improvement, a strategy must be chosen. There is nothing like tangible, visible success to persuade and carry the day. Too much change causes confusion, so it is best to focus on just one or two efforts over a period of a few months. Many organizations choose some combination of TQM efforts (such as cost-effective ways to increase customer satisfaction, reengineering, or empowerment) or information technology, along with one or more accounting-based strategies. The former strategies are often highly invasive, whereas many accounting-based strategies require little staff involvement.

It is not necessary to fret too much over which strategy to use. Managers can start with whatever they feel comfortable with, recognizing that many efforts take several months to show bottom-line results. The key to success is ensuring awareness, involvement, and maintenance (AIM). Employee input improves the quality of decisions and increases employee commitment. It also helps managers to find employees willing to try something new. Success requires consistency, and managers will need to integrate the new efforts into their offices' operating processes. Through consistency and persistence, managers increase the productivity of nonprofit organizations.

References

Berman, E., *Productivity in Public and Nonprofit Organizations*, Thousand Oaks, CA: Sage, 1998.

Berman, E., "Professionalism among Public and Nonprofit Managers: A Comparison," *American Review of Public Administration* (June 1999): 149–66.

Bramson, R., *Coping with Difficult Bosses*, New York: Simon and Schuster, 1992.

Brown, M., D. Hitchcock, and M. Willard, *Why TQM Fails and What to Do about It*, Chicago: Irwin, 1994.

Coates, N., "A Model for Consulting to Help Effect Change in Organizations," *Nonprofit Management & Leadership* (winter 1997): 157–69.

Drucker, P., *Managing the Nonprofit Organization: Principles and Practices*, New York: HarperCollins, 1992.

Eadie, D., *Changing by Design: A Practical Approach to Leading Innovation in Nonprofit Organizations*, San Francisco: Jossey-Bass, 1997.

Elliott, B., M. Katsioloudes, and R. Weldon, "Nonprofit Organizations and the Internet," *Nonprofit Management & Leadership* (spring 1998): 297–303.

Glasser, W., *The Control Theory Manager*, New York: Harper Business, 1994.

Herman, R., and D. Renz, "Multiple Constituencies and the Social Construction of Nonprofit Organization Effectiveness," *Nonprofit and Voluntary Sector Quarterly* (June 1997): 185–206.

Kanter, D., and P. Mirvis, *The Cynical Americans: Living and Working in an Age of Discontent and Disillusion*, San Francisco: Jossey-Bass, 1989.

Katz, R., "Quality Management Approaches and Their Influence on Nonprofits and the Public Sector," in T. Daniels (ed.), *The Nonprofit Handbook*, 2nd ed., New York: John Wiley, 1997, pp. 58–70.

Larson, J., and G. Ellis, "The Myths of Customer Satisfaction," *Nonprofit World* (November/December 1998): 54.

National Council of Nonprofit Associations, *A Greater Voice: Nonprofit Organizations, Communications Technology and Advocacy*, Washington, D.C.: Author, 1998.

National Strategy for Nonprofit Technology, *A Blueprint for Infusing Technology into the Nonprofit Sector*, 1999, available at http://www.nten.org (January 5, 2000).

Nonprofits' Policy & Technology Project, *1998 NPT Award Winners*, 1998, http://www.ombwatch.org/npt/activity/awards/1998awds.htm.

Nonprofit World, "Four Part Series: Quality Management" (March/April 1993): 18–24; (May/June 1993): 29–31; (July/August 1993): 28–33; (September/October 1993): 30–34.

Nonprofit World, "101 Things to Do before the New Millennium" (May/June 1999): 50–52.

Remenyi, D., A. Money, and A. Twite, *Measuring and Managing IT Benefits*, 2nd ed., Oxford: Blackwell, 1993.

Sandler, M., and D. Hudson, *Beyond the Bottom Line: How to Do More with Less in Nonprofit and Public Organizations*, New York: Oxford University Press, 1998.

Steckel, R., and J. Lehman, *In Search of America's Best Nonprofits*, San Francisco: Jossey-Bass, 1997.

Wallace, N., "Charities Receive Awards for Innovative Ideas," *The Chronicle of Philanthropy* (June 17, 1999). Also available at http://www.philanthropy.com (January 5, 2000).

Werther, W., and E. Berman, "A Conceptual Framework for Overcoming Resistance to the Measurement of Productivity and Quality," in D. Sumanth, J. Edosomwan, R. Poupart, and D. Sink (eds.), *Productivity & Quality Frontiers IV*, Norcross, GA: Institute of Industrial Engineers, 1993, pp. 1027–35.

7

Evaluation and Accountability

How well are nonprofit programs and organizations doing, and what have they accomplished? Funders and other stakeholders increasingly expect providers to show the outcomes or impacts of their expenditures and efforts: What did program efforts achieve? What impact did they have? How effective and efficient are organizations and programs? Which target populations benefited most from efforts? How can these results be improved in future years? Although some accountability takes the form of anecdotal testimonials, modern approaches use systematic, objective, and verifiable methods. The United Way and other funding agencies, including many public agencies, are powerful agents forcing providers to take these outcome questions seriously and to implement various forms of program evaluation (Cutt et al., 1996; Newcomer, 1997; United Way, 1999; Vogt, 1999).

Modern, real-time evaluation approaches hold several promises for managers. Weekly, monthly, or quarterly progress reports help to avoid surprises later and allow managers to monitor progress toward program goals. Such meetings also help to focus on ways to improve the efficiency of service delivery and thereby increase stakeholder satisfaction. The nature of program evaluation data—hard, objective facts—helps to validate and refine managers' own sense of program progress; it can even refine managers' sense of program goals and priorities. It can also help track client satisfaction and inquiries. Evaluation provides comparison between different components of programs, thereby helping to determine which ones need improvement. The availability of data is also useful in public relations campaigns and provides a vehicle for keeping stakeholders informed and committed to the program.

Evaluation and accountability are bedrock concepts that need to be relied on at every stage of a nonprofit's life cycle. Start-ups need accountability and evaluation focused on outcomes as a way of establishing the credibility of the organization, its programs, and its leadership. Education and accountability are hallmarks of a professionally led nonprofit. Moreover, the feedback generated can be used to engender further support among funders, board members, clients, and other stakeholders, while lapses in evaluation and accountability might be excused in a start-up operation. As the nonprofit develops into growth and mature phases of its life cycle, stakeholders, particularly funders, expect evaluation and accountability. Their absence reflects poorly on the organization and its leadership.

Misconceptions abound about program evaluation. Some managers believe that program evaluation only can be used to prove program success. Rather, evaluation increases the stream of feedback about program performance, providing a balanced picture. Traditionally, leaders have used informal feedback such as client complaints to learn of program problems, but such feedback is unsystematic and seldom includes much information about positive outcomes. Evaluation methods provide a more complete picture of program performance. Although evaluation should be systematic, it is not designed to prove scientifically, beyond reasonable doubt, the success or failure of programs. Another misconception is that program evaluations simply document the obvious and generate reports that gather dust. In the past, program evaluations were performed by outside consultants, which were both expensive and untimely. Today, program evaluation is conducted in-house, in real-time fashion, with an eye toward monitoring and managerial relevance, rather than determining ultimate social impacts (McNamara, 1999).

This chapter discusses both program evaluation and organizational assessment. The first part discusses the fundamentals of evaluation. Whether nonprofit organizations are sufficiently accountable is very much in the eye of the beholders, its stakeholders, who often demand that specific and credible information be made available. In the second part of the chapter we discuss performance measurement, which has gained in importance in recent years. Performance measurement is a form of program evaluation that is now mandated by numerous public and private funding agencies. In the third part we discuss strategies of data collection. Specifically, this chapter focuses on practices for valid surveys. In the fourth and final section this chapter provides information about the evaluation of organizations rather than their programs. Approaches are discussed for evaluating the board's functioning and organizational leadership in nonprofits.

Fundamentals of Evaluation

Program evaluation serves multiple purposes. Through evaluation, agencies and managers give *accountability* for their results, show *responsiveness* to clients and constituents, provide *cost-justification* for expenditures, demonstrate commitment to *performance improvement*, and improve *planning and budgeting* of programs by obtaining an objective assessment of what is working, what is needed, and the effectiveness of delivery processes. Finally, evaluation is also used for *oversight* of contracted services (Rossi, 1999).

Determining What to Evaluate

Traditionally, accountability has focused on two important aspects: (1) showing which activities have been undertaken and that they are consistent with the purpose of received moneys ("We counseled 689 clients over a three-month period. . . ."), and (2) justifying the appropriateness of expenditures ("We determined that all expenditures reflect program priorities. . . ."). Nitterhouse (1997) notes that many small religious nonprofits lack financial management expertise to provide even this level of accountability. Yet as difficult as these items are for some small nonprofits, in recent years a strong emphasis has been placed on documenting outcomes, which is a two-step process. First, nonprofits are asked to develop a comprehensive understanding of how and why their activities cause project outcomes to occur. This is called the program model. Second, they must identify the range of outcomes to be measured (Sustainability Network, 1999).

The United Way is a forceful leader in getting member organizations to think through the relationship between program activities and outcomes. In the past, nonprofit programs sometimes adopted lofty goals that could not be achieved with the limited means at hand. For example, although after school programs may affect truancy and scholastic achievement, they might have only limited, if any, impact on neighborhood crime. It probably would be wrong (or at least incredulous) to assume that they do because most efforts to reduce crime require a multifaceted, coordinated array of programs. Organizations therefore should carefully consider their goals and develop programs that can affect these goals.

A program flowchart (or "logic model," in United Way terminology) is a visual approach to show these linkages. Figure 7-1 shows a

Figure 7-1 **Program Flowchart**

Resources → Activities → Outcomes → Goals

Program Example: "Meals on Wheels"

Resources		Activities		Outcomes		Goals
Staff vehicles other expenses	→	Picking up and delivering meals; identifying persons in need of service; seeking community support for program; identifying and referring problems to agencies, including follow-up	→	Improved nutrition of clients; early detection and referral of medical and other problems facing homebound clients; community support for program	→	Increased independence of clients (reduced institutionalization); improved recovery

brief program model, which can be expanded for more complex programs. The model, consistent with the strategic framework discussed in chapter 1, distinguishes between outcomes and goals. *Goals* are the ultimate, long-term aims of the program that, in many ways, are the rationale for the program. *Outcomes* are the immediate results of completed activities, which support the ultimate aims. For example, consider a home nutritional program for elderly individuals:

> The Meals-on-Wheels program may have a goal of increased independence by ensuring that homebound clients have receive adequate nutrition. This program also provides early detection of other problems that might affect this goal of independence; although the agency does not take on itself to resolve other problems, it does provide referral and follow-up. Figure 7-1 also shows outcomes and goals are limited to its client population; the agency does not, for example, seek to claim these outcomes for the entire city.
>
> By focusing on outcomes, managers can hope to better deal with determining what these activities and resources accomplish. Focusing on outcomes gives managers timely information about trends that affect goal attainment. Indeed, it is only somewhat useful to know whether homebound, ill clients are having a speedy recovery (a goal); it far more useful to know whether workers are picking up on early signals about problems that affect recovery and are effective in making necessary referrals (outcomes).
>
> Evaluation is attuned to unintended or secondary outcomes. Undoubtedly, the need to detect medical problems was derived from the goal of ensuring independence; other problems than meals affect this outcome. Likewise, managers should keep a watchful eye for other outcomes, intended or unintended, positive or negative. For example, clients might become financially dependent on subsidized meals, which is an undesirable outcome. However, other unintended outcomes might be that as a result of home delivery and interaction, some clients begin to attend better to their grooming—this is a desirable outcome.

Needs assessments focus on outcomes of individuals within existing resources or conditions. For example, a needs assessment for elderly individuals might focus on frequent obstacles and challenges in daily routines, indicating the need for household help, including support in cooking. Then the needs assessment might focus on the client's familiarity with existing community and other resources. Which resources has she contacted? How did she come to contact these resources? What was the outcome of these efforts? Did it resolve the problem? Answers to these questions may indicate the need for services.

Organizing for Evaluation

An important purpose of program evaluation is to provide accountability and foster program improvement. For these reasons, key decision makers and stakeholders who affect the future of programs are well-advised to be involved in program evaluation efforts. Their needs and concerns matter. Evaluation often is also improved by getting the input of program clients, who offer important insight into possibly important secondary outcomes and other factors that affect program success. Finally, employees and supervisors should also be involved. Many employees value the opportunity to shape evaluation objectives; it gives them an opportunity to obtain hard evidence of program success and an opportunity for recognition. A study of 300 nonprofit organizations shows that those that use stakeholder involvement report a greater likelihood of programmatic changes being made (Fine, Thayer, and Coghlan, 1998).

Some managers choose to integrate these constituencies into evaluation efforts by forming evaluation-working groups, whereas others build on existing advisory groups or solicit input in an ad-hoc manner. The point, of course, is to improve evaluation and obtain commitment from important stakeholders for program goals. Some practical interview questions that might be used to help identify program objectives and accountability expectations are these: From your perspective, what is the program trying to accomplish? What accomplishments are targeted for the next few years? Which other objectives would you like to see? What are the largest problems faced by the program at this time? How are these problems being worked on? What are the major activities of the program? Is more effort needed? What kind of information do you get on program results?

Evaluation requires time and resources. Many efforts require surveys of program clients for whom costs must be budgeted. Additional costs may be involved in collecting and analyzing administrative program data. The failure to plan for these expenses, especially survey research, dooms many evaluation efforts. In some cases, employees are asked to conduct surveys, but in most instances this is impractical or inappropriate. Rather, nonprofits should negotiate with funders about their evaluation expectations. Many funders require evaluation, and expect 5 or 10 percent of program costs to be directed toward this purpose.

Ethics

Evaluation should be conducted according to high professional and ethical standards. The American Evaluation Association (1998) has developed such standards; for example, evaluators should adhere to the highest appropriate technical standards to increase the accuracy and credibility of information that is produced. They should also communicate their methods and any shortcomings of their study accurately with the clients. Study participants should be informed of any risks that participation might bring and about any limits to the confidentiality of their information. Evaluators should avoid conflicts of interests, disclosing the source of financial support when appropriate. When findings negatively affect the interests of stakeholders, the results should be presented in ways that promote the stakeholders' dignity and self-worth.

Design

In most cases, evaluation involves the collection of data about the program and its clients. In a few instances, funders may wish providers to go beyond this strategy and compare outcomes against a control group of individuals who did not receive program benefits. This is akin to the concept of medical drug trials, in which some individuals receive a treatment drug and others only a placebo. At best, this clinical trial model can only be approximated in program evaluation; for example, people can seldom be denied services. Still, the idea of identifying a control group is useful, such as when comparing the effect of pregnancy education on the behavior of teenage women: Were those who received education more likely to give birth to healthy babies? Of course, evaluators will have to consider various control variables that might distinguish between the groups, such as drug use, income, level of education, and the like.

Performance Measurement

Performance measurement begins with developing a program model but focuses on the second step of evaluation: identifying a range of outcomes and developing strategies for measuring them.

Performance measurement distinguishes between *outputs* and *outcomes*. In nonprofit management, outputs are defined as the extent that activities are successfully completed. For example, the number of meals that have been successfully delivered is a relevant output measure for the Meals on Wheels program (see Figure 7-1). The number of completed briefings to community leaders about the Meals on Wheels program is another output measure. Outcomes are defined as the extent that goals are successfully achieved, such as the percentage of the target populations that receives daily warm meals. Productivity improvement in nonprofit organizations requires the measurement of outputs, outcomes, and goals.

Measurement Indicators

Some creativity is needed to measure outputs, outcomes, and goals. To this end, managers identify measurement indicators that encompass all of the important dimensions of the outcomes being measured. For example, Table 7-1 shows that the outcome of "improved nutrition" might be measured through three measurement indicators: the number of daily warm meals, the level of calorie intake, and by measures that reflect balanced nutrition (such as daily consumption of fruit, vegetables, carbohydrates, and so on). Measurement indicators should be chosen to represent and to be comprehensive of that which is measured.

Table 7-1 **Performance Measures**

Outcomes	Measurement Indicators
Improved nutrition	• Daily warm meals • Calorie intake • Balanced nutrition
Detection of medical and other problems	• Completed weekly checklist of medical and self-care issues • Assessment of physical exercise
Community support for program	• Statements by elected officials and community leaders • Contributions by local governments

Another example concerns outcomes to increase awareness. For example, disease-prevention programs for sexually transmitted diseases often have as outcomes the increased awareness among target groups of the dangers of disease and prevention methods. Awareness is assumed to affect behavior, but how might "increased awareness" be measured? Some measurement indicators should focus on the aspects about which target clients are aware: For example, exactly what do the clients know about the disease or methods of prevention? To what extent do they know these facts—do they believe these facts to be accurate and important? Other measurement indicators might focus on identifying which target groups have become aware of this information, how they have become aware of it, and sources of information that different target groups use. Other indicators might focus on other information that is needed but not presently provided.

Measurement indicators typically reflect program priorities. For example, the detection of medical and other problems seem to require two indicators: a weekly checklist and an assessment of physical exercise. Many elderly people may suffer from a lack of exercise, and this is an important priority for this program, perhaps suggested by funding agencies. Measurement indicators are also needed to measure outputs and goals. A rather simple indictor of delivering meals is the number of meals successfully delivered. For this program, that may involve completing a checklist. The measurement of increased independence is more complex, requiring multiple indicators and perhaps a survey of clients themselves.

Derived Measures

Outputs, outcomes, and goals are fundamental to performance measurement. *Efficiency* is defined as outcomes or outputs per dollar or per person. For example, the Meals on Wheels program might be concerned with the efficiency of delivering meals—that is, the cost per delivered meal. On tracking these costs, the program might decide to try to improve its efficiency. Another efficiency measure is the per-person cost of improved nutrition. After making some reasonable assumptions about nutrition in the absence of this program, a measure can be constructed of the cost of improving nutrition.

Efficiency measures are different from workload measures. *Workloads* are activities, and *workload ratios* are defined as activities per worker or unit (for example, number of referrals per month or worker). The difference between these two measures is critical because it is important to increase workloads only when outcomes are maintained or also improved. For example, increased workloads in social services are only desirable when outcomes can be maintained or improved. If caseloads grow but outcomes decline, the caseload increase may be a false economy when measured against outcomes. For example, if the number of meals per driver increased but the need for fast delivery prevented drivers from observing other indicators of client well-being, the caseload or deliveries per driver would increase, but the number of elderly people maintaining their independence (desired outcome) might decline over time.

Benchmarks are standards for comparing performance. External benchmarks offer performance standards set by leading programs ("best practices") or professional organizations. Such standards frequently are absent or unknown, as in the case of meals that are delivered per driver. Internal benchmarks are standards based on the past performance of a program. These should be set aggressively but realistically to motivate continued program improvement, though such historical data are lacking among start-ups.

Lessons Learned

Performance measurement is increasingly used, and a number of studies suggest some best practices. First, performance measurement should be mission-driven. That is, measures should help stakeholders and managers monitor how programs are contributing to the mission and its supporting goals. They should reflect some real needs of leaders, employees, and other constituents. For example, Schuster (1997) discusses how performance measurement in arts organizations has sometimes been affected by the need to appeal to funders. Second, measurement should be feasible. It is unlikely that performance measurement will be undertaken when leaders feel that the costs and time for doing so are too high: Information technology has greatly increased the use of performance measurement in recent years. Likewise, managers need a good sense of how and when productivity improvement will be used. Third, performance measurement is a matter of continuous improvement. As priorities change over time, new measures are adopted. Organizations also improve their measures over time. This typically results in some measures that are baseline and trend data and other measures that reflect momentary priorities.

Fourth, performance measures are best when accompanied by qualitative or interpretative information. The numbers seldom speak for themselves but usually require some context. Both the numbers and context should be communicated to stakeholders.

Data Collection

Data for performance measurement come from many different sources: management information systems, activity logs, service requests, incident reports, inspection reports, inventories, time reports, grants management, licenses, complaint logs, claims, customer surveys, financial reports, audits, and other sources. Generally these sources can be grouped as follows: administrative records, surveys, focus groups, and experts (Berman, 1998).

Administrative Records

Much information produced by program management is for the purpose of control rather than evaluation. Budgets, inventory control, and employee activity logs are typical examples of information that are regularly produced to ensure that expenditures are appropriate, that an organization's assets are accounted for, and that employees account for time and effort. Yet with minor additions these data can be used for evaluation. For example, logs of employee activity can be used to estimate the time and cost of delivering services. Inspection reports can be used to determine error levels in service delivery. In human services, analyzing employee activity logs by client treatment problems can give an estimate of the time and cost in dealing with different types of problems.

Administrative data are for measuring resources, activities, and outputs. These data often are readily transformed into workload ratios and efficiency measures. They also have value in assessing outcomes and goals, but outcomes and goal assessment typically also require feedback from clients that is seldom captured by administrative data. For example, assessments of increased nutrition and independence should include clients' own assessments, often requiring a survey as discussed later. Unless such input is captured in administrative records (for example, requiring staff to collect this information), an additional effort will be necessary.

Administrative records are also often less than perfect. They may have inaccurate or incomplete data and are sometimes based on inconsistent record-keeping definitions or practices over time. Fortunately, these problems often are of little consequence, though in some cases these problems may require organizations to reconsider their data collection practices. Information technology helps to analyze data that is based on many records, as if often the case in social services, hospitals, or education. In these instances, manual analysis is often too burdensome. When information technology is not available, a random sample may be drawn from many records to estimate the performance measures.

Surveys

Surveys are increasingly used to collect information from clients, which is essential to outcome and goal assessment. For example, following financial counseling, clients are asked about the effectiveness of the service that they received: Did the service help resolve the problem? Did the problem reappear after treatment? What aspects of the treatment were most useful? What aspects of the treatment were unsatisfactory? Such information is seldom provided through administrative records. Today, many surveys are telephone surveys because they allow for faster data collection than mail surveys, which often require multiple mailings.

Standards for conducting surveys are on the rise. Managers are now expected to be familiar with four important problems of surveys: (1) determining survey size, (2) drawing representative samples, (3) addressing problems of nonresponse bias, and (4) ensuring valid questions.

First, managers seldom gather data from all clients; rather they take a sample. The appropriate sample size depends on the *sampling error*—that is, the margin of error by which sample results vary in 95 of 100 repeated samples. Samples of 384 have a sampling error of 5 percent. Large samples have smaller sampling errors because they better mirror the population from which they are drawn. Samples of 800 have a sampling error of about 3.5 percent, whereas samples of 200 have errors in excess of about 7.1 percent. Usually, samples of 300 to 400 provide a reasonable balance between accuracy and cost. However, when many subsamples are analyzed (for example, performance measures by type of client problem), then an overall larger sample must be drawn. (Note: These sampling errors are based on large populations. When the population is only 1,000, a 5 percent sampling error is obtained for samples of only 278 (rather than 384). Very small populations (of, say, fewer than 300) require a census rather than sample.)

Second, samples should be randomly chosen. A *random sample* is defined as one in which each client or interviewee has the same chance of being chosen. Such samples are representative of the population. A practical problem is sometimes the lack of a reliable sampling frame—that is, the list of clients from which the sample is drawn. A case in point is walk-in clinics that do not even have the names or addresses of their clients. In these instances, a random sample is obtained by randomly choosing several dates and times for interviewing. A random sample can also be drawn from patient or client files. Perhaps the most frequent violation of random sampling is the use of voluntary responses—for example, customer service response cards that are given to all clients or left on reception counters to be picked up and completed by whichever client wants to. Such samples of respondents are often greatly biased toward those who have complaints: They are not representative of all clients.

Third, survey results may be affected by nonresponse bias. Even though the initial sample is representative of the population, a low response rate (say, 20 percent) may make the respondents unrepresentative of the sample. Typically, when response rates fall below 50 percent, further efforts must be undertaken to make certain that respondents are representative of the sample. Comparing demographic or service characteristics of respondents with known characteristics of the sample or population can do this. Typically, the age, gender, or service needs of population or sample are known. Note that the sample sizes discussed refer to completed samples. If, for example, a final sample of 400 and a 35 percent response rate are assumed, then a sample of (400/0.35=) 1,142 must be drawn from the population. In practice, telephone surveys among clients often have a 35 percent to 50 percent response rate.

Ensuring the accuracy of telephone numbers or addresses can increase response rates. They are also increased by correctly informing respondents of the purpose of the survey. Many people are reluctant to participate in surveys that solicit purchases. However, they are more likely to participate when they are informed of the evaluative purpose of the survey; that they are not being asked to buy anything;

that their responses are held in confidence; that they may skip items that make them feel uncomfortable; and that can call a supervisor to verify the purpose of the survey. These procedures markedly cut down on refusal rates in telephone and mail surveys.

Fourth, survey questions (also called "items") must be unbiased. It is well-known that researchers can bias responses by the phrasing of their questions. The ethical principle, as well as practical usefulness, of "adhering to the highest appropriate technical standards to increase the accuracy and credibility of information" suggests managers must avoid this pitfall. The general criteria for the phrasing of questions are that they should be unambiguous, avoid double meanings (that is, not asking two questions as a single one), be relevant to respondents (they should be sufficiently knowledgeable to answer), avoid biased or negative terms, and be as short and simple as possible. Applying these criteria helps refine proposed survey questions; most survey questions are drafted several times before they are found to be acceptable. Questions that telegraph the desired answer, for example, should not be allowed. In other words, they should not be prefaced with something like, "Don't you agree?"

Fifth, the length of telephone surveys can be considerably longer than many people assume is possible. Telephone surveys often have as many as 60 to 80 items. This is accomplished by structuring questions around a common response structure. For example, the introduction to a series of questions might be, "I will read you a series a statements. Please state for each whether you strongly agree, agree, disagree, or strongly disagree." This allows the interviewer to quickly read as many as 15 to 20 items. Thus telephone surveys of 60 to 80 items often take fewer than 15 minutes.

Focus Groups

Focus groups are used to better understand client needs and reasoning. They are used to gather in-depth information through structured interviews. As such, they complement the use of surveys and administrative records, which provide systematic but seldom in-depth information about problems and responses. Focus groups are often used in designing surveys to ensure that all relevant questions are asked. They are also used as management tools to identify problems and suggest solutions. However, a downside is that focus groups are exploratory in nature. The obvious drawback is, of course, that focus groups are not representative of the population; most groups are only 8 to 15 persons.

It is highly recommended that focus group members be selected from the same target groups. Focus group members should be homogeneous in their problems or responses. This helps avoid problems of "crowding out" among participants or some participants imposing the importance of their problems on others. Today, focus group participants are usually paid for their time. Such payments are necessary to ensure that they show up, and food should be available, too. Many communities have professional facilities with two-way mirrors and recording capabilities. By observing participants, managers often get a sense of "hot buttons" that might not otherwise be evident from transcripts or conclusions.

Experts

Evaluation is enhanced by the assessments of known experts. Like the use of focus groups, experts add qualitative information to the evaluation process. Experts are appropriate when objective, factual data are insufficient to make judgments. This often is the case in program management or medical interventions. The accreditation of many graduate programs in higher education often involves a site visit by a panel of experts. Although it is obvious that experts must have appropriate credentials, the use of experts is complicated by the fact that they are often paid by the organization that they are evaluating. Obviously, this can influence their opinions. Another problem is that experts do not always agree with each other. The use of a single expert may have little credibility, but the use of multiple experts can complicate matters. One approach is to have multiple experts operate as a panel, thereby requiring them to submit a collective, consensus-based report.

Organizational Evaluation

Nonprofit evaluation also concerns matters of organizational performance and effectiveness, such as board leadership. The nature of organizational evaluation tends to be qualitative, often focusing on the subjective assessments of individuals. Objective, quantitative indicators often are absent, or play a supporting, corroborating role at best. Assessment instruments vary, but most have common elements that are mentioned in the discussion that follows. Surveys are typically used to structure the data collection process, even though the number of officials is often small (such as board members). Perhaps the only large-scale survey efforts are those involving employees in large organizations.

Organizational Assessment

Effective organizations are defined as those that (1) have clear goals and missions that make significant contributions to their environments that, in turn, recognize and reward organizations; (2) reinforce and coordinate activities that promote these goals in effective and efficient ways; (3) seek out information and feedback from many internal and external sources to evaluate goal attainment and share such information liberally among those who might be affected by it; (4) are able to attract and retain people who are skilled and motivated to accomplish these goals (Kolb, Osland, and Rubin, 1995, as adapted). These basic points are easily expanded into various checklists of organizational effectiveness (for example, Harrison, 1994). Some checklists emphasize decision-making processes such as the frequency and openness of communications between managers and different levels of staff. Other checklists examine matters of coordination and control and interactions with external stakeholders, including clients.

Organizations that lack one or more of these elements often experience ineffectiveness; for example, organizations that lack efficient execution waste resources and therefore accomplish less. Inefficient execution can be caused by ineffective leadership, antiquated technology, or confusing policies, each of which distorts the ability to effectively use new information from internal and external sources. These conditions may also cause a sharp drop in employee motivation, which in turn causes retention problems. The range of organizational pathologies that can be observed is large. Research suggests that organizations that score high on organizational effectiveness are also more likely to adopt management practices and processes such as strategic planning, measures of customer satisfaction, and employee empowerment that, in turn, keep them productive (Herman and Renz, 1998).

Organizations vary, and in this regard Bardwick (1995) develops a typology of organizational cultures. Organizational culture is defined as the pattern of shared values and beliefs that lead to certain norms of behavior (Schein, 1985). Bardwick distinguishes cultures of entitlement, fear, and revitalization. Cultures of entitlement are characterized by job security, a lack of rewards for accomplishment, and complacency about improvement. High levels of stress about job security and punishment characterize cultures of fear; rewards are often political and uncertain. Cultures of revitalization are those in which employees feel empowered and energized by challenging work; they are judged and rewarded by their accomplishments. These cultures are not totally exclusive; for example, cultures of fear may be present in cultures that have only modest levels of revitalization. Berman (1999) provides empirical evidence of these cultures in large social services and museums. He finds only modest levels of revitalization in these organizations, but these orientations are associated with efforts to promote organizational effectiveness. Cultures of fear and entitlement work against professionalism in management. Table 7-2 shows some diagnostic questions that are used for determining organizational culture.

Board Leadership

Jackson and Holland (1998) provide a useful assessment instrument for assessing the board's effectiveness. Their six categories address the extent that board members (1) understand the culture norms and values of the organization; (2) are informed about the organization, the professions that work there, and its own roles and procedures; (3) work to foster cohesiveness among board members; (4) recognize complex issues and work to get multiple perspectives and input on such issues; (5) make healthy relationships a priority among key constituents; and (6) work together to formulate and shape the strategic vision of the nonprofit organization. The Jackson and Holland study includes a 65-item diagnostic instrument. Examples of items are, "The board sets clear organizational priorities in the years ahead," and "This board periodically sets time aside to learn more about important issues facing organizations such as the one we govern."

Processes of board assessment may be as important as the actual results. Earlier comments about the participation of stakeholders in evaluation are especially important. A proper board assessment process would start with obtaining the commitment from the chair of the nonprofit board for the assessment, undoubtedly for the purpose of furthering dialogue and team building among board members. Then the chair would request other members to complete the instrument

Table 7-2 **Organizational Culture Assessment**

Entitlement Culture

Often, ineffective people aren't fired.

There are too many rules and regulations in this organization.

My time at the office is consumed with shuffling paper, getting signatures, writing reports, and going to endless meetings.

Employees are more worried about making retirement than about serving the customer.

Employees have so much job security that they don't have to earn their rewards.

Employees just act busy rather than doing meaningful work.

Fear Culture

People are careful what they say around here.

People pay a price for their mistakes.

Employees talk about fear of losing their jobs.

Employee cynicism is high.

There seems to be a lot of confusion and rivalry among employees or managers.

There is a general feeling of mistrust among organizational members.

Employees have no control over what is happening to them at work.

Revitalized Culture

People who are productive and add value don't have to worry about losing their job here.

Employees feel empowered.

Most employees and managers are driven by the need for accomplishment.

Most employees and managers look forward with optimism.

Most employees and managers are willing to see things in a new light.

Risk taking is encouraged in our organization.

Employees are highly motivated to achieve goals.

Adapted from Berman (1999); Bardwick (1995).

and participate in a board workshop for the purpose of identifying improvements in the board's functioning.

Management Performance

The previous chapter touched on the idea that many employees have gripes about their supervisors and managers. Against what criteria should managers be evaluated? The literature is clear that different types of organizations, problems, and environments require different types of managerial leadership and that different managerial levels vary in their tasks and hence criteria for evaluation. Yet there are some common underlying themes, reflecting the perspectives of subordinates, employers, and activities to ensure their own well-being.

From the perspective of subordinates, managers should do the following: (1) Set goals for staff; (2) provide resources and remove barriers that affect employee performance; (3) provide feedback in ways that encourage and provide support; and (4) support employee development and be understanding about employees' personal needs (Werther, 1989). Goal setting is especially affected by the nature of work and organizations. In hospitals and universities, managers are expected to follow the lead of doctors and researchers, whereas in shelters and community health organizations, directors are expected to set clear goals for those who work for them. In many instances, subordinates also expect managers to have open communication about their managerial performance in the previously mentioned areas— hence a fifth criterion.

Employers have rather different expectations about managers. Managers are expected to (1) contribute to organizational goals and meet specific performance targets; (2) develop a vision for their units; (3) achieve goals with tightly constrained resources; (4) avoid bringing individual employees' problems to the attention of higher managers; and (5) be available to higher bosses at their command. Failure to meet any of these expectations causes managers to lose their jobs. In addition, some management jobs have considerable paperwork burdens.

These expectations of employers and employees are, at times, stressful for managers. To ensure their mental and physical health, some additional goals are therefore to (1) develop personal and career goals and strategies; (2) maintain physical fitness; (3) maintain a clear sense of the controllability of factors, putting energy in those that can be affected by managerial actions; and (4) understand their own personal strengths and weaknesses, improving both and avoiding unnecessary risks. Organizations that assess managerial performance often emphasize these criteria.

The evaluation process typically has the manager evaluated by superiors, with the executive director being evaluated by the board of directors. Increases in the use of 360-degree evaluations is growing in popularity. In a 360-degree evaluation, supervisors, peers, and subordinates or clients evaluate the individual. Multiple points of view reinforce the stakeholders' approach and ensure multiple points of feedback.

Employee Effectiveness

Organizations often conduct employee surveys to assess items that may affect organizational performance. Employee surveys vary, covering the following wide range of topics: (1) motivation and morale; (2) working conditions; (3) supervisory relations; (4) client relations; (5) career development and job training; (6) benefits and compensation; (7) performance appraisal and rewards; (8) ethics and legal compliance; (9) coordination and collaboration; and (10) other issues (e.g., race relations, team work, human resource management). In recent years, surveys include an emphasis on matters of employee empowerment: Figure 6-2 in the previous chapter provides some useful questions.

To ensure an adequate response rate, employee surveys are frequently conducted simultaneously among all employees of a work group or department. Although voluntary, the collective presence of coworkers during regular work hours creates an environment in which many surveys are completed and returned. To ensure the confidentiality of individual responses, employees are instructed to complete surveys, return them in a blank envelope, and not mark their names on them. To build trust, results are often posted on the organization's internal website or otherwise widely distributed.

Conclusion

Funding agencies and other stakeholders increasingly demand program evaluation. Effective evaluation uses input from many sources to shape and guide these efforts, and the results of evaluation are often broadly shared among stakeholders. Modern evaluation efforts focus on performance measurement, which provides real-time monitoring of program accomplishments. Performance measurement requires managers to think through the connection between activities and goals and to specify outcome and output indicators from which, often, efficiency measures are constructed. Performance measurement uses both administrative data as well as information that is gathered from focus groups and surveys. The latter requires technical expertise that is increasingly expected from nonprofit organizations and their managers.

The purpose of all evaluation is to make organizations function better. Organizational assessments help managers focus on missions and goals and examine the extent that their processes, decision making, and resources are consistent with goal attainment. Whether overall assessments are conducted or those that focus on managers, employees, boards, or clients, all assessments are important steps toward getting reliable, systematic information around which organizations can rally to improve their organizations. A hallmark of modern organizations is that they seek out evaluative information of interest to various constituencies and share it widely with stakeholders; that is the essence of accountability.

References

American Evaluation Association, "Guidelines for Evaluators. A Report from the AEA Task Force on Guiding Principles for Evaluators," 1998, available at http://www.eval.org/EvaluationDocuments/aeaprin6.html (October 31, 1999).

Bardwick, J., *Danger in the Comfort Zone*, New York: AMACOM, 1995.

Berman, E., *Productivity in Public and Nonprofit Organizations*, Thousand Oaks, CA: Sage, 1998.

Berman, E., "Professionalism among Public and Nonprofit Managers: A Comparison," *American Review of Public Administration* (June 1999): 149–66.

Cutt, J., D. Bragg, K. Balfour, V. Murray, and W. Tassie, "Nonprofits Accommodate the Information Demands of Public and Private Funders," *Nonprofit Management & Leadership* (fall 1996): 45–67.

Fine, A. H., C. E. Thayer, and A. Coghlan, *Program Evaluation in the Nonprofit Sector*, Washington, D.C.: Innovation Network, 1998, available at: http://www.innonet.org (November 5, 1999).

Harrison, M., *Diagnosing Organizations*, 2nd ed., Thousand Oaks, CA: Sage, 1994.

Herman, R. D., and D. Renz, "Nonprofit Organizational Effectiveness: Contrasts between Especially Effective and Less Effective Organizations," *Nonprofit Management & Leadership* (fall 1998): 23–38.

Jackson, D. K., and T. P. Holland, "Measuring the Effectiveness of Nonprofit Boards," *Nonprofit and Voluntary Sector Quarterly* (June 1998): 159–82.

Kolb, D., J. Osland, and I. Rubin, *Organizational Behavior*, Englewood Cliffs, NJ: Prentice-Hall, 1995.

McNamara, C., *Evaluation Activities in Organizations*, St. Paul, MN: Management Assistance Program for Nonprofits, 1999, available at http://www.mapnp.org/ library/evaluation/evaluatn.html (October 29, 1999).

Newcomer, K. E., *Using Performance Measurement to Improve Public and Nonprofit Programs*. San Francisco: Jossey-Bass, 1997.

Nitterhouse, D. "Financial Management and Accountability in Small, Religiously Affiliated Nonprofit Organizations, *Nonprofit and Voluntary Sector Quarterly* (Suppl. 1997): 101–21.

Rossi, P., H. Freeman, and M. Lipsey, *Evaluation*, 6th ed., Thousand Oaks, CA: Sage.

Schein, E., *Organizational Culture and Leadership*, San Francisco: Jossey-Bass, 1985.

Schuster, M., "The Performance of Performance Indicators in the Arts," *Nonprofit Management & Leadership* (spring 1997): 253–69.

Sustainability Network, *Evaluation*, 1999, available at: http://sustain.web.net/resourc/eval.htm (October 29, 1999).

United Way of America, *Achieving and Measuring Community Outcomes: Challenges, Issues, Some Approaches*, April 1999, available at: http://www.unitedway.org/outcomes/ (October 29, 1999).

Vogt, J. A., "Is Outcome Measurement Dead? Not at All," *Nonprofit World* (July/August 1999): 40–44.

Werther, B., *Dear Boss*, New York: Meadowbrook Press, 1989.

8

Building Bridges

Many nonprofit organizations find it beneficial to form alliances with other organizations. From the environment to education, and from health to homelessness, many examples of alliances exist. The purposes of these partnerships vary greatly, ranging from resource pooling and coordination to undertaking collective lobbying and engaging in community-based planning. Finding the right partners and purposes are essential, as are finding answers to the following questions: Is the proposed partner credible and effective? Is a partnership essential to fulfilling our mission and goals? Is the proposed partnership carefully thought through? Does the proposed structure best fit the purpose? Can we work with the other organization? How will inevitable moments of disagreement be dealt with? How much top management involvement will be necessary to sustain the partnership? Are adequate resources committed to the partnership? How will personnel turnover affect the partnership? The decision to form an alliance is decidedly strategic in nature, shaping the future of organizations.

Though partnerships can occur at any stage in a nonprofit's existence, they are most common among mature ones. Mature nonprofits have a better reputation, more resources, and greater capability to nurture and manage an alliance. Start-ups and even fast-growing nonprofits often lack the reputation, resources, and capabilities—even though they too can benefit from alliances.

This chapter examines different types of alliances and partnerships. It first develops a general framework for managing partnerships, examining key benefits and research-based lessons of success. It then examines partnerships involving three sectors: nonprofit organizations, partnerships with business, and those involving the public sector. Although partnerships with similar purposes are often found in these sectors, they are greatly shaped by the unique expectations and needs of partners in these different sectors.

The terms *alliance* and *partnership* often are used interchangeably. Legally, though, an important distinction exists. An alliance is a state of mind that exists between two or more organizations to collectively engage in some effort. It is an open-ended arrangement. A partnership is a formal, legal agreement to do the same, but with the purpose of generating measurable gains. Similarly, a joint venture is like a partnership but with a single purpose. Nonprofits form partnerships and joint ventures (for example, a museum that contracts out its coffee shop to make a profit), but these activities do not always enjoy tax-exempt status, and they must be established in ways that comply with various tax code provisions so that nonprofits do not lose their tax-exempt status. In this chapter, the terms *alliance* and *partnership* are used in the everyday meaning as "a state of mind" arrangement, except when explicitly otherwise noted (Arsenault, 1998; McLaughlin, 1998; Schwartz and Horn, 1999).

Framework

This section looks at the reasons for forming alliances and some important practices in managing them well. Typically, an economics perspective drives the assessment of benefits.

Benefits

Alliances offer numerous advantages to nonprofit organizations. First, perhaps the most common form of alliance is for the purpose of coordination. Nonprofits have different areas of specialization, and it may be necessary to jointly plan and coordinate services to deal with broader problems. A typical example is community health care alliances, which require diverse abilities such as nursing, crisis management, education, and even economic services. Few nonprofits have all of these abilities, and they may need to coordinate their resources. Nonprofits are sometimes brought together by local governments or umbrella organizations that have received or provide grants to address community problems. Examples of public involvement are commonly found in such coordinated activities as those that address crime, economic development, and health care crises such as AIDS and tuberculosis. In each case, coordination is viewed as essential.

Second, nonprofit organizations form alliances for the purposes of joint bidding, service procurement, and marketing. The purpose of joint bidding alliances is to increase market power and, possibly, economies of scale to get better bids from vendors. For example, private schools may wish to bundle their procurement needs for supplies to obtain lower prices, similar to central purchasing by larger public school systems. Organizations can also join together in responding to requests for proposals (RFP) from funders, without necessarily involving other forms of partnering. This may entail resource pooling as well. For example, two small nonprofits that provide counseling services might team up in response to a school RFP for counseling services. Bundling is also present when, for example, museums join together to market annual passes that are valid among several museums.

Third, nonprofits provide services to other organizations that might be considered a partnership rather than a transaction. For example, some nonprofit organizations monitor environmentally sensitive sites and provide this information to the federal government, for which they receive a grant from another nonprofit foundation, which may or may not cover the actual costs of monitoring. This service involves more than a voluntary information exchange but neither is it a marketplace transaction. Businesses team up with nonprofits to promote causes such as environmental protection or women's health. They may ally with nonprofits simply to create a favorable image or access to upscale customers. This helps the nonprofit promote the cause and allows business to better align itself with a customer segment. Other examples are drawn from cooperation among nonprofits, for example, when social service agencies agree to help each other in some ways, such as making client referrals to each other.

Fourth, organizations form alliances to share information, such as about general developments in the community, new regulatory requirements, treatment approaches, and sharing experiences about common management problems such as employee training or new uses of information technology for inventory or client management. Although professional associations sometimes provide some of these means of information sharing through their local chapters, the development of local chapters often is uneven. Thus managers' proactively seek out other organizations to more fully develop these advantages.

Making It Work

A variety of lessons learned apply in keeping alliances viable. Although each partnership is unique, successful partnerships share many common features (Berman, 1998). At the heart of every enduring partnership is the belief that it is a win–win situation. As a voluntary association, partnerships would otherwise not form. But the reality of changing environments implies that managers must assess the viability of their partnerships; they often need to make adjustments to ensure that they remain win–win situations.

The reality of working with different organizations means that some compromise is necessary: Participating in alliances entails giving up some control of mission and decision-making processes. The actual mission of a partnership might not fully reflect the preferences of each organization. Also, organizations open themselves up to scrutiny by other partners because each wants to ensure that others are living up to their commitments. Thus before entering into partnerships, managers must carefully assess the pros and cons of the partnership. Partnerships often work best for activities that are important because they do tie up management time, but not for those that are critical to the survival of organizations.

Partnerships require a clear division of responsibilities. Members must be clear about each other's strengths, contributions, and responsibilities. These roles must be spelled out at the onset of partnerships to avoid misunderstanding and hence conflict. Sometimes, partnership may increase legal liabilities: For example, joint ventures among hospitals have been subject to antitrust action by the Justice Department, raising concerns about diminished competition. Legal concerns also arise about possible wrongdoing by partners. Usually, these fears can be allayed, but they emphasize the need for a clear understanding of roles and responsibilities.

Clearly, trust is the ultimate commodity in maintaining partnerships. Leaders must inspire and reinforce trust through their actions. Commitments must be honored. Trust and leadership are also present in how managers deal with conflict—a true test of leadership. Maintaining successful relations involves a need to emphasize areas of agreement and commitment rather than division. Disagreement must be resolved, such as among technical persons at different nonprofits, but this cannot be done by creating losers, without risking participation. Partnership is an act of consensus building. Rather, leaders must act tactfully, acknowledging different purposes and the working styles of others and working toward win—win situations.

Alliances among Nonprofits

Many of the purposes discussed in the previous section are found in alliances among nonprofits. Alliances often involve two or three nonprofits working together in joint marketing or procurement. Nonprofits also form alliances to help other nonprofits. Alliances with more than three members are often called coalitions, such as those that work on matters of homelessness, teenage pregnancy, and AIDS. Another example is the California Community Foundation in Los Angeles, which sponsors an online giving website that lets individuals contribute $25 or more to any of nine foundations (Cohen, 1999).

Alliances often address specific, critical needs, such as space dilemmas, which are common among nonprofits. In the early 1990s, Wayne County Alcoholism Services (Wooster, Ohio) had outgrown its building. Facing high rents and inadequate resources to purchase its own building, the executive director soon discovered that other nonprofits experienced similar problems. By joining forces with the Every Woman's House, a local women's shelter, these two organizations collectively purchased a 32,000-square-foot building, reducing the facility costs for each (Kohm, 1998). In other examples, nonprofits that work together are found to get good deals on land and real estate that are targeted for redevelopment.

Start-ups and small nonprofits often struggle to adequately meet their information technology and payroll needs. Small nonprofits sometimes team up with larger nonprofits that manage their payroll and administration for them. Nonprofits that collaborate in this manner typically do not view themselves as competitors, and they are able to work out arrangements safeguarding the proprietary nature of information. These agreements are key to the success of joint marketing efforts. For example, many regions now have arts alliances that collectively market their shows and activities. Tickets for theaters are sold at multiple outlets, without incurring the fees and discounts of wholesalers. However, this requires sharing membership lists and similar matters that require considerable trust.

Successful joint marketing and real estate arrangements may lead to further collaborative efforts, notably capital and other fundraising campaigns. Joint fundraising also reduces costs of special events and mailings. Wayne County Alcoholism Services and Every Woman's House later joined in a successful joint capital campaign: Donors felt that they were helping two nonprofits, rather than one, and gave generously. Arts organizations sometimes establish local nonprofits whose purpose is fundraising: Received moneys are distributed to individual organizations according to participatory formulas. Collaborating nonprofits are also attractive to foundations because they increase the impact of funding.

Coordination is an urgent need, especially the need to avoid overlap and duplication of services that causes ruinous competition. In the absence of regional cooperation, food banks sometimes find themselves in competition with each other for food and distribution facilities. Public relations messages begin to sound alike, and funding agencies receive duplicating proposals. In these cases, the threat of destructive competition forces coordination.

Many funders are moving away from single issues programs in favor of broader areas that require geographic and functional collaboration (*Philanthropy Journal,* 1998). Rapp and Whitfield (1999) discuss how in Rochester, New York, settlement houses and family resource centers were begun to provide similar services in response to the priorities of funding agencies for comprehensive services. Historically, settlement houses provided recreational, early childhood, and social services, whereas family resource centers provided services that promote the wellness of families, such as parent education and preventive counseling. Such differences became minute over time, and funding in the area eventually asked these organizations to increase their collaboration.

Foundations also support other nonprofits whose missions help foster alliances with other nonprofits. For example, many foundations sponsor innovative demonstration programs. Resource centers are sometimes funded by the same foundations to ensure that these positive outcomes find wide distribution. To succeed, resource centers form alliances with nonprofits to help them use these new efforts: They provide information, know-how, and access to funding (Netting, Williams, and Hyer, 1998). In an innovative effort, Community Partners provides financial, administrative, and legal services and management training to new nonprofit start-ups in the Los Angeles area. Community Partners is self-funded from a small administrative fee that it charges to start-ups (Kohm, 1998).

Another example is the Alliance for Justice. This nonprofit organization attracts lawyers to donate their time to other nonprofits that have a need for legal expertise. They also help nonprofits meet their advocacy and lobbying needs. Similarly, some nonprofits seek out doctors and dentists who might donate some of their time to work with indigent or other populations, sometimes through other nonprofits.

Lessons from such partnerships show that they can be time-consuming for managers. Often, considerable time is needed to persuade board members and others in their own organization of the desirability of the partnership. Leaders answer an endless array of questions such as, Is the partnership appropriate for us? How do we know that the other organization will live up to its promises? What happens if the partnership does not work out? How can we safeguard proprietary or critical information? What happens if we lose our employees to the other organization? Often, it seems that leaders spend about as much time on persuading their own board members and staff as on working with prospective partners.

Although driven by urgent needs, partnerships represent strategic choices. Therefore, they should be mission-driven and, by definition, help nonprofits achieve their goals. These examples also show that successful partnerships represent good business sense for the long-term. Partnerships are not quick fixes but a way of laying a structure for future success. It is because of this strategic importance that they can justify the management time that is necessary to maintain them and work out inevitable conflicts over programs or duties that threaten the win–win relationship. Organizations have choices and may be able to select partners and shape alliances in ways that best meet their needs. Figure 8-1 provides a checklist to assist in evaluating partner choice.

Partnerships with Business

Nonprofit organizations often have a simple motivation to form partnerships with business: access to money. Many nonprofits experience revenue shortfalls that cause an acute need for money. Whether it is because of changes in government funding priories, the end of a contract, or the growth of a social or health problem, more resources allow for more good deeds to be done. Creative nonprofit executives often search for ways to open up the coffers of businesses to deal effectively with these funding problems. In so doing, they discover

Figure 8-1 A Checklist for Partnerships

- How does the partnership address our mission?
- Which strategic issue does the partnership help resolve?
- Is this proposed partner credible and among the best possible?
- Can the partnership be characterized as a win–win relationship?
- Are the required resources commensurate with the anticipated benefits?
- Is the distribution of responsibilities clearly laid out and agreed on by all?
- Can I get along with the people in the other organization?
- How do others in my organization feel about the proposed partnership?
- Is there a workable process for ensuring accountability?
- Is there a process for period review of the partnership?
- Are there any legal entanglements?
- What is the strategy for resolving inevitable moments of discord?
- What contingency plan exists if one of the partners drops out of the partnership?
- Are future managers bound by the partnership?

Source: Adapted from Berman (1998).

other business assets, too: expertise and human resources. Businesses can help nonprofits handle their payroll, printing, or information technology needs, for example. Very large companies often encourage their employees to serve as volunteers for nonprofit causes. Corporate philanthropy is an important source of nonprofit income, albeit not as important as individual giving. Sometimes, however, corporations can donate more than money, as an example from Xerox in *PR News* suggests.

> This week, Xerox Corp., will announce the latest ambassadors in its Social Service Leave program—an annual initiative that grants year-long paid sabbaticals to select employees so they can lend their expertise to the nonprofit sector. Xerox marketing executive Cheryl Hitchcock will spend the year developing a strategic plan to boost endowments at the historically black college Morgan State University, while engineer Bruce Genut plans to set up computer networks and provide IT training for Science Linkages, a Rochester, N.Y., organization that builds community-based computer centers. (Bernstein, 2000)

But a partnership is a two-way street: What do nonprofits offer to business? What is the basis of the win–win relationship? Often, the answer is cause-related marketing, in some shape or form. One of the first and best known of these examples involves American Express. In 1982, it launched a local campaign whereby it donated five cents for arts organizations in San Francisco each time someone used its card in the area, and $2 for each new card member who signed up. The campaign was hugely successful and was promptly replicated nationally in 1983. The national campaign involved donating one cent per transaction and giving $1 per new card member who signed up to the Statue of Liberty restoration project. According to Andreasen (1996), the use of American Express cards increased 28 percent over the previous year. People like to be able to buy and do good at the same time.

In short, cause-related marketing ties purchasing with doing well. Although cause-related marketing has found much appeal in recent years, a balanced assessment of pros and cons is in order. On the positive side, cause-related marketing can be a source of revenue and opportunity for reaching a broader audience by using the marketing channels of for-profit companies. On the negative side, cause-related marketing ties the good name of nonprofit to that of the for-profit. Some members of the nonprofit may have negative feelings toward certain firms and may not wish to be associated with them (for example, those that do medical research using laboratory animals or human fetuses). The reputations of nonprofits may also be affected by actions of for-profit firms during the partnership—for example, subsequent allegations of child exploitation in foreign sweatshops by the for-profit involved in a partnership. As noted by an anonymous reviewer, "If a corporation is looking for the good name and integrity associated with the nonprofit logo, it's worth asking why."

Despite these cautions, cause-related marketing arrangements have proliferated since the American Express example, involving such well-known nonprofits as the YMCA and the American Red Cross. American Express renewed its campaign in the 1990s with its Charge against Hunger campaign. Recently, Hewlett-Packard promoted its printers by giving purchasers up to $150 discount when they donated their old printer, fax, scanner, or copier to a charity of their choice. Sometimes, local nonprofits partner with local business in the same way. For example, some department stores promote their wares through similar campaigns to local food banks and charities. Some fast food outlets and supermarkets promote local educational causes. Many people are familiar with the *Entertainment Guides* that include discount coupons to area restaurants, sales of which support local charities.

These partnerships can also increase business access and appeal to more defined, targeted market segments. For example, Teledyne WaterPik donated $350,000 to a Susan G. Komen Breast Cancer Foundation program "Race for the Cure," which included the distribution of shower cards (plastic cards that are hung around shower taps that instruct when and how to do breast exams). The shower cards carry the WaterPik logo. In competitive markets where consumers have an array of choices and the price and quality of products are equal, many consumers report that they would rather buy a product that is associated with a cause. WaterPik does not promote specific products with the shower card, only its support and alignment with a cause that is significant to many of its potential customers. Research shows that success of such efforts depends on sustained and multiple efforts; one-shot promotional efforts have little lasting sales impact.

A related example is many computer makers and software companies have donated equipment to schools in part to build brand loyalty. In the 1980s, Apple was among the first to donate computers to schools. Microsoft donated software to schools in the 1990s, in the expectation that students would become loyal to Microsoft products. As a sign of the times, Microsoft recently donated $1 million to Senior Net, a nonprofit organization that provides computer training and Internet access to senior citizens in 150 computer learning centers throughout the country (*Philanthropy Journal Alert,* 1998). It also gave $700,000 to Green Thumb, another nonprofit organization that provides computer training to seniors. Seniors are among the fastest growing population segment, and many use computers to stay in touch with family members.

Donations also occur in-kind. EDS Corporation, which provides data services, donated information technology services to the Detroit Symphony Orchestra for its finance, marketing, and development needs. In return, the orchestra visibly promotes EDS through its brochures, mailings, and while on tour. In a rather unique use of corporate human resources, players from the Oakland A's baseball team participated in the Oakland Ballet Company's *Nutcracker* production, some even with choreographed solos. Promotion helped to regularly sell out these performances, and also brought other corporations to sponsor the nonprofit ballet company (Scheff and Kotler, 1996).

Businesses also help nonprofits when they ask their vendors and partners to participate in funding nonprofits. The grocery store Food Lion allowed vendors to participate in in-store promotions bearing the Children's Miracle Network logo. Ten manufacturers participated, thus producing a benefit for this nonprofit. Without the role of Food Lion, it is unlikely that these manufacturers would have contributed. In short, businesses can ask other businesses to participate in their favorite charities (Swanson, 1999).

Becoming Like a Business

Nonprofits are becoming increasingly more entrepreneurial. Universities have long merchandised their logos for use on t-shirts, mugs, and the like. Similarly, many environmental organizations have benefited from similar sales of their trademarks. Girl Scout cookie sales are well-known, too. Recently, the Edyth Bush Charitable Foundation and the Minneapolis-based National Center for Social Entrepreneurs helped fund a program in which nonprofit organizations examined their operations and missions to become less dependent on government grants and charitable contributions. In Orlando, the Girl Scout Council decided to become less dependent on annual cookie sales, which accounted for 70 percent of its revenue. After a market analysis, it decided to create a separate tax-paying company that will purchase and operate a Mail Boxes Etc. franchise. The company is appropriately named "Just For Profit," and its goal is to generate $500,000 in after-tax earnings in five years (*Orlando Sentinel,* 1999).

In other instances, businesses lend their expertise to nonprofits. Many museums find that they can generate revenue by aggressively marketing their meeting space for rent. Universities have increasingly marketed their cafeterias and bookstores to national chains that pay a fee and percentage of sales. Such "auxiliary" income amounts to millions of dollars. Many schools have also revised their licensing practices for soft drink vending machines, demanding additional revenues for placement of these machines. In other cases, nonprofits are now buying office buildings, using the rental income to finance the mortgage and provide nearly free facilities for themselves.

Business partnership can produce benefits for both. To form such a partnership nonprofits must first do screening and background research of potential partners. The business partner must be reputable. In the late 1990s, some apparel companies gained adverse publicity from engaging in sweatshop labor practices; this is clearly embarrassing—and offensive—to most socially conscious nonprofits that, in turn, could lose credibility and membership support. Business partners must be carefully selected. Nonprofits must also articulate how the nonprofit mission is consistent with the business interest. What is the partnership? Why is it a win–win situation? How, specifically, will it help the business? What are the defined goals, benefits, and costs? It may be necessary for the nonprofits to be persistent to determine this information.

Alliances Involving Government

Partnerships with government are more varied and complex than those with business. Nonprofits are participants in program planning and policy development, in issues that range from the community health concerns of neighborhoods to national concerns of environment and consumer product safety. They are partners in the public policy process. Nonprofit organizations participate alone, as well as through their associations (O'Connell, 1997). Nonprofits are also contractors to government for many services in which they sometimes shape the goals and implementation processes of public policy.

The philosophical debate about the role of government in nonprofit governance and management is mixed. Although government–nonprofit relations are inevitable, many observers are concerned about a range of negative consequences. Nonprofit managers often are well aware of many restrictions and requirements that accompany public resources. Public grants frequently limit activities that nonprofits may undertake while requiring others. In many states, for example, private schools that receive public funding are held to the same requirements as public schools for special education, bilingual education, nutrition, and equal educational opportunity. Freedom of choice on these matters is restricted or denied. Government grants also include detailed, often burdensome accounting practices. Nonprofit social services that receive Medicare funding often require very lengthy accounting, taking away staff time from direct service delivery. In addition, government funding is notoriously unstable, and sometimes government reimbursement fails to cover actual program costs. Such uncertainties cause many nonprofits to diversify their revenue sources to reduce their dependency on government funding.

Nonprofits may also find themselves in competition with government. Nonprofits are sometimes unwanted critics, for example, as advocates for the poor or unrecognized minority groups. Coston (1998) notes that in some countries nonprofits are severely repressed because of outspokenness. Nonprofits may be required to register (which can be administratively denied or delayed forever) and they are limited to operations that are restrictively defined and that require case-by-case approval by governmental agencies. These restrictions are found, in varying degree, in Japan, Egypt, and Indonesia. In some developing countries, nonprofits are also seen as causing credibility problems for government agencies by providing superior services, hence adding to the antagonism between the voluntary and public sectors.

But there are also positive consequences to the role of government, especially when the public and nonprofit sectors are viewed as complementary, as in the United States (Salamon, 1995). Nonprofits provide services in areas that lack adequate public consensus for support and they often are at the forefront of new social and medical problems, as indicated by early involvement in AIDS prevention and treatment programs. Their advocacy and support help propel these concerns into national awareness and, often, public policy. Such a role is consistent with a pluralistic society. Nonprofits also offer government a cost-effective and innovative way of implementing public programs. Public resources help nonprofits advance their mission—even if limited by various restrictions. Nonprofit participation in service delivery increases credibility in public policy debates, increases access to decision makers, and provides the nonprofit with a forum for advocacy.

Whatever the ultimate judgment about the role of government in nonprofit governance, current trends suggest that it is increasing. The transfer of federal responsibilities to state and local governments (known as "devolution") increases the role of nonprofits and foundations in service delivery and planning. Many local and state governments lack adequate staffing to fulfill their new responsibilities and find in nonprofit organizations a willing and affordable partner. Nonprofits also assist local and state governments in their planning by contributing information and know-how and by generating effective community-based responses. It is interesting to note that these trends also provide large businesses with opportunities. For example, in

Miami-Dade County (Florida), Lockheed Martin was hired to administer the county's welfare-to-work program; nonprofits lacked adequate administration, information, and billing services for such large contracts. However, Lockheed did subcontract to 30 nonprofits various transportation, training, and job placement services (Ryan, 1999).

Additional Examples

Some partnerships are designed to bring volunteers to public objectives. For example, BayKeepers is a nonprofit organization supported by foundations, grants, and gifts that supplements public agencies' efforts to find and stop illegal polluters. Most state and federal agencies lack adequate inspectors to monitor bays and waterways; BayKeepers's volunteers seek out polluters and take water samples for testing. They provide evidence of polluting to public agencies, thereby helping their activities. BayKeepers also has lawyers on staff who help pursue cases in court (Wood, 1999). Other examples of volunteer collaboration include nonprofits for elderly individuals that make them available as volunteers to local governments. For example, some local bicycle paths are now "patrolled" by retirees who report safety and infrastructure problems to parks' departments. Retirees are also used in staffing recreation centers and the like.

Some government–nonprofit partnerships are financially oriented. A problem in land conservation is that state and federal agencies often are slow to react to opportunities for acquiring land with important environmental value. Such land sometimes comes available with little advance notice and requires quick action to avoid development. Nature Conservancy and Trust for Public Land help governments by providing seed money and loans that enable public agencies to buy land for conservation. According to the Land Trust Alliance, almost 1 million of the 4.7 million acres that is held by land trusts is conserved as park land, wildlife refuges, and green space in partnership with public agencies (*Planning*, 1998).

Of course, many partnerships involve contracting of some sort. Charter schools are a case in point about the complementary nature of the public and nonprofit sectors, about pluralism and choice. Charter schools allow for innovation in ways that are not presently possible in public schools. A review of studies finds that charter schools enjoy considerable autonomy in developing their own curricula and selecting their instructional methods and teachers (Hassel, 1997). They have a high degree of flexibility in spending their money. However, they are held to a relatively high degree of compliance accountability: They must file all of the same reports that school districts do, but without those resources or administrative infrastructure. Also, in some states charter schools are eligible only for state funds; they do not receive any funds that are locally raised and distributed through local school boards. This funding gap is difficult to make up because most charter schools have fewer than 200 students, but some charter schools receive support from private foundations. They are also viewed as being in competition with mainstream public schools for resources, and it appears that this aspect is closely watched by public schools, while the public schools have not much interfered with curricular innovation by the charter schools. On balance, then, charter schools experience little goal diversion as a result of receiving public funding, but they do experience paperwork and financial burdens.

But historical experience of kindergartens in the United States shows that goal diversion may result.

> At the end of the nineteenth century, many nonprofit kindergartens were church-based and focused on the children's general development, moral and religious training, and concern for the family's well-being, including parenting training. As the demand for kindergarten grew, many sought public funding. This caused the kindergartens to pursue child-based outcomes with emphasis on dexterity, socialization/obedience and academic outcomes. Moral development, reference to religion, and family visits were dropped, including parenting education: sectarian values, especially those based on religion, find little acceptance in U.S. public decision-making processes that must seek a broad-based consensus. (Montes, 1997, pp. 409–14)

Finally, managers of nonprofit organizations often approach government officials on matters of public contracts or services that might lead to future contracts. Although this does not make them lobbyists of political processes, many of the same rules and practices apply. Local governments vary regarding the rules and practices for such encounters and discussions. In some jurisdictions, visits with senior government officials follow the same practices as for lobbyists. Nonprofit managers must register in a publicly available log and disclose the purpose of their visit. They should also know that public officials are severely limited in their ability to receive gifts. Increasingly, gifts of any kind are restricted to $25, and even these may be subject to public disclosure. They are often required to pay for their own meals, for which they receive limited reimbursement.

What, then, is a nonprofit manager to do? Nonprofits that want government contracts will have to make the case that they can be trusted to fulfill a public need at a reasonable cost. Typically, this is best demonstrated by a prolonged commitment to dealing with the problem, as evidenced by enduring service delivery and participation in various boards and panels that address the problem. Having a credible reputation among leading organizations is essential. Having a direct "in" with elected officials is helpful but less important than is sometimes popularly conceived. In a few jurisdictions, elected officials are even prohibited from interfering with contract award decisions or making "suggestions" to staff. Of course, this practice varies. In short, having a credible reputation among a broad range of organizations is important.

Coalitions and Consensus-Building

Some of the most important examples of government–nonprofit alliances are those that bring a broad range of public and private organizations to bear on complex problems such as preventing contagious diseases or addressing stagnant local economic development, teenage pregnancy, or crime in low-income neighborhoods. Resolution of these problems often resists the best efforts by single jurisdictions, nonprofits, and foundations; only well-coordinated efforts are able to make headway on these issues. For example, the restoration of neighborhoods requires crime prevention efforts, local financing, new economic development, and improved educational opportunities.

Such intractable issues often require leadership by elected officials, typically in consort with influential community leaders. The reason is that these leaders can readily assert credibility as acting in the public interest. Elected officials are also able to influence public spending priorities and mobilize considerable staff hours and expertise as might be needed. Other leaders might have good ideas, but few can mold disparate agencies and organizations to work in consort. Nonprofit foundations can raise the salience of issues but cannot force organizations to work together.

Of course, not all problems are found to attract collaboration and consensus-building. In general, issues must be sustained, salient concerns among a broad segment of the population and leadership;

they must be consistent with the political agendas of leaders; and leaders must have know-how in forming broad-based coalitions for change.

Broad-based efforts take on many forms. The simplest of forms is a summit of local leaders vowing to increase their individual efforts to attack some continuing problem. An example from Orlando illustrates its use:

> During the late 1990s, Orlando attracted more than 30 million visitors annually, making it a tourist destination of global significance. What is less well-known about Orlando is that it also became a known heroin market. To avoid imminent damage to its main industry, the county manager, Linda Chapin, convened a local summit of county, municipal, educational, criminal justice, and community leaders. Following this summit, many agencies increased their budgets for fighting drug crimes and also stepped up their coordination and collaboration. Schools increased their prevention efforts, working with police and counseling agencies. Since then, this drug problem has stabilized, and—although it has not disappeared—it has not inflicted manifest damage on tourism.

Many problems require somewhat more coordination and planning to solve them, especially those that are even more multifaceted. Community-based strategic planning is a process that can involve hundreds of leaders over a six-month process. During this time, leaders develop goals, objectives, strategies, and time tables for a comprehensive effort to abate some problem. The process is typically led by a well-known community or elected leader, assisted by a facilitator (Berman, 1998). In the early stages, leaders agree about the scope of the effort and the nature of their voluntary participation. They develop trust through collective examination of the issues and data at hand. Later, they develop goals, objectives, and strategies. Although participation by organizations is voluntary, most are willing to commit their organizations in important ways.

Local economic development is a typical example that benefits from coordination. In stagnating economies, spurring economic development requires improved efforts to rehabilitate neighborhoods and housing, ensure adequate education and vocational training, secure available investment incentives, establish or improve redevelopment districts, develop business and shopping centers, improve transportation bottlenecks, address crime, and support existing industries. Such a comprehensive plan requires participation of many leaders of government, as well as schools, banks, social services, neighborhood associations, and leading businesspeople. Many of these leaders do not know even each other, however, because their daily activities do not put them in contact with each other. For example, few business leaders know the directors of area vocational training schools. Thus a facilitated process is necessary to develop a working relationship to improve linkages and develop new action strategies.

Homelessness is another example that requires coordinated, shared leadership. Homeless services require a "continuum of care" that goes beyond emergency shelter. Because the causes of homelessness are varied, the services for homeless people must include medical and mental health care, social services, income assistance, job placement, housing assistance, and case management. This issue is also different in that nonprofit leaders often carry the burden of leadership for coalitions because homelessness is seldom viewed as a priority among government officials. Recognizing this, many nonprofit leaders have teamed together to create homelessness coalitions that keep homelessness an issue in the public consciousness and that coordinate service delivery and grant applications to higher governments and foundations.

Nonprofit leaders play important roles in shaping community-based action. As advocates, nonprofits maintain public awareness. Leaders may not be able to shape which issues get broadly addressed, but they can support the environment that makes it likely that the issue will be addressed. Sometimes only a minor crisis is needed to spur the attention of senior community leaders and elected officials. As participants, their role is to build new partnerships among different organizations. By sharing information and working together, new relations are formed that can positively shape the nonprofit mission in the years ahead. Collective action builds trust and often produces important outcomes addressing difficult problems. Such teamwork might even lead to future grant applications by nonprofits bidding together.

Conclusion

Nonprofits benefit from using partnerships in fulfilling their mission. Partnerships are common with other nonprofits, businesses, and governments, and vary greatly in their intent. When only a few partners are involved, partnerships among nonprofits often concern joint bidding on contracts, collective joint purchasing of office space, or sharing of administrative tasks. Partnerships with businesses frequently center around an exchange of money for access to a nonprofits' name, logo, or membership list for marketing. Government partnerships often involve contracting for service delivery. When many organizations are involved, partnerships among nonprofits often involve coalitions, sometimes with support of foundations, to provide coordination and advocacy. When government also is involved, they may become broad-based efforts at consensus-building, along with substantial resources for addressing complex issues, and involving diverse organizations brought together by public leadership.

Partnerships help nonprofits address important strategic issues. For small nonprofits, these issues often stem from having inadequate resources: Partnerships allow nonprofits to bundle their strengths, for example, by bidding together on larger contracts or office buildings. For large nonprofits, partnerships help extend their mission without diluting it and losing focus. Thus foundations and agencies such as the United Way team up with local nonprofits to increase services and resolve important issues but without building their own capacity in this area, which could prove to be unwieldy and unsustainable. Whatever the purpose, the decision to use partnerships involves important strategic considerations about the future of organizations.

Some managers of nonprofits have limited experience in working with partnerships, and many organizations have only a few partnerships. This is in part because partnerships are time-consuming to build and maintain and in part because they do diminish control. The art of crafting partnerships is to create win–win relationships. The range of partnership purposes is limited only by the creativity of finding new, innovative ways of meeting their strategic needs. Managers who seek to build partnerships must engage in an open dialogue with other organizations, building commitment and consensus on working toward common goals.

References

Andreasen, A., "Profits for Nonprofits." *Harvard Business Review* (November–December 1996): 47–59.
Arsenault, J., *Forging Nonprofit Alliances: A Comprehensive Guide*, San Francisco: Jossey-Bass, 1998.

Berman, E., *Productivity in Public and Nonprofit Organizations*, Thousand Oaks, CA: Sage, 1998.

Bernstein, P., "Philanthropy, Reputation Go Hand in Hand," *PR News*, January 17, 2000, p. 1.

Cohen, T. "Donor Service Foundations Relying on Technology," *The NonProfit Times* (November 1999): 58

Coston, J., "A Model and Typology of Government–NPO Relationships," *Nonprofit and Voluntary Sector Quarterly* 27 (September 1998): 358–82.

Hassel, B., "Balancing Acts: What Charter Schools Teach Us about Government–Nonprofit Contracting," *Nonprofit and Voluntary Sector Quarterly* 26 (December 1997): 442–65.

Kohm, A., "Cooperating to Survive and Thrive," *Nonprofit World* 16, (May–June 1998): 36–44.

McLaughlin, T., *Nonprofit Mergers and Alliances*, New York: John Wiley, 1998.

Montes, G., "Public Funding and Institutional Reorganization: Evidence from the Early Kindergarten Movement," *Nonprofit Management & Leadership* 7 (summer 1997): 407–21.

Netting, F., F. Williams, and K. Hyer, "Resource Centers: A Foundation's Strategy to Support Nonprofit Grantees," *Nonprofit Management & Leadership* 8 (spring 1998): 261–74.

O'Connell, B. (1997). *Powered by Coalition: The Story of Independent Sector*. San Francisco: Jossey-Bass.

Orlando Sentinel, "Nonprofits Turn to Business to Boost Bottom Line—and Mission," November 15, 1999.

Philanthropy Journal, "Nonprofits Seek Control Over Turf" (October 19, 1998), available at http://www.seflin.org/nsfre/npc.11.html (January 5, 2000).

Philanthropy Journal Alert 3 (October 7, 1998).

Planning, "Land Trusts and Partners Add to Protected Inventory," 64 (November 1998): 23–25.

Rapp, C., and C. Whitfield, "Neighborhood-Based Services: Organizational Change and Integration Prospects," *Nonprofit Management & Leadership* 9 (spring 1999): 261–76.

Ryan, W., "The New Landscape for Nonprofits," *Harvard Business Review* 77 (January–February 1999): 127–37.

Salamon, L., *Partners in Public Service*, Baltimore: Johns Hopkins University Press, 1995.

Scheff, J., and P. Kotler, "How the Arts Can Prosper through Strategic Collaborations," *Harvard Business Review* 74 (January–February 1996): 52–62.

Schwartz, J., and H. C. Horn, Jr., *Health Care Alliances and Conversions*. San Francisco: Jossey-Bass, 1999.

Swanson, K., *Who Cares* (September–October 1998), available at http://www.whocares.org/sepoct98/cover.htm (June 30, 1999).

Wood, D., "A Citizen Armada Searches Waterways for Pollution," *Christian Science Monitor* 91 (August 18, 1999): 3.

9

Fundraising

Fundraising is a critical function for nonprofits. The demands on many nonprofits exceed—sometimes greatly—the resources available. The result is often insufficient funds. When the need is to feed hungry individuals, house homeless people, or treat sick patients, limited resources mean turning away truly needy individuals. The resource challenge for nonprofits has increased in recent years, caused by many factors, including changing federal funding priorities, the emergence of new social problems that make demands on already scarce resources, and increased responsibilities of nonprofits to secure their own funding.

Fundraising helps nonprofits ensure adequate resources, and it depends on leadership involvement. Indeed, fundraising should be tied to the strategic priorities of nonprofit organizations, and leaders need to ensure that fundraising supports the strategic development of their organizations (Kelly, 1998).

Leaders include executive director, board members, and development staff, if any. Start-ups seldom have professional fundraising staff, so this responsibility falls on the executive director and the board—especially the board chair and the chair of the development committee. Donors need to be identified and cultivated and other forms of fundraising planned and executed.

From a strategic perspective, one often-unanswerable question may be, Is the lack of funding a problem or a symptom? Ask most executive directors and they will tell you it is a problem, as evidenced by the lack of funds to meet the needs of their many constituents. However, another perspective that should not be overlooked is whether the vision is sufficiently articulated and ennobling to attract the energies of board members, leadership, staff, volunteers, and donors. Is the mission crafted carefully enough so that it clearly delineates the efforts of the nonprofit? Is the strategy optimal? Is the nonprofit staffed with the right leaders, workers, and volunteers in the right positions? Are currently available resources being effectively and efficiently used? A negative response to any of these questions may suggest that a lack of resources is a symptom of a larger, more strategic concern. Regardless of the reason, few leaders of nonprofits believe they have sufficient funding, making fundraising a crucial issue in the life of virtually every nonprofit.

Fundraising is decidedly broader in scope than artfully asking people for their money. Rather, fundraising is foremost about enabling the execution of the nonprofit's mission, strategies, and operational plans. Through fundraising, external constituents are provided the opportunity to participate in the nonprofit mission. This allows donors to become part of the noble enterprise through their giving. As one author notes, "In their best moments, fundraising professionals translate noble beliefs and worthy purposes into giving *opportunities*" (Greenfield, 1997, xiv; italics added). In a very real sense, fundraisers give people and organizations with resources an opportunity to do good and feel good about themselves and their contributions. Fundraising, then, is about the opportunity of association. Fundraisers offer a broad range of opportunities for participation, reflecting their assets and specific interests. Some donors may even wish to contribute their talents as well as their assets.

In recent years, the environment for personal giving has been quite good. In 1998 Americans contributed $174.5 billion to nonprofits, a 10.7 percent increase over 1997. Personal giving and bequests represent 85.1 percent of all giving, with the remainder coming from foundations and corporations. Research shows that low-, middle-, and high-income households contribute about the same percentage of their income (1.5 to 2.0 percent), though very wealthy households contribute somewhat more (3 to 5 percent; Shervish and Havens, 1998). In recent years, aggregate giving has increased by 10 to 15 percent annually, and some key recipient groups such as health care organizations have seen annual increases of more than 20 percent (AAFRC, 1999). Much of this increased giving reflects the strong economy of the late 1990s. Foundations have also increased their giving, buoyed by unexpectedly large investment returns on their assets.

Despite this recent surge in opportunity, the challenge remains for individual organizations to ensure that they benefit from these revenue streams. Nonprofits cannot assume that the present largess will continue. Reversals in financial markets, even if temporary, might dramatically curtail giving. The future is even more clouded by the continuing devolution and shedding of federal financial funding. Even worse, changes in the tax deductibility of charitable donations under flat tax and other proposed tax reforms potentially could be devastating to the trends of increased giving by individuals, corporations, and foundations. States also have an uneven record in using nonprofits as a vehicle for implementing their policy objectives. They are subject to political changes and their accountability can be intrusive in the management of programs. Finally, with the growing sophistication of leaders and development officers in nonprofits, competition for funding sources grows more intense, ensuring that those nonprofits that do not continuously upgrade their fundraising skills may well find themselves losing ground in the battles for funding. Thus nonprofit leaders need to understand and fully use the latest strategies in fundraising from private and public sources.

Strategic Linkages

Top management leadership in fundraising is crucial. The strategic development of nonprofits is closely linked to their fundraising capabilities. New initiatives often require fundraising activities, and, increasingly, some donors demand that nonprofits match their grants through in-house fundraising. The executive director, chief development officer, and board members must ensure that fundraising capabilities are adequate to meet new initiatives and requirements. In turn, the capabilities require the allocation of adequate resources for fundraising—another strategic task of top management.

The resources and sophistication of the fundraising activity, of course, will vary widely. New or struggling organizations may not be able to afford a chief development officer, let alone a support staff. In these cases, the success of fundraising falls heavily to the executive director and the board. So important is board involvement that the chair of the development committee is often the stepping stone to becoming chair of the nonprofit's board. With greater sophistication and maturity, resources can be devoted to hiring a chief fundraiser (commonly known as the chief development officer) and building a fundraising staff. With this degree of sophistication in more mature organizations, the executive director and the board are still involved with networking and fundraising, particularly when the "ask" is made.

Leaders are also important to the success of fundraising in other ways. They lead by example in making fundraising appeals, and they are able to commit the organization in ways that are important to donors. For example, at the kickoff of a fundraising drive, board members are often asked to provide a "lead" (and therefore rather substantial) "gift." The use of lead gifts enables the kickoff to begin with some serious progress toward the goal already in hand. Finally, revenue diversification is often an important concern of nonprofit leadership. Many organizations experience overdependence on a few revenue sources and changing funding priorities. Fundraising should open up new sources of funding, thus sheltering the organization from abrupt resource shortages when donor priorities shift. In this way, fundraising figures into the strategic planning of nonprofits by providing a broadened and, presumably, more stable base of funds.

Yet these linkages between development and fundraising are sometimes lost in practice. Many social services organizations are led by presidents with backgrounds in providing services, not business development. Their day to day activities often overlook the need for ongoing, hands-on involvement in fundraising. In other cases, business managers lead health care organizations yet lack adequate medical knowledge to have credibility with potential funding sources. This problem is exacerbated when they are unable to team up with those with this expertise. In other instances, top managers simply do not take to external networking; they prefer to focus on matters of internal operations management. The need for integration at senior management levels is clearly expressed by the following senior fundraiser for a local United Way:

> I think the chief reason that we are able to be successful at fundraising in our local community is that our CEO has a campaign fundraising background. He knows what is needed to raise money, and he is willing to lead by example. He has a business background and knows how to commit our organization to fundraising. He motivates our managers to go out and ask for money. I think we have been very fortunate. (personal communication, M. Engar, October 4, 1999)

Not all organizations can count on the individual orientations of their managers to ensure strategic integration. In this way, CEOs have been urged in recent years to lead in fundraising. At a minimum, top managers should set aside some time each week to contact potential donors and strengthen relationships with existing ones. Networking, following up on leads, and providing support for board members and the nonprofit's chief development office are other minimum areas of involvement. A CEO should also personally thank important donors.

Executive directors are also encouraged to better use their board members as assets in marketing their organization. Not only are board members expected to personally contribute to fundraising campaigns, they should take an active role in cultivating relationships with other leaders who are important to the organization. Board members should be selected who are willing to enthusiastically ask their peers to support the organization in thoughtful ways and offer to make fundraising calls to important prospects. The CEO and chair of the board should lead, setting the example for other board members and senior managers. The fundraising abilities of potential board members are a legitimate criterion for their selection. Indeed, in recent years some large nonprofits have cut back the number of board members, focusing instead on board members who can assist in fundraising. "Give, get, or get off" is still a common understanding in start-up as well as mature boards. Being a member of the board should be something more than just an honorary position or title.

The executive director also plays a strong role in ensuring the climate for effective fundraising. In this regard, perhaps the largest strategic asset of nonprofit organizations is the past success of its programs. Fundraising offers donors the gift of participation and of making an impact on society. The ethics of fundraising requires that donors are told about the result of past efforts, when asked (Anderson, 1996). Few donors take kindly to being duped by gifts that are ill-used. Such donors will not likely repeat their donations. Large donors and foundations are likely to require detailed evaluation of program results. Entrepreneurs who give to philanthropy often want to see "focused missions, concisely articulated problems, proposed solution, strategies for getting it done and benchmarks for evaluating accomplishments"(Leader to Leader, 1999). Simply put, these business people expect the nonprofit to act more like a business in its policies, procedures, and feedback mechanisms.

The National Society of Fundraising Executives has developed a "donor bill of rights" that sets standards for ensuring that donors retain their trust in philanthropic giving (NSFRE, 2000). Such confidence is in the interest of all—the public, donors, and nonprofits. The rights of donors include being informed of the nonprofit's mission and intended use of donated resources; being assured that gifts are used for purposes for which they are given; knowing the identity of board members and expecting the board to exercise prudent judgment in its stewardship; being informed whether those seeking donations are volunteers, employees, or hired solicitors; expecting that all relationships are professional in nature; having access to financial statements of the organization; having their names deleted from mailing lists; and receiving acknowledgment and recognition for their donations. Leaders help ensure the long-term effectiveness of their organizations' fundraising by emphasizing their importance and monitoring adherence to the standards by those who interact with donors.

Strategic integration requires that fundraisers have good stories to tell about the organizations' accomplishments. Donors, board members, volunteers, and staff want to be associated with a successful organization. The executive director, perhaps more than any other person associated with the nonprofit, must convey pride and confidence in the organization, its mission, its people, and, most important, its accomplishments. CEOs shape the future by protecting and nourishing these achievements as a strategic fundraising asset.

Most important, the executive director and the chair of the board shape the overall level and strategic direction of fundraising. It is ironic, but fundraising does not come cheap. The cost of telethons, for example, is often $.75 to $1.25 for each dollar raised from first-time donors and about $.25 to $.40 for repeat mail and telephone donors (hence justifying the cost of acquiring first-time donors). Special events such as galas often cost $.20 to $.50 for each dollar raised. Add to this the sunk cost of staff salaries. It follows that organizations need a realistic, strategic plan of their fundraising objectives. Indeed, sometimes questions arise about the value of fundraising: Are these moneys better spent on direct service provision to client groups? Top managers, then, along with fundraisers, must articulate the contribution of the fundraising function to the nonprofit mission and determine the overall level of fundraising efforts as well as the trade-offs between spending money on current constituent needs and investing in raising more funds for the future.

Finally, top management leadership is necessary to support the overall strategy of the fundraising itself. An important perspective in fundraising is viewing donor cultivation as a strategic process. Most donors make many small contributions before they feel comfortable in making large gifts. The "pyramid of giving" is an important concept that suggests that most people first contribute through an annual giving campaign to a specified organization, perhaps through a telethon, direct mail campaign, or appeal. Then some people may go on to later contribute larger amounts through endowments, capital, or major gift campaigns. Eventually, some donors may even establish bequests or planned gifts. Nonprofits must work with donors to increase their comfort level and ensure that their gifts serve the needs of both. It is a myth that major, unrestricted gifts often occur without much prior contact: Such examples are very much the exception, so much so that they typically make news (Greenfield, 1997). It is for this reason that fundraising requires different activities for different levels of giving, and these must be strategically integrated and planned.

In sum, fundraising requires the involvement of top managers who can link it to the strategic development of their organization. The following sections in this chapter discuss fundraising activities that are commonly found in nonprofits: annual campaigns, acquiring large donations, events, grants, Internet soliciting, capital campaigns, and planned giving.

Annual Giving Campaigns

Annual campaigns are designed to attract new donors and to maintain existing ones. Likely activities include direct mail, telethons, and other forms of direct solicitation. The term "annual" refers to the frequency of giving: Most donors give once per year, but most campaigns involve multiple mailings and efforts, perhaps as many as six per year. Multiple mailings remind donors of the nonprofit, help keep donors appraised of the work of the nonprofit organizations, and serve other fundraising purposes.

Market segmentation is used to ensure that giving opportunities and messages are appropriately tailored. Frequent mailings are necessary for keeping existing donors informed of the impact of their past contributions, thereby addressing issues of accountability. Multiple mailings also provide the means for reminding donors of the need to renew and prompting them to do so, often with requests that they consider increasing their donation to the next level of giving.

Individuals, who typically write small checks of $10 or $25, do most of the giving. Giving campaigns are typically designed to support operational expenses rather than major expenses such as new buildings or major programs. Even by total amount of giving, corporations and foundations play a minor role in this area: They are more likely to provide grants or respond to requests for major gifts (for example, facilities that can be named after them). The number of existing donors greatly affects the effectiveness of annual campaigns. As previously noted, the cost of acquiring new donors through annual campaigns is about equal to their contribution; the fundraising payoff comes from repeat donors. Organizations that lack substantial numbers of existing donors may spend three to five years conducting campaigns to acquire an adequate number of donors, who then generate substantial payoff from fundraising efforts.

Donor Base

Having a large donor base is a strategic asset for nonprofit organizations. Recognizing the importance of maintaining existing donors, substantial effort is expended to ensure that past donors renew their pledges. Organizations often target renewal rates of about 70 to 90 percent; certainly, renewal rates below 50 percent are problematic given high acquisition costs of new donors. A low renewal rate would indicate problems with either the campaign effort or the image of the nonprofit. Frequent mailings, then, are a strategy for ensuring that a positive image of the organization is kept in the mind of donors. It also allows nonprofits to show how donors' $10 or $25 contributions make a difference (e.g., feeding a child). Mailings over the course of a year typically include brochures; newsletters and newspaper clippings that highlight the organization's achievements; stickers, calendars, bookmarks, and other related token of thanks that can be displayed; membership benefits if applicable; appeal for renewal; and a questionnaire. The latter is a useful vehicle for identifying donors who may be interested in a higher level of support.

Telethons and direct mail are also used to reach new donors; getting new donors is a sine qua non for the growth of the campaign effort. Various marketing companies provide targeted lists of potential donors. However, many lists are inaccurate: They are dated and contain many errors. The effectiveness of annual campaigns requires some list cleaning to ensure that materials are sent appropriately. Some organizations also ask their employees and board members for lists of individuals to be included in campaigns. In some instances, nonprofits successfully ask major donors to fund these new member acquisition efforts or at least get donors to defray some costs, such as getting a board member to use his or her firm's in-house print shop to publish brochures or handle the postage expense.

Campaign Duration

Major university fundraising programs, for example, are ongoing, punctuated with major capital campaigns that may last for five years. Community nonprofits often have campaigns that last eight to ten weeks—starting with setting up the mailing or telephone lists, printing materials, mailing, making telephone calls, receiving donations, ensuring follow-up. Organizations that undertake three to six campaigns yearly in effect commit themselves to fundraising throughout the year. Recognizing the challenges of getting new donors, ensuring renewal, and allocating adequate resources to this effort, it comes as no surprise that many small and medium nonprofits have mixed records in giving campaigns. Many local United Ways overcome some of these barriers by getting major employers to commit themselves to asking their employees to contribute to the United Way. In such a campaign each year employees are asked by their employers to give to the United Way. This approach ensures a broad targeting of communities and substantially multiplies the fundraising resources of the United Way.

Consultants

Today, consultants often play a significant leadership role. The expertise of consultants is helpful in doing feasibility studies, developing campaign strategies, training board members and staff, managing or providing technical expertise to campaign activities, developing new prospects, and evaluating fundraising activities. Consultants are hired to do such tasks as cleaning mailing lists and providing attractive mailing materials or videos, recruiting fundraising managers and staff for fundraising, and conducting telethons. Nonprofits are sometimes reluctant to invest in the cost of an experienced fundraising consultant, but technical and strategic expertise may be worth it.

Nonprofits should be sure that the consultant's expertise and work style fits the needs of the nonprofit; sometimes the chemistry or past experience just does not provide the right fit, for example, involving a consultant who has worked in an unrelated nonprofit field or only with large organizations. An important issue also is compensation. Nonprofits sometimes try to pay consultants on a contingency basis. Although this may appear to be in the organization's interest (it minimizes potential losses), contingency contracting may cause consultants to make inaccurate representations to potential donors to increase the initial donor base. Such gains mask later problems of retention. As noted, nonprofits must ensure that their work is seen as truthful and effective, and creating long-term, stable relationships between donor and nonprofit is an important focus of giving campaigns. Working on commissions may induce unethical behavior. For this reason, many fundraisers prefer to work on a reimbursable expenses-plus fixed-fee basis.

Success Difficulties

Various trends have raised the difficulty of succeeding with annual campaigns. Donor fatigue from multiple mailings and from the competition among nonprofits may cause donors to withdraw their interest and involvement. At the same time, cost escalation for postage, printing, staff, and professional services all eat away at the effectiveness of annual giving campaigns. Even intergenerational preferences in giving must now be taken into account.

Special Events

Many nonprofits host outdoor festivals, sporting competitions, and gala-type banquets. Special events provide visibility for the nonprofit and offer donors who have contributed in the past and provide the opportunity to contribute again, perhaps at higher levels. Events present an occasion for those donors and others to better familiarize themselves with the organization—for example, by meeting some of its managers and employees in person. They also meet others who share similar commitment to the organization. Special events are very much the middle step in the "pyramid of giving." Those who give to special events may be candidates for higher levels of giving discussed in the next section. Organizations frequently host various events during the year to provide multiple occasions for donors and others. Many ballet and opera companies hold annual galas, as well as open rehearsals and special shows that aim to attract various audiences to its causes.

Many small and medium-size nonprofit organizations find it advantageous to participate in existing special events or even combine their efforts and host a joint event. Collective efforts increase attendance, which reduces costs and makes them more attractive to potential sponsors. Joint sponsorship might lead to a large enough event that sponsors may be attracted to lend their name and resources.

Sponsorship is an important source of event income. Events increase sponsorship appeal by attracting persons with common interests.

> For example, art galleries in districts that contain other galleries often band together to host special events such as "art nights," during which they collectively extend their show hours and welcome participants. These participants often have upper middle to high incomes and are an attractive target group for sponsors such as luxury car manufacturers and dealers, upscale department stores, national travel agencies and their chains, as well as local gourmet shops and upscale restaurants. Their sponsorships offset event costs and may provide revenue for lasting improvements. (See also Hopkins and Friedman, 1997.)

Likewise, some social service agencies collectively hold events, sometimes in partnership with the United Way, to promote awareness and support (for example, "help our children" or "walk for a cancer cure"). These events may include festival-type activities, sporting events, and evening galas during a two- or three-day period, complete with corporate-sponsored, logo-emblazoned shirts, prizes, trophies, and other giveaways. Fundraising may occur through sponsorship (e.g., Health Maintenance Organizations or hospitals that want to increase their image), merchandising (e.g., booths where sponsors can tell their story and provide refreshments or t-shirts, buttons, and the like), event fees ("walking for life"), and solicited donations (such as through concurrent telethons). The profit from selling food and drinks often is another source of income.

Event management is obviously a major undertaking, with an event manager–producer being responsible for overall coordination. Some of the main activities are marketing and media relations, coordination of participating organizations, volunteer management, finance and accounting, legal aspects relating to contract management and liability insurance, and on-site management (electrical, sanitation, audio, waste, traffic, security, and related issues). Although many nonprofits are able to organize small events, larger events often require professional event management organizations. Large events often have significant costs because of equipment and stage rentals, security, liability insurance, and pre-event marketing. Nonprofits will need to choose strategically the special events in which they participate because rain outs or other unforeseen problems can make the event a source of costs, not fundraising (Freedman and Feldman, 1998).

Fundraising activities for special events include targeting existing donors and others who support the organization to participate in the event. These persons must be given ample warning of the upcoming event and encouraged to show their support by participating in it. During the event, fundraisers should identify walk-ins and others new to the organization who are to be targeted in subsequent campaigns. After the event, donors who have participated must be thanked for doing so, especially those who have given their time or money. These before and after activities that involve donors provide a tie-in with campaign activities.

The strategic importance of special events in the pyramid of giving suggests that their success should not only be assessed by the amount of money raised but secondarily in terms of "friend-raising." Special events are opportunities for solidifying the donor base. Through interactions with donors, nonprofits use special events to increase the personal commitment of individuals to the organization and its causes. Special events are an occasion for making new friends, for example, among those who are not yet donors. It is difficult to quantify the extent that increased relationships increase fundraising, but it stands to reason that those who feel a close connection to the organization and its managers are more likely to give more than those who feel less of a bond.

Major Giving

Major giving encompasses bequests, donations for capital buildings, corporate giving, and major giving from individuals. Such giving typically starts at $1,000 and includes donations of $1 to $40 million for buildings or naming institutions such as law, business, or architecture schools after those who give millions of dollars in endowments. Recently, for example, Ted Turner (founder of CNN and related companies) gave $1 billion to the United Nations. Bill Gates (founder of Microsoft) created a scholarship fund of $1 billion for minorities, which will fund many nonprofit activities. With the considerable wealth being accumulated by corporate leaders and founders of Internet and other organizations, the future of large-scale philanthropy holds considerable promise in the twenty-first century. Although unusually large gifts make headlines, one need only to read the donor plaques in hospitals and universities to appreciate the depth of giving among American individuals and corporations. Some social service agencies are also recipients of giving largess.

Most major giving comes from affluent individuals. Research suggests that those who give large gifts often have a sincere and long-standing commitment to the cause of the organization. Many have had an active involvement in the organization itself. They respect the officers of the organization, whom they often like in a personal way. Some reasons for large-scale giving are pride of association with prestigious organizations, social status that comes with major giving, gratitude, creating a sense of immortality (for instance, when a university building carries one's name), and psychological satisfaction that comes from giving back to society (Cook, 1997).

Sometimes a precursor to major giving is the death, or pending death, of a family member; a large contribution is seen as a sign of respect to that person's wishes or memory. Donors may have believed in a cause or have been grateful to an organization for its support or services (e.g., hospital, higher education, or church). Donors sometimes seek to aid their direct family through increased access to the facility or organization that they are helping to fund or simply by having the family name associated with the organization. Among donors who are still living, the latter often is a primary motivation. Although those who give do receive tax benefits for doing so, the cost of giving is of course always greater than these benefits.

The cultivation of prospective, affluent individuals is critical. Often, prospects are identified from those who already give to the organization or are otherwise known to support the organization's cause. It is a myth that many large grants arise from those who are unknown to the organization. The success of capital campaigns, fellowships, and endowments is greatly enhanced by having a network of individuals who are likely to give. Some criteria for screening prospects for major giving are that they own a business or have inherited or married into family wealth; have a history of philanthropic giving; have recently received a financial windfall from, for example, sale of a business; are nearing retirement or are 55 years old or older; and have few heirs. Religious commitment is an important criterion for religious organizations seeking major giving.

Executive directors play an important role in ensuring that the nonprofit has a structure in place for screening and following up with prospects. They must also involve board members and volunteers who have connections. Some members and volunteers feel uneasy about cultivating and eventually asking prospects for their major gifts. Asking people for their money is not about begging or asking for charity; it is about providing them with the unique opportunity of making a difference and leaving a mark on society or the organization. Few fundraisers directly ask for money. As the saying goes, "Ask for money, and you'll get advice; ask for advice, and you'll get money" (Lawson, 1997) Whatever the outcome, the result should always be the strengthening of the prospect's ties with the organization.

Capital fund appeals offer a good opportunity for affluent individuals to give. Few buildings are paid for by numerous small donations; the success of building campaigns typically depends on having one or more gifts of $1 million and more, and five to ten individuals giving substantial gifts of $400,000 to $1 million. Then smaller gifts help buy equipment or special features. Capital fund appeals provide vehicles for satisfying the giving needs of affluent individuals. Non-profits facilitate such giving by helping affluent individuals pay over time or by setting up planned giving opportunities, such as charitable trusts or the transfer of partnership interests, stocks, real estate, and patents. A variety of software programs help donors who are considering donating parts of their estates: These programs compare the benefits and tax consequences of different types of trusts and other forms of giving. As a result, large donations are often intertwined with family estate planning and taxes.

Stories of organizations coming into major gifts are numerous and varied, but many support a strategic model of cultivation and follow-up. Hospitals frequently receive large gifts from patients who feel grateful for how they were treated. Immediately following treatment, patients are told of the hospital's need for a new center. It is ironic, but even those who die (or their families) often are grateful for final aid received and therefore give generously to hospitals or hospice organizations through their wills. Many cancer centers often are very well-endowed, for example. Likewise, institutions of higher education sometimes receive large bequests from those who were not particularly close with the institution, though most donors have a record of giving and other affiliations with the institution; however, they also receive major gifts from large organizations and affluent individuals who, in one way or another, benefit from the university in the community. Similarly, many local United Way organizations receive large gifts from leading, affluent citizens in a community. Often, these relationships have been cultivated and sustained over many years, despite management turnover and inevitable ups and downs of the organization (Sturtevant, 1997).

Although corporations play a small role in giving, some may be inclined to make a major gift. Corporations are often reluctant to give because of uncertain business payoff and negative effects on their bottom line. Many business executives also feel uneasy about nonprofit management; they do not really understand why these organizations are necessary. They also view small gifts as a waste of staff time. Yet large corporations may be willing to make a gift for marketing purposes. For example, they often donate to business schools in U.S. higher education to increase access to their graduates. Some are willing to give $1 million for an endowed chair or toward capital expansion. But it may be more difficult to attract such funding for social purposes. Some large building corporations and food chains are known to associate themselves with local social causes to create community goodwill. Corporate giving increasingly is tied to a real or perceived benefit for the organization. Though this attitude may seem crass, such give and take may be necessary for corporate management to convince their board members of the value of giving. Nevertheless, business owners, rather than corporations, are more often inclined to engage in major giving.

Grants

Grant directories are full of private foundations and public agencies whose purpose is to provide grants for work that is typically performed by nonprofit organizations (e.g., Annual Register, 1997; Brewer, 1998). Both private foundations and public agencies often make grants available for testing and evaluating innovative strategies. For example, experimental programs involving elderly individuals deal with ensuring that they stay fit, take the right medication, and avoid social isolation. Both private foundations and public agencies often are willing to sponsor model programs in these areas, such as using volunteers to tend to these tasks. Virtually no social area exists for which grants are not available for testing some innovative idea, provided that the problem is viewed as important, the approach novel and appropriate, and the credentials of the nonprofit provider acceptable. Of particular note are the fast-growing community foundations. By 2000 there were 547 community foundations, up from fewer than 200 twenty years earlier. As their name implies, these grant-making organizations target causes within their local communities (Fitzsimons, 2000).

Private foundations and public agencies also use nonprofits for service delivery, and public agencies are increasingly doing so. In many communities nonprofits now provide school counseling, parent education, maternity services and counseling, criminal justice rehabilitation, consumer credit counseling, and so on. These often are ongoing grants and contracts for services, unlike those for experimental programs. Nonprofits are limited in applying for grants only by their capacity to meet service standards and loads. Typically, public sector funding for these activities is quite large and may even include quasi monopolies for some services; for example, some small and medium cities have only one Medicaid provider for mental health services. The role of private foundations often is to fill the gap of services not funded by the public sector. For example, the public sector often has limits in providing services; many religious organizations provide for additional health, nutrition, shelter, and schooling needs.

In recent years, there has been increased grant writing as a means of fundraising. However, it is largely a myth that large grants can be obtained simply by completing an organization's grant application form. The relationship between the grantor and grantee is everything: Agencies must have confidence in the nonprofit organization's abilities to deliver. Many organizations that receive large grants have steadily built this relationship by starting with small grants, gradually working toward larger commitments. Exceptions exist, but they are not the rule.

Public agencies and private foundations operate rather differently and often have separate purposes. Public agencies often have extensive accountability procedures that many nonprofits find too cumbersome. Public funding can also be notoriously fickle because of political decisions. Yet the selection process and level of public funding often conveys prestige to the nonprofit organization receiving it. Private foundations often have more relaxed accountability standards, but their level of giving is often smaller. In social services, private foundations are more likely to support experimentation and testing, whereas public organizations support direct services on a large scale. However, private organizations that support service delivery are now becoming tougher in their accountability standards. The United Way, for example, is now requiring many local organizations to increase their outcome evaluations.

The importance of achieving outcomes cannot be overlooked in the grant process. When nonprofits fail to deliver as promised in their grant proposals, future funding may be jeopardized. In some cases, state licenses of health care or social service organizations may be suspended or revoked. Criminal investigations and allegations of fraud are not uncommon in recent years. For these reasons, nonprofit organizations must be realistic about the capabilities in the grant process, track and report outcomes, and honor their fiduciary and social responsibilities.

Grant proposals typically require the following information: the nonprofit's tax exemption certification, mission, background and prior accomplishments; current budget and major programs; number and qualifications of staff; accreditation and affiliations. The main body of the proposal discusses the proposed project or program. This aspect should address the need for the program; specific contributions of the program; program goals and specific objectives; strategies and activities for achieving the objectives; unique capabilities and qualifications of the nonprofit organization to do the proposed work; and proposed standards for measuring the organization's success in performing the project. The proposal should also have a detailed budget that specifies the number, type, and cost of personnel, office, and equipment costs, and travel and consulting expenses. It may also include income generated from the project, such as reimbursements for services delivered. Finally, the proposal should provide more information about key staff as well as organizations whose contribution is critical to the project's success. In this case, letters from these other organizations in support of the proposal should be included (Miner, 1998).

Writing a grant proposal often is labor intensive. It is obvious that proposals will be more successful when the donor has already indicated substantial interest in the proposal's goals and strategies—or better yet, when the donor has already set money aside for it. Therefore, grant writers do well to first contact prospective donors and engage in a conversation with them about the donor's goals and objectives. Such dialogue can help indicate the prospect for success or lead to substantive changes that will facilitate a successful outcome. Even though often little is promised by the donor before receiving the proposal, grant writers can determine whether the likelihood of acceptance is realistic or merely remote and learn of the key considerations in evaluating grant proposals by this giving organization. If success seems unlikely, grant writers and leaders might want to consider other projects or other donors. In any event, unsolicited proposals will usually have a far lower chance of success than those whose submission precedes such dialogue and agreement (Golden, 1997).

Conclusion

Fundraising helps the nonprofit organization obtain resources for managing its programs. Acquiring and maintaining donors is an important focus in fundraising; the pyramid of giving describes how the sequencing of fundraising activities is used to target different amounts given by individuals. Specifically, annual campaigns are used to raise small contributions from donors, whereas events such as galas are used to encourage existing and some new donors to make more substantial gifts. Major gifts are solicited from affluent individuals, and grants are sought from foundations, corporations, and public agencies.

Different fundraising strategies require different tactics, but all require the leadership from top managers, board members, and the chief development officer. Fundraising requires dedication and, certainly, the commitment of resources. Annual campaigns require frequent mailings. Special events are costly, too. Major gifts require targeted efforts to build relations with wealthy individuals. Grant applications take time and, hence, money. Thus leaders must decide to what extent they will commit their organizations to fundraising. They must decide which specific fundraising activities are targeted, and relate these to the long-term development of their organizations. Guiding these decisions should be an overall strategic plan that furthers the mission of the nonprofit.

Evaluation is increasingly part of fundraising. The cost of acquiring new donors through campaigns is expensive, sometimes more than their first-year contribution. Even efforts at friend-raising are subject to scrutiny of the goals set for these programs. Although managers cannot overlook the importance of fundraising for nonprofit organizations, neither can they ignore the need for evaluating its effectiveness.

References

American Association of Fund-Raising Counsel/Trust for Philanthropy, "Giving USA 1999" (May 25, 1999), press release.

Annual Register of Grant Support: A Directory of Funding Sources, New Providence, NJ: Bowker, 1997.

Anderson, A., *Ethics for Fundraisers*, Bloomington: Indiana University Press, 1996.

Brewer, E., *Finding Funding*, Thousand Oaks, CA: Corwin Press, 1998.

Cook, W., "Surveying the Major Gifts Literature: Observations and Reflections," *Nonprofit Management & Leadership* 7 (spring 1997): 333–47.

Fitzsimons, K., "Giving to a Fund that Does the Giving," *New York Times* (East Coast ed.), January 30, 2000, p. 14CN–17.

Freedman, H., and K. Feldman, *The Business of Special Events: Fundraising Strategies for Changing Times*, Sarasota, FL: Pineapple Press, 1998.

Golden, S., *Secrets of Successful Grantsmanship*, San Francisco: Jossey-Bass, 1997.

Greenfield, J. (ed.), *The Nonprofit Handbook: Fundraising,* 2nd ed., New York: John Wiley & Sons, 1997.

Hopkins, K., and C. Friedman., *Successful Fundraising for Arts and Cultural Organizations,* 2nd ed., Phoenix, AZ: Oryx Press, 1997.

Kelly, K., *Effective Fund-Raising Management*, Mahwah, NJ: Erlbaum, 1998.

Lawson, C., "Capital Funds Appeals," in J. Greenfield (ed.), *The Nonprofit Handbook: Fundraising,* 2nd ed., New York: John Wiley and Sons, 1997, pp. 442–74.

Leader to Leader, *The New Face of Philanthropy*, available at http://www.pfdf.org/leaderbooks/l2l/summer99/toc.html (October 13, 1999).

Miner, L., *Proposal Planning and Writing*, Phoenix, AZ: Oryx Press, 1998.

National Society of Fundraising Executives, *Donor Bill of Rights*, available at http://www.nsfre.org/welcome/donor.html (May 11, 2000).

Shervish, P., and J. Havens, "Money and Magnanimity: New Findings on the Distribution of Income, Wealth and Philanthropy," *Nonprofit Management & Leadership* (summer 1998): 421–34.

Sturtevant, W., *The Artful Journey: Cultivating and Soliciting the Major Gift*, Chicago: Bonus Books, 1997.

10

The Third Sector Reconsidered

Nonprofit organizations exist to do social good. Though collectively nonprofits are much smaller than the for-profit and government components of the economy, the third sector addresses issues left undone by the other two. For-profits must contribute to the wealth of the owners, the stockholders; government has a wider mandate but faces policy and electoral constraints. There is overlap among the sectors: For-profit businesses operate theaters and governments own museums, for example, even though nonprofits are a mainstay of the arts, especially at the local level.

Nonprofits play an important role in society—meeting religious, educational, health, cultural, welfare, humanitarian, and other needs. Though other societies have nonprofit organizations, the third sector finds its greatest expression in the United States' economy. In other societies, many of the activities associated with nonprofits in the United States are lacking in developing countries or are addressed in these countries by their governments—for example, through extensive welfare benefits or socialized medicine. In some cases nonprofits are severely regulated to prevent them from pointing out deficiencies in government programs.

Nonprofits also play a more central role in the U.S. economy because of a culture of giving and a willingness to form associations of common interest (de Tocqueville, 1969). "And while 43% of French and 44% Germans said they gave money to charity [in 1999], 73% of Americans reported doing so. Charitable gifts by Americans totaled $190 billion in 1999—equivalent to . . . 2% of our national income" (Greenfeld, 2000, p. 49). Favorable tax treatment and a long history of philanthropy further encourage the spread of nonprofits. Favorable tax laws exempt nonprofits from taxes and make contributions to them deductible from income taxes. Philanthropic organizations, large and small, provide grants totaling billions of dollars annually to tens of thousands of nonprofits. Corporate and individual philanthropy adds billions more to the coffers of religious, educational, health, cultural, welfare, and other nonprofits (Lerner, 1999).

From this willingness to give and this ability to form associations, nonprofits arise. Each is formed to pursue its own vision and mission. They are embedded operationally in a culture that promotes business-like efficiency, so the pursuit of goals and objectives is done productively, with success measured in terms of outcomes. When barriers to the mission arise or when efficiency dictates, nonprofits often form alliances with each other, governments, or businesses.

Vision/Mission-Driven Nonprofits

The vision and the mission serve as the central organizing principle of the nonprofit. Incorporation papers and bylaws will set forth the operating structure and the formal legal requirements for a nonprofit to exist. But its purpose is intertwined with its vision and mission. The vision tells the nonprofit's multiple constituents why it exists, what it hopes to achieve, what it hopes to become. The mission communicates what the nonprofit will do to pursue its vision.

Though sometimes forgotten in the day to day race to survive and deliver service to clients, the vision and mission serve as a template against which the organization's efforts can and should be gauged. If time, money, or other resources do not fit with the mission or move the nonprofit toward its vision, leadership needs to question the appropriateness of those actions. Otherwise, the board, clients, donors, volunteers, and others may become unclear about what role the nonprofit is undertaking. Ambiguity about the role of the nonprofit weakens its ability to attract board members, volunteers, donations, grants, and other resources. Vision and mission define what the organization seeks to be and what it proposes to do. "How" the nonprofit achieves its mission and pursues its vision is the scope of strategy.

The Strategic Connection

Strategy defines how the nonprofit will use its resources to attain its mission. Strategy formulation (or reformulation) generally takes place within the context of long-range planning. The goal is to determine what the nonprofit's deliverables will be and what the organization will be at some point—usually three to five years in the future. Then an assessment of the available resources and organizational strengths are made. It is the organization's strengths that serve as its tools for meeting those future objectives. If strengths are insufficient to meet the external opportunities, then goals and objectives need to be scaled back or organizational strengths enhanced.

Adding strengths to the nonprofit's tools may mean developing needed skills internally or acquiring them externally. For example, future success may depend heavily on a planned fundraising drive. If the nonprofit lacks the talent needed to conduct the fundraising drive, the drive may be put off for a year or longer while the nonprofit develops its fundraising staff. Or a more expedient route—resources permitting—may be to buy the needed talent by recruiting the skilled staff.

Building strengths to meet future opportunities is not the same as overcoming weaknesses. A weakness in the accounting department caused by a lack of automation, for example, does not necessarily give the nonprofit a new strength in delivering its mission when manual systems are replaced with computer-based ones. Accounting will be more efficient and timely as a result, and that may be helpful in operating the nonprofit more efficiently. But a strong accounting department does not necessarily add strengths to the nonprofit's ability to raise funds or deliver services.

Likewise, identifying potential threats to the nonprofit's success and eliminating them does not further the mission or deliverables of the nonprofit. More effective nonprofits remain aware of these threats, monitor them, and then put their resources into building strengths that are most likely to further the vision and mission. Only when the potential threat becomes real are resources taken away from mission-critical areas and devoted to reducing external threats.

By setting long-term goals and short-term budget priorities, non-profit leaders define how they are going to achieve their mission. Equally important, these goals and priorities define what the nonprofit is *not* going to do.

Most nonprofits face limited resources and near unlimited demands for their services. Balancing resources with results is a difficult task because there is almost always "so much more to do." The trap for boards and leaders is a temptation to try to be all things to all people. Though noble, such goals are unattainable. Worse, by failing to identify what the nonprofit is not, vision and mission become unfocused, creating ambiguity about its role and potentially diluting its support among key constituents.

Effective organizations develop a strategy to achieve their mission by devoting resources primarily to building strengths. Then its strengths are combined to meet the mission-related opportunities that exist in its operating environment. Weaknesses and threats are tolerated until they impinge on attaining the mission.

The Life Cycle of Nonprofits

A nonprofit's vision, mission, and strategy, however, are dramatically shaped by the nonprofit's stage of development. Newly created nonprofits find the start-up phase particularly challenging. The need to translate a vision into a mission and strategy is daunting by itself. However, a start-up often has extremely limited resources, particularly financial and human ones. Constrained by money and talent, the nonprofit is often trapped in a potentially lethal, downward spiral: Lack of talent makes attracting more talent and funds difficult. Without additional funds and talent, mission objectives are limited and perhaps unattainable. With only limited prospects, volunteers and donors are scarce.

In the start-up phase, the nonprofit may have little to "sell" but its vision, its possibilities. That vision may be sufficient to attract a few board members, who in turn may be able to attract others. The vision of start-up nonprofits is often one of their most important assets, encouraging members (volunteers, staff, and board members) to go all out and make a difference. Indeed, the limited resources force the board to be hands-on, and the members undertake activities that would typically be left to staff in more mature nonprofits. Still, some nonprofits find the start-up phase involves a curious mix between noble visions and missions and the mundane business of ensuring survival. Though vulnerable, start-ups do have the great advantage of passion for the vision and mission among the founders, board, volunteers, and staff. Small nonprofits that successfully make the transition from start-ups to mature organizations can and do make a difference by changing society.

As the mix of vision, mission, strategy, financial, and human resources improves the start-up makes the transition to a developing or growing nonprofit. Resources remain scarce, and future funding is often uncertain. But professional staff, past accomplishments, and greater visibility make attracting financial and human resources easier, which helps ensure the future. The focus moves from mere survival to a more reactive mode in which the nonprofit is able to respond to demands, often in a reactive mode.

With maturity often comes dedicated (or at least more predictable and reliable) sources of funding and a professional staff. The increasingly prestigious board shifts from operating concerns to policy matters. With both a track record and greater resources, professional leadership in the form of a paid president or executive director also becomes typical, as does the appearance of a professional development staff. Greater funding also enables long-range planning that puts the nonprofit on a proactive course, better able to anticipate future needs and opportunities through planning and goal setting.

The Success Triangle: Board, Leadership, Staff

A nonprofit's success is measured by its outcomes. What did it accomplish? How effectively, and efficiently did it accomplish its mission? Is it moving toward its vision? How do clients, staff, volunteers, donors, board members, and the larger community view the nonprofit? Although nonprofits seek to achieve surplus revenues or at least break even from their operations, they lack the marketplace evaluation of their performance that sends powerful messages to the leadership of for-profit organizations. Nonprofits even lack the evaluation of voters, which drives virtually all levels of government. Instead, nonprofits develop internal goals and objectives against which to measure their success or failure.

The foundation for that success rests with people. Specifically, the board members, nonprofit leadership in the form of the president or executive director, and staff form a success triangle. Each is interdependent, with the extent and importance of each shaped by the nonprofit's vision, mission, and stage of development. Collectively, they attain the results for which the nonprofit is known. They craft the vision, mission, strategies, goals, and objectives that guide the nonprofit. Though financial resources are an obvious element of success, monies are best seen as a byproduct of success, not its foundation. Ample financial resources without competent human resources is an even more certain recipe for failure than the reverse.

Efficiency and Effectiveness

Deploying resources to pursue the vision and mission should be done with two constraints in mind: effectiveness and efficiency. Effectiveness focuses on doing the right things. The pursuit of well-defined goals that further the mission of the nonprofit suggests effectiveness. Efficiency is concerned with doing things right. That is, efficiency addresses the need to conserve resources so that goals and objectives are attained with the greatest productivity. The fewest resources (inputs) should be used to achieve a given level of results (outputs). However, the pursuit of efficiency must not stifle creativity and the development of new programs. Nor should the pursuit of efficiency be allowed to stifle risk-taking. Efficiency is a means to an end—the fulfillment of the vision. The management task is to strike the right balance between effectiveness and efficiency.

Beyond mere efficiency, high productivity challenges members of the success triangle to improve not just their results but also the means they use to attain those results. Pursuit of high productivity draws attention to finding better ways of achieving the same results. Although the vision, mission, strategies, goals, and objectives change slowly over time, effective leadership constantly seeks to improve the processes used to attain desired outcomes.

Key to success, however, is the need to produce results. Outcomes should be visible, measurable, and relevant to the vision/mission. Funders increasingly expect to see outcomes, which may explain why many are reluctant to finance day to day operations with grants, preferring to target their grants to projects with identifiable, measurable, and relevant outcomes. Outcome measures are, perhaps, the single best way to demonstrate to multiple constituents that the nonprofit is successful.

Besides effectiveness and efficiency, however, there are processes. Nonprofits have a special concern with the connection between processes and outcomes. Like all organizations, nonprofits are goal seeking. Goals or outcomes are crucial in justifying the existence of nonprofits. However, nonprofits need to pay particular attention to the processes they use to attain the desired outcomes. Not only must the processes be appropriate to attaining success; they must also be acceptable to multiple constituents. Often this means that nonprofit management must not only live up to the letter of laws, but they must avoid even the appearance of violating the spirit of laws and the community standards expected of them. For example, allegations of wrongdoing, law violations, ethical lapses, discrimination, or other societal prohibitions that might go largely unnoticed by the public if done by a private business can cause uproar when done by nonprofits. Because nonprofits exist only from the support of donors and other contributors, nonprofit leaders need to be process-sensitive. Successful outcomes and good intentions may not be sufficient if constituents see the processes used to achieve those outcomes as inappropriate or wrong. Although the ends seldom justify the means, in the third sector even greater sensitivity is needed to this means–end distinction.

Alliances and Partnerships

Efficiency and effectiveness also demand creative ways to leverage limited resources. Although the degree of cleverness found in the nonprofit sector would fill many books, one common source of leveraging limited resources is through alliances. As de Tocqueville observed in the early 1800s, "Better use has been made of association and this powerful instrument of action has been applied to more varied aims in America than anywhere else in the world" (1969, p. 189). His observation remains true today.

Most nonprofits can be viewed as a spontaneous association of people attracted by a common purpose. Taking this cultural characteristic a step further finds many nonprofits forming alliances with other nonprofits, governments, and for-profits. Alliances allow nonprofits to use the strengths and resources of others to accomplish mutual goals. For example, a nonprofit opera company may find a natural ally in a bank's trust department because both need to attract high net-worth individuals. Opera patrons might look favorably on a trust department that cosponsors opera-related events. Not only does the opera gain a source of funding, but also the bank's trust department gains exposure among a select group of potential clients. Or several nonprofits might join together to increase their ability to influence public opinion by pooling their talents and public relations benefits. Government alliances also work to further the mission of nonprofits. Consider an example from a private–public partnership:

In Miami-Dade County, Florida, a consensus among business, political, and community leaders was reached to build a pair of performing arts center buildings. A nonprofit Center for Performing Arts Trust was created to manage this private–public partnership largely funded by private donations to the Performing Arts Center Foundation and tax revenues. By joining in a public–private alliance, the major nonprofit performing arts groups appear assured of a world-class venue (furthering their individual visions and missions) while furthering the goals of government and the private sector to enhance the quality of cultural life in the Miami metropolitan area.

The Great Funding Crisis

Time and time again, nonprofit leaders report that their biggest problem is funding. Many conversations between the executive director and the board begin, "If we had more funding. . . ." This concern is understandable because executive directors and boards see a never-ending set of needs and possibilities that fall within the vision–mission of the nonprofit. If they did have more money they could do more to address the needs to which the success triangle is committed. Thus the only barrier to continued success often appears to be funding. Although efforts might be better devoted to getting the funding than lamenting what could be done, the demands facing a nonprofit are likely to exceed resources in all but the most unusual cases. A change in perspectives may be needed, which is not easily attained (Coates, 1997).

Another view is to see the lack of funding as a symptom—a symptom of the nonprofit's effectiveness in a variety of areas. Too often nonprofits measure their success exclusively in terms of outcomes. Clients served, students taught, patients cured, and other outcome measures do point to the accomplishments of the nonprofit. Moreover, these accomplishments help justify its existence and requests for future funding or volunteer help.

But if insufficient funding is seen as a symptom of deeper problems, then boards, staff, and executive directors can ask what needs to be done to be more effective in fundraising? The answer has two parts. First, there are technical and procedural approaches to fundraising that were mentioned in this book. Professional groups, such as the National Society of Fund Raising Executives, specialized degrees and training, and countless books and articles on the subject offer virtually unlimited advice on how to design and implement one-time or ongoing fundraising efforts. Improving the technical abilities of the nonprofit to raise funds would seem to represent a potentially good return for the effort.

Second, beneath these important tactical concerns lies a deeper strategic issue. How is the nonprofit positioned to raise funds? Is the vision appropriate and exciting to those whose support is crucial? Do current and potential donors (including board members and volunteers who are important donors, too) understand the mission and the outcomes that have been achieved? Do they understand the scope of the issues that the nonprofit is addressing? How are they involved besides giving time or money? Do key supporters feel that they have a vote in the organization's direction and activities, whether they exercise their vote or not? How are staff, volunteers, board members, donors, and other key constituents involved in the decisions that affect the direction of the nonprofit? Are they advocates of the organization? What would it take for them to become active advocates?

At the core of fundraising is a competition for limited philanthropic and charitable dollars. Merely having a good cause is just the starting point. Other nonprofits have equally valid views of their importance and the urgency of their cause. What are the attributes and outcomes that make donors in all their forms want to support one particular nonprofit versus other, equally deserving ones? Perhaps the issue is not a lack of funds but poorly articulated vision and mission statements; poorly publicized outcomes; insufficient orientation and involvement among board members, staff, volunteers, or key donors and foundations; ineffective strategies, goals, and objectives; poorly selected, informed, or motivated board members; inappropriate staff; low productivity; insufficient outcome measures; weak or ineffective alliances; or simply poor fundraising tactics and strategies. Restated, does the fundraising effort rest on a solid foundation of a strategically oriented and professionally managed nonprofit?

One partial answer to these questions is to benchmark with other nonprofits and for-profits, seeking better approaches to operations and fundraising (Hiebeler, 1994). Returning to the largely unexplored international issues of nonprofits, much can be learned from how nonprofits are handled in other countries, especially given the diversity nonprofits encounter in the United States.

Fundraising is essential to the success of nonprofits. When problems with fundraising exist, failure may rest on the lack of a strategic approach to the management of the nonprofit that severely hampers the fundraising capabilities of the organization.

The Future of Nonprofits

Nonprofits are here to stay. Like governments and for-profits, nonprofits fill too many needs in society to go away. Moreover, there are a variety of trends that suggest the third sector will grow in both size and importance in coming decades. But the sector is not without its problems. One particularly nagging issue is that nonprofits exist to do social good, but information about them (their accounting practices, and their general management) is not as transparent to the general public as publicly traded private corporations. Nonprofits need to become more transparent to the general public. Institutes, centers, and even the IRS help by publishing some financial records (Tempel, 1999). The recent IRS requirement that nonprofits have to file Form 90 disclosure forms that will be available to the general public is a beginning (Rankin, 1999). More is needed to ensure that the public retains its faith in nonprofit organizations (McIlquham, 1999).

Since the early 1980s, the political rhetoric and (to a much lesser extent) action has been to reduce government involvement in the arts, welfare, and other areas of social services. Nowhere is this trend more evident than in "welfare to work" programs, aimed at giving welfare recipients time limits on their benefits, forcing many off the welfare roles into jobs. Along the way, the social net for many poor families has been torn, with nonprofits struggling to patch the holes.

> Within these concerns . . . there is an even deeper issue about . . . the social contract that interweaves business, government, and nonprofit organizations together into the societal fabric. That contract is changing as government retreats from responsibility but sometimes tries to stop nonprofits from speaking out, and as corporations align their giving programs to support their strategic interests rather than community-defined needs. (Young, 1997)

Cutbacks facing nonprofits are not limited to just the United States. In one study, 237 Australian managers of arts nonprofits reported contending with cutbacks through a variety of traditional means more commonly associated with for-profit organizations—including the use of cost reductions, downsizing, refinancing, commercialization, relocation, political, and cooperative strategies (Palmer, 1997).

Compounded by a limited trust in government and scandals at national and local levels, few politicians talk about raising taxes to meet social needs. Instead the great social debate at the beginning of the twenty-first century seems to be whether to reduce the national debt, strengthen social security, or cut taxes. Yet the needs for universal health care, education, food for hungry people, and other social services continue; likewise, the desire for art and other cultural activities seems to rely increasingly on the nonprofit sector, with support from foundations and the for-profit sector. Simply stated, the needs and desires for the types of services provided by nonprofits appear to be growing, offering them even more opportunities to pursue. Moreover, this trend toward self-reliance and less dependence on government appears to be part of a culturally imbedded trend, of which the Depression- and World War II-induced dependence on government is a deviation (de Tocqueville, 1969).

If this assessment is accurate, these trends merge with a historical growth of greater wealth, leading to greater consumption of health, education, arts, and cultural offerings. In short, the need for the types of services provided by nonprofits appears to be growing and is likely to continue to do so into the future.

At the same time, philanthropy in the United States is at an all-time high at the individual, corporate, and philanthropic foundation levels. Some of these favorable trends are, no doubt, attributable to a long-running "bull" market in stocks, also begun in the early 1980s. At the same time, powerful concentrations of wealth are being formed in the hands of investors and entrepreneurs. Bill Gates of Microsoft fame (who has created a $17 billion foundation) and Ted Turner (who committed $1 billion to the United Nations) have pledged funds to nonprofits measured in the *billions* of dollars. Others have pledged hundreds of millions of dollars. All this is at the beginning of the largest wealth transfer in history, as successful parents of baby boomers begin leaving estates to family and nonprofits. Estimates suggest that over the next 55 years, the intergenerational wealth transfer may exceed 55 trillion dollars. When those over 50 are included, the numbers shoot to $136 trillion. Among the very wealthy, a higher proportion of their estate goes to nonprofits (Carpenter, 1999). Sprinkled in between are large numbers of entrepreneurs and investors who have created 36,000 foundations in the United States (*PNN Alert,*

1999). The result is that both the need for nonprofits and the potential resources to fuel them appear to be creating a golden age of nonprofits.

The Golden Age of Nonprofits

To expect the first decades of the twenty-first century to be a golden age for nonprofits is not unrealistic. Besides the tremendous wealth already acquired by seniors and successful entrepreneurs and a seemingly never-ending demand for the services of nonprofits, the baby boomer generation represents the largest age cohort in the history of the country. This cohort has a strong record of social consciousness that dates back to the 1960s. As the group moves from careers to retirement in coming decades, there is little to suggest that they will abandon social activism. Although the trillions of dollars being shuffled from one generation to the next is impressive, the potential volunteer efforts of 78 million affluent, well-educated, and socially active baby boomers may make an even larger impact on nonprofits, which are prepared to enlist these young retirees into their nonprofit's vision. Even before counting the swelling ranks of retirees, 56 percent of adults 18 years old and older volunteered in the past year (Sinclair, 1999).

Added to these impressive numbers are a new generation of extremely wealthy entrepreneurs. As the editors at *Philanthropy News Network* observed,

> American philanthropy has grown into a multi-billion dollar industry fueled by new wealth—money from both inheritances and high-tech/entrepreneurial fortunes. This has translated into more donors, more foundations and a growing number of charities. (*PNN Alert,* 2000, p. 2)

A writer for the *New York Times* observed that there are a

growing number of technology entrepreneurs and financiers who are embracing philanthropy at a relatively young age. The group is led by Microsoft Corporation chairman, William H. Gates, 44, the world's richest man and the benefactor of a $17 billion charitable foundation. It also includes Jim Clark, 55, the founder of Netscape; Steve Kirsch, 43, the founder of Infoseek, and Jeff Skoll, 34, the founder of eBay. (Sack, 2000, p. A-13)

Successful nonprofits will take advantage of these demographic trends by creating ways to tap this vast pool of human talent. Clever nonprofits will engage potential volunteers before they formally retire, offering them a direction, purpose, and, most important, a legacy for their talents. Though the outlines of these programs are not precise, they are likely to form around two patterns. One will be the traditional approach in which nonprofits will seek out volunteers among retirees and meet with growing success as the pool of retirees grows. Another approach will be employer-based. Recognizing the benefits of maintaining liaison with retirees as substitute workers and sources of organizational history, large employers are likely to set up retiree clubs, presumably with more attractive names. These employer-based groups will not only be sources of temporary talent for the organization, these groups may become an extension of the employer, providing a small army of volunteers that can help with community issues and nonprofits, either on a one-to-one basis or en masse. One example that has existed for decades is the Pioneer Clubs, created for retirees of AT&T before its breakup into local operating companies. Besides the benefits to retirees and nonprofits, the employer may well benefit from the favorable publicity such civic-mindedness can generate.

Beyond the availability of volunteers, it is even conceivable that the nonprofit sector's fast growth rate may enable it to stand as an economic equal with government, especially if the dollar value of in-kind and volunteers is counted (Vantil, 1999). To the extent that nonprofits are successful at meeting societal needs, their successes are likely to attract more financial and human support, creating a virtuous cycle of growth and mission-related outcomes.

Global Trends

A growing trend is the emergence of supragovernmental organizations. Funded by governments, organizations such as the United Nations, the World Court, the World Trade Organization, and others assume responsibilities for issues that cut across national borders. Many of these quasi government organizations set a pattern for worldwide organizations to address global issues. Though organized on a country-by-country basis, the Red Cross and the Red Crescent are examples of nonprofits that also act globally when calamities exceed the resources of any one group. When it comes to disaster relief, health care, and other issues, the line between government and nonprofits blurs—

especially when operating on a global basis. Though nonprofits remain largely a national phenomenon wherever they are found, an increasingly global society suggests that nonprofit issues are likely to span borders, and this phenomenon is likely to be accelerated by the boundaryless Internet (Elliott, Katsioloudes, and Weldon, 1998). Globalization of research and practice in the areas of nonprofit management is sure to grow as well (Young, 1997).

Perhaps the major export of the United States is its culture, for better or worse. United States–based trends in entertainment, fashion, and even eating have already swept the globe, whether in the form of U.S. music and movies, tennis shoes and blue jeans, or the increasingly ubiquitous colas and franchise hamburger joints. Perhaps attitudes toward philanthropy and nonprofits are buried no deeper. The spread of U.S. culture and corporations brings with it U.S. attitudes in these areas. Cultures that are used to the government or religious groups filling the needs met by nonprofits in the United States may have little interest or incentive to change. But as old religious patterns break down, especially in developing nations, and governments everywhere face demands that exceed their resources, there is an opportunity for nonprofits to take root.

If patterns of emulating the United States lead to a growing philanthropic viewpoint, nonprofits may begin to emerge in larger numbers in developed countries, which have the resources to support these organizations. With the suspicion about the integrity of many developing nations' governments, large international philanthropic organizations (such as the Ford Foundation) may increasingly prefer to deal with local nonprofits in the belief that a greater part of the grant will reach the targeted population. When the potential clout of a multibillion-dollar foundation is considered, the tens of millions of dollars of grants may be used to help needy individuals as well as to create or reshape the nonprofit sector of developing countries.

Moreover, spreading nonprofit behaviors need not be altruistic or even begin with nonprofits. Consider the situation Amoco faced when it began drilling in Angola. According to the *Wall Street Journal* (Deutsch, 1999, pp. 1, 18),

> When Amoco started drilling for oil in Angola a few years ago, Exxon and Chevron had already landed some of the richest oil fields and could easily outbid their smaller rival for others. Lately, though, Amoco has been the successful bidder on several oil tracts.

Why? The company, which is now BP Amoco, realized that Angolan government, torn by civil war, was ready to favor any company that was also willing to assist with social projects. So in an alliance with the United Nations Development Program, Amoco offered $800,000 to assist local fisherman revive their industry and an abandoned fishing port. About a dozen boats have been replaced or repaired.

Certainly the logic of nonprofits is compelling: People or organizations contribute according to their perceptions of what matters, clients benefit, and there is little expense to government—except the lost taxes resulting from tax-deductible gifts. To the extent that governments outside the United States see nonprofits as a viable way to meet social needs with limited government interference or costs, legal, tax, societal, and other barriers to their formation may lessen.

Conclusion

The societal fabric consists of three sectors: government, for-profit, and nonprofit. Each plays a unique, at times overlapping role. Lacking the profits of business or the taxation abilities of government, nonprofits exist only so long as they are able to attract financial and other resources needed to carry our their missions. To be successful, nonprofits need a vision and a mission to guide their efforts and to attract the resources needed to achieve both.

How they achieve the vision and mission will be greatly influenced by a number of factors, including the degree of maturity the nonprofit has achieved in its life cycle and the strategies it follows. Success generally rests on a platform created by the board of directors, staff, and the leadership of the nonprofit. It also depends on distinguishing between efficient and effective actions. Although effectiveness is crucial, effective actions can fail if not executed with great efficiency, especially in the world of limited resources nonprofits continually encounter. Without a clear vision and mission; without a platform of directors, staff, and leadership dedicated to the vision and mission; without the needed strategies to support the mission; and without executing the mission efficiently, funding is apt to be an ongoing problem.

Demographic patterns combined with philanthropic patterns of giving suggest that the United States may be entering a golden age of nonprofits. Funded by foundations and private giving; trends toward alliances among nonprofits, government, and for-profits; and an aging but active population suggest that financial, human, and other resources available to nonprofits are likely to grow dramatically.

Nonprofits are a unique solution to meeting social needs while allowing decentralized decision making among those most affected. Though they exist in other societies, they have received their most widespread impact in the United States. Recognizing that other cultures are unique, but also recognizing that the United States has had a tremendous impact on the rest of the world, it is conceivable that the good nonprofits may gain a similar popularity elsewhere in the world. As the world gets "smaller" because of advances in communications satellites, the Internet, and instant media, more of the world will be exposed to the U.S. approach to a three-sector economy. Though cultural, legal, and religious barriers will prevent a wholesale adoption of nonprofits around the world, it seems equally likely that their benefits will cause nonprofits to grow in other cultures—calling for a growing third sector and the need to improve the art of nonprofit management.

References

Carpenter, C., "Wealth Transfer May Be More than Expected," *The NonProfit Times* (December 1999): 4.

Coates, N. "A Model for Consulting to Help Effect Change in Organizations," *Nonprofit Management & Leadership* (winter 1997): 157–69.

de Tocqueville, A., *Democracy in America* (Edited by J. P. Mayer) New York: HarperCollins, 1969.

Deutsch, C. H., "Unlikely Allies with the United Nations," *Wall Street Journal* (Eastern Edition), December 10, 1999, pp. 1, 18.

Elliott, B., M. Katsioloudes, and R. Weldon, "Nonprofit Organizations and the Internet," *Nonprofit Management & Leadership* (spring 1998): 297–303.

Greenfeld, K. T., "A New Way of Giving," *Time* (July 24, 2000): 49.

Hiebeler, R., "To Compete Better, Look Far Afield," *New York Times* (National Edition), September 18, 1994, p. T1.

Lerner, J. "Philanthropy Made Modern," *Hemispheres* (November 1999): 48–50.

McIlquham, A., "Polishing the Sector: A Shining New Century and Image," *The NonProfit Times* (December 1999): 14.

Palmer, I. "Arts Management Cutback Strategies: A Cross-Sector Analysis," *Nonprofit Management & Leadership* (spring 1997): 271–90.

PNN Alert, August 25, 1999, p. 2.

PNN Alert, January 14, 2000, p. 2.

Rankin, K. "Expect Media Scrutiny on 90 Filings," *The NonProfit Times* (August 1999): 12.

Sack, Kevin, "Ex-Official of Netscape Starts $100 Million Drive for Literacy," *New York Times* (East Coast Edition), January 20, 2000, p. A-13.

Sinclair, M. "IS Reports Volunteers at a 12-Year High," *The NonProfit Times* (December 1999): 5.

Tempel, E. R., "Let's Make Nonprofit Operations Transparent to the Public," *The NonProfit Times* (October 1999): 54.

Young, D. R., "The First Seven Years of *Nonprofit Management and Leadership*," *Nonprofit Management & Leadership* (winter 1997): 199.

Vantil, J. "The Nonprofit World 2025: From a Magic Carpet," *The NonProfit Times* (December 1999): 46.

Index